THE THEORY OF INTEREST

FRIEDRICH A. LUTZ

THE THEORY OF INTEREST

D. REIDEL PUBLISHING COMPANY / DORDRECHT-HOLLAND

ALDINE PUBLISHING COMPANY / CHICAGO

ZINSTHEORIE

Published by Polygraphischer Verlag AG, Zurich, and

J. C. B. Mohr (Paul Siebeck), Tübingen, 1967 (2nd edition)

Translated from the German by Claus Wittich, Columbia University

SOLE DISTRIBUTORS FOR U.S.A. AND CANADA

ALDINE PUBLISHING COMPANY / CHICAGO

Library of Congress Catalog Card Number: 67–17604

Printed in The Netherlands by D. Reidel, Dordrecht

PREFACE TO THE ENGLISH EDITION

This volume is a translation of the second edition of my book, *Zinstheorie*. The original publication was for a German speaking audience. Had it been intended for "Anglo-Saxon" readers, certain phases of the discussion – particularly a few of the passages dealing with Keynes' work – might have been presented in a somewhat shortened form, since American and British economists could reasonably be expected to be more familiar with such topics than most German economists. Even so, it may be useful for many students to have it "all there".

I am very much indebted to the translator, Mr. C. Wittich. His enquiries about certain passages in the German text frequently prompted me to rewrite them and clarify the meaning. For this help, as well as for the accuracy of his translation of a book not easy to render in English, I must give sincere thanks.

Professor R. C. Bernhard of the University of Utah read the English translation and made a number of very valuable suggestions. I appreciate his kindness in undertaking this work.

The English version occasionally deviates slightly from the German, but the meaning of the German text has at no point been altered by such changes.

FRIEDRICH A. LUTZ

Zurich, September 1966

FROM THE PREFACE TO THE SECOND GERMAN EDITION

In this second edition of my *Zinstheorie*, Chapters 1–12 have been taken over from the first edition essentially unchanged. Occasionally the style has been improved and the meaning of certain passages clarified. Chapters 13–16 have been added to the part of the book dealing with the history of doctrines. The presentation of the theories of the term structure of interest rates (Chapters 17–19) is also new. The positive part of the book, with the exception of a few passages, has been completely rewritten and greatly enlarged. It now contains an analysis of the influence of the banking system on the interest rate. The positive part ends with a treatment of the problem of the interest rate in the framework of a general equilibrium analysis.

I was greatly helped by my assistant, Dr. Verena Bachmann. She has drawn my attention to a number of passages which needed editorial revision; she was always ready to discuss the problems with me; and she has read the proofs with great diligence. Above all, § 6 of the Mathematical Appendix is her work. In this she was helped by Dr. D. Onigkeit, to whom thanks are also due. My participation in the work now incorporated in § 6 of the Mathematical Appendix was only that of a consultant. It is a pleasant duty to express here my sincere thanks to Dr. Bachmann.

The work on the manuscript was finished in Autumn 1965, so that no account could be taken of the literature which appeared after November 1965.

TABLE OF CONTENTS

PART ONE / INTEREST THEORIES FOR A STATIONARY ECONOMY

PART TWO / INTEREST THEORIES FOR A PROGRESSIVE ECONOMY

PART ONE

INTEREST THEORIES FOR A STATIONARY ECONOMY

In this book the theories of interest are divided into three groups. The first is represented by attempts to explain the interest rate in a stationary economy. The second comprises theories that proceed from a dynamic economy in which new investment and saving take place. The third covers the so-called monetary theories of interest. Strictly speaking, this third group is merely a subdivision of the second, since the monetary theories also assume an economy in which investment and saving occur. It is desirable, however, even at the expense of strict logic, to put monetary theories of interest into a separate group, not only because it has become accepted practice to regard them as a particular species of interest theories, but also because it contributes to the clarity of exposition to have those theories which put greater stress on the significance of the monetary factor considered separately. Theories of the structure of interest rates will be discussed in Part IV.

In this first part of the book we shall deal with theories of interest for a stationary economy. The protagonists of the theoretical analysis presented in this part are Böhm-Bawerk, Wicksell, Åkerman, and Hayek. The last-named, however, can be included in this group only with important qualifications.

CHAPTER 1

EUGEN VON BÖHM-BAWERK

In his *Positive Theory of Capital*[1], Böhm-Bawerk expounds his theory of interest in two parts. In the first part, he deals with the origin of the phenomenon of interest on capital. During his own lifetime, discussion of his interest theory was largely concentrated on this first part – that is, on his thesis that interest exists because future goods are valued less highly than present goods. He gave three reasons for this supposition; namely, the differences in the relationship between wants and the means for their satisfaction in different periods of time, the systematic subjective undervaluation of future goods as compared with present goods, and, finally, the superiority, due to technical reasons, of present goods as means for the satisfaction of our wants. In the second part of his theory of interest, Böhm-Bawerk examines the determinants of the level of the interest rate.

It is evident, however, that this division of the subject into two parts is artificial, since any exposition of the determinants of the level of the rate of interest must also contain, implicitly, the causes of the phenomenon of interest. Moreover, there is a quite definite break between the first and second part of Böhm-Bawerk's work. The analysis in the second part is conducted without any reference to the higher valuation of present goods relative to future goods. Since this second part is undoubtedly central for Böhm-Bawerk's theory of interest, we shall concentrate in our exposition on that section of his work. Thus we gain the additional advantage of being able to avoid a long-winded discussion of the three reasons for the undervaluation of future goods. Accordingly, the sections of the *Positive Theory* important for the following discussion are Books I and II, which contain Böhm-Bawerk's theory of capital, and the third section of Book IV which deals with the level of the rate of interest on capital, as well as those 'Further Essays' in Volume II which elucidate these sections.

[1] Eugen von Böhm-Bawerk, *Capital and Interest*, Vol. II: *Positive Theory of Capital*, trans. G. D. Huncke (South Holland, Illinois, 1959).

I. The Theory of Capital

Two concepts are important for the understanding of Böhm-Bawerk's theory of interest: the "period of production" and the "subsistence fund". Let us start with an explanation of the first.

With a given quantity of services provided by the two original factors of production, labour and land, it is possible to produce more (or, alternatively, better) consumption goods, the longer is the time period which elapses, on the average, between the moment when these services are first applied and the moment when the consumption goods become available. After a certain point, however, the rate of increase of the output of consumption goods will become smaller, and at a further point the increase will completely cease.[2] This is Böhm-Bawerk's law of the greater productivity of the more roundabout methods of production.

Let us consider the simple case, which is assumed in Böhm-Bawerk's theory, where there is only one original factor of production, labour – the productive services of land being regarded as free. In this case the average period of production is calculated as follows: each unit of labour used in the production process is multiplied by the time which elapses between the moment of its application and the completion of the product; the resulting figures are added up and their total is divided by the number of labour units. In this way we arrive at a weighted arithmetic average as the measure of the average period of production. If, for instance, three labour units are applied two unit periods of time and another two labour units one unit period of time before the consumption good is finished, then the average period of production is calculated as $[(3 \times 2) + 2]/5 = 1.6$ unit periods. It is clear that in this method of calculation those labour units which were applied earlier influence the length of the average period of production much more strongly than do the units which were applied later.

Two special cases may now be considered. One is characterized by the fact that all inputs are applied simultaneously at the beginning of the period of production and no further inputs are needed between this point of time and the time when the consumption good becomes available. This case played an important role in capital theory; it is usually illustrated by

[2] This last proposition is to be found in *Capital and Interest*, Vol. III: *Further Essays on Capital and Interest*, trans. H. F. Sennholz (South Holland, Illinois, 1959), p. 6.

the example of trees which grow of themselves once they have been planted, or by the example of wine which matures of itself once it has been stored. Here the *absolute* period of production – the time which elapses between the first input of productive services and the point when the goods are ready for consumption – is identical with the *average* period of production as calculated by Böhm-Bawerk's method. It is not on this case, however, that Böhm-Bawerk has based his discussion of the determinants of the rate of interest.

The second special case is that of the "even flow" period of production (in Böhm-Bawerk's terminology, the *gleichmässig ausgefüllte Produktionsperiode*). Here the application of productive services is spaced uniformly through the absolute period of production: in each unit period throughout the process of production the same quantity of productive services is added. Böhm-Bawerk usually has this case in mind. The average period of production is here equal to exactly half the absolute period of production, a fact which can be established as follows: Suppose that the same quantity l of labour inputs is applied at each stage of the production process and that the last stage is one unit period distant from the moment at which the product is ready for consumption, the penultimate stage two unit periods and the first stage t unit periods distant from this moment. Then the sum of the products of the labour inputs and their respective time distances from the moment of completion of the consumption good is equal to

$$l + 2l + 3l + \cdots + tl = \tfrac{1}{2}lt(t + 1).$$

If we divide this expression by the total input of labour units lt, we obtain $\frac{1}{2}t + \frac{1}{2}$. Finally, if we conceive of the unit period as small enough to be able to neglect the half period in this expression, we may say that $t/2$ is the average period of production.

Böhm-Bawerk also uses the concept of an "average social period of production", without, however, explaining how this average of the production periods of individual goods is to be calculated. He seems to think that this is merely a problem of practical measurability, and that the logical precision of the concept would not be affected if the problem should in reality be insoluble.

Böhm-Bawerk does not altogether neglect durable goods. He distinguishes between durable production and durable consumption goods.

With respect to the latter he claims the validity of a rule similar to – but not identical with – the law of the greater productivity of longer production periods. This rule, incidentally, had already been stated by John Rae. The more services of the original factors of production are used, for instance, in the construction of a house, the longer will be the useful "life" of this house. Moreover, the "lifetime" of the house will increase at a faster rate than the total input of factor services. If 30 man-years are necessary to build a house which will last, say, 30 years, then 50 man-years may build one which will last perhaps 60 years. To avoid misunderstanding it should be stressed that the application of these 50 man-years need not necessitate a longer construction period for the house than that of 30 man-years; 50 man-years can be applied during one single calendar year, exactly as can 30 man-years. However, in the case of waiting for the services of such consumer *durables*, the concept of the "waiting period", which Böhm-Bawerk uses in this context, has a meaning quite different from that in the previously discussed case of the production of non-durable consumer goods. In the case of a durable consumer good, such as a house, one does indeed wait for *future* services; this waiting, however, is here accompanied by the enjoyment of the *present* services of the house, which are true consumer goods, while in the previously treated case of the production of non-durable consumer goods real "abstinence" is required since the consumer goods do not become available until the period of production has been completed.

Although it is quite true that the useful life of durable production goods follows the same rule as that of durable consumption goods, Böhm-Bawerk subsumes this case under the rule of the greater productivity of more roundabout methods of production. The extension in the useful life of durable *production* goods he considers to be simply one of the ways in which the period of production can be extended. To him, waiting for future services of durable production goods is identical with waiting longer for consumption goods, a kind of waiting which is not accompanied by a concurrent yield of consumption goods.[3] The objection immediately arises that such distinction between durable production goods and durable consumption goods is not justified. A shoe-making machine, exactly like a house, produces consumer goods as long as it remains in

[3] Böhm-Bawerk, *Capital and Interest*, Vol. II, p. 93.

use, and waiting for its future services is accompanied by a continuous receipt of consumption goods in the form of shoes. In fact, Böhm-Bawerk includes in *both* cases in his average period of production the average period of waiting for the services or the consumer goods which are yielded by the durable goods.[4] Thus his method of calculation in fact contradicts his theoretical distinction. However, as Böhm-Bawerk leaves durable goods out of account in his discussion of the determinants of the level of the interest rate, we can disregard them in the following exposition.

Böhm-Bawerk's law of the greater productivity of more roundabout methods of production is valid at every point in time. He does not deny the possibility of technical inventions which might have the effect of shortening the average production period, but he asserts that any known technical methods which are not in use, even though they yield a greater product, must entail longer periods of production than the processes actually used; for if such were not the case, they would be applied instead. According to Böhm-Bawerk there exists at any time a long list of known technical processes which, because they involve longer production periods, yield more output than the methods actually used. It is the level of the rate of interest which makes it unprofitable at a given moment to adopt these processes.

How does Böhm-Bawerk "prove" the existence of his law? The "law" is in fact an empirical rule which he undertakes to prove from the observation of reality. At the same time he supports it with arguments of a general character. He repeatedly stresses that the law cannot be derived

[4] In 'Einige strittige Fragen der Kapitalstheorie' (*Kleinere Abhandlungen über Kapital und Zins*, edited by F. X. Weiss, Vienna, 1926, p. 202, footnote) Böhm-Bawerk takes the case of a durable production good having a useful "life" of twenty years and which is itself produced by 100 workers in one year. The production of consumption goods by means of the durable production good is also assumed to require the work of 100 workers for one year. Böhm-Bawerk then proceeds to calculate as follows: the services provided by the workers who made the machine reappear, on the average, "a little more than 10, say, 11 years later" in the form of consumption goods. During each year of utilization of the durable production good the work of 5 workers is being amortized. In addition, 100 workers are currently employed on the machine whose services mature on the average within half a year. Consequently the average production period of the consumption goods is $[(5 \times 11) + (100 \times \frac{1}{2})]/105$ = one year. Exactly the same method can be applied to calculate the production period of the services rendered by durable consumption goods. We do not need to decide the question whether the whole approach is meaningful or not.

logically from a given set of premises, and he admits the impossibility of concretely measuring the period of production.

A collation of all the arguments which Böhm-Bawerk brought to bear on this question yields the following result. In the first place, he endeavours to "prove" his law by reference to a great number of specific examples. These are typified by the famous fishery example: the transition from fishing by hand to fishing with a hook and then to fishing with a net from a boat is a transition representing the adoption of ever longer and ever more productive roundabout techniques. Secondly, he analyses the technical nature of the process of production. Each lengthening of the production process with a given input of original productive services signifies the harnessing of additional powers of nature, he says, and therefore it should be only natural that such lengthening would lead to an increase in output. However, there is a limit to everything; and it would have to be assumed that, from a certain point on, the increases in output would become smaller and finally would cease entirely. Thirdly, he points out that even though we may be unable to measure the average period of production, we do know, in every concrete case, whether a particular process tends to lengthen or to shorten it. When, for instance, a tailor instals a sewing machine and thereby sets free two workers at the final stage of production – workers who now become employed at an earlier stage in the production of sewing machines – then quite obviously the production process has become longer. Numerous such examples offer themselves to the observer, and it is also quite obvious that the output per unit of productive service is increased as a result of such lengthening of the period of production. Fourthly, as mentioned earlier, if other things remain the same, an increase in the capital stock causes a reduction in the rate of interest which renders investments profitable which formerly were not. But why were they formerly not profitable? There can be no doubt that the new methods of production do yield a larger physical product than the methods which were in use when the interest rate was higher, for otherwise they would not now be chosen. The only reason why it did not pay to use them at the higher rate of interest is, as Böhm-Bawerk tries to prove by arithmetical examples [5], the fact that their average period of production is longer; this, in his opinion, demonstrates the existence

[5] Böhm-Bawerk, *Capital and Interest*, Vol. III, p. 20ff.

of his law. Fifthly, Böhm-Bawerk asserts that his law is nothing but a particular interpretation of the generally accepted fact that the productivity of labour increases with the amount of capital combined with it. An increase of capital per worker in the process of production he holds to be identical with the adoption of a longer, more roundabout productive method. Böhm-Bawerk does not claim that this applies unconditionally if the production processes of any two different goods are compared, but he maintains that the identity holds for the social period of production. Nor is a perfect correlation between capital per worker and the length of the period of production to be expected. An increase in capital per worker by 10% does not necessarily connote an increase in the length of the production process by 10%; all that is claimed is that when capital per worker employed in the economy increases, the length of the average social period of production increases also. Böhm-Bawerk tries to prove this assertion in several ways. The simplest justification he derives from an analysis of the saving process. With a given labour force, saving increases the *per capita* capital stock of an economy by lessening the demand for consumer goods and diverting it to capital goods. Labour is redirected from the production of consumption goods to that of capital goods, which means nothing other than a lengthening of the average process of production.[6]

As soon as the identity of "capitalist" production with "roundabout" production has been recognized, we can, following Böhm-Bawerk, view the stock of goods existing at any moment of time as consisting of goods which have reached varying stages in the process of production. The composition of this stock – which Böhm-Bawerk calls the *subsistence fund* – with respect to the time distance of each component from the moment at which the consumption good is ready, indicates the time structure of the production process. The subsistence fund may be regarded from two points of view. On the one hand, looking backward, we can regard it as the result of roundabout productive processes which have been started upon but are not yet completed. On the other hand, looking forward, we can regard it as the necessary condition for the continuance and completion of roundabout processes which have already been started upon and for the starting of new such processes. The in-

[6] Böhm-Bawerk, *Capital and Interest*, Vol. III, p. 16ff.

complete production processes as well as the newly starting ones require, week by week, the application of services of the two original factors of production, for the subsistence of which a continuous stream of consumption goods must be available. It is the subsistence fund which provides these consumption goods. They can be continually drawn from it to the extent that the goods of which it consists are made ready for final use through the addition of productive services. Thus it is the function of the subsistence fund to make possible longer productive processes by releasing the stream of consumption goods which is required for the maintenance of the productive factors employed in those roundabout processes. The greater this fund, the longer are the productive processes which can be chosen.

The subsistence fund does not, of course, need to have the form of goods ready for consumption, for the goods will not be used at once but only gradually. It is easy to see that in the above-mentioned case of an "even flow" production process, in which the same amount of productive services is applied at each stage of production, the total subsistence fund need amount to only one half of the subsistence which the productive factors require during the production process. To support those workers who are beginning a new process it is necessary to provide subsistence for the whole of the absolute period of production t, because only after that length of time will the product of their work appear in the form of consumption goods. To support those workers who are engaged in the second stage of the production process, subsistence must be provided for the time $t-1$, and so on, down to the workers at the last stage of production who produce, so to speak, their own consumption goods. It follows from this that the existing subsistence fund must contain the means of subsistence for the workers engaged in the process of production for exactly one half of the absolute period of production or, in other words, for the whole of the *average* period of production. For this particular case, which underlies Böhm-Bawerk's exposition of the theory of interest, the subsistence fund may be illustrated as in Figure 1. During the first unit of time (numbered 1 in the left hand diagram) the workers are paid a sum which is represented by the rectangle constructed over this unit period. This sum of wages is equal to the value of the raw materials produced at the first stage of production, which thus is also represented by the first rectangle. During the second unit period an equal amount of

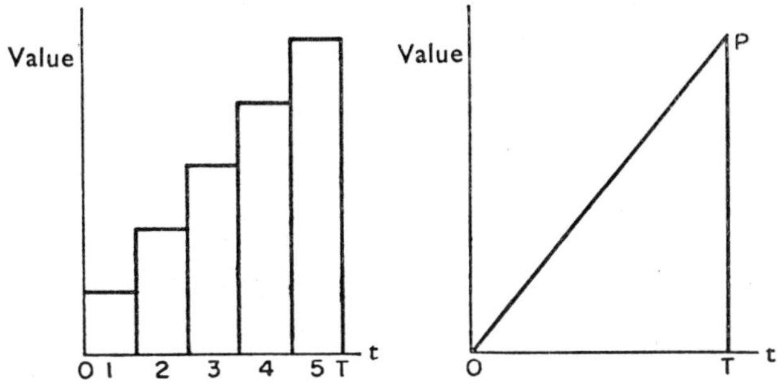

Fig. 1.

labour is added; the value of the goods at the second stage of production, which contains the value of the raw materials from the preceding stage, is represented by the second rectangle – and so on, up to the rectangle over the fifth unit period which represents the value of goods at the final stage of production. When the production process is in full swing there will be goods at all stages simultaneously. The workers do not accompany their product as it is being gradually transformed into a consumption good, but remain at their stage in the process and continually pass products of this stage on to workers at the next stage. Clearly, the value of the total subsistence fund at any given moment of time is then equal to the sum of the area of all rectangles (interest being disregarded). If we make the unit period very small the bar diagram on the left hand will approach the form of a triangle, as in the right diagram, and the total value of the subsistence fund can be represented by the area *OPT*.

The value of the consumption goods which are taken out of the subsistence fund and paid to the workers as wages during each small unit of time is equal to *PT*. The total value of consumption goods which accrue during the absolute period of production *OT* would be represented by a rectangle (not actually drawn) with the sides *OT* and *PT*, with an area twice that of the triangle which represents the subsistence fund.

If the function of the subsistence fund is to make roundabout production possible, the function of the interest rate is to induce entrepreneurs to choose roundabout processes of such length that the fund will be sufficient to maintain the original factors of production during this period. How this result comes about is the subject of our next section in which the determinants of the rate of interest are considered.

II. The Level of the Interest Rate

In his discussion of the determinants of the interest rate, Böhm-Bawerk makes the following simplifying assumptions:

1. There are no durable production goods.

2. Labour is the only factor of production. The services contributed by land are assumed to be free goods. All labour services are homogeneous.

3. Competition exists between entrepreneurs as well as between workers.

4. The law of greater productivity of more roundabout methods of production is valid.[7]

5. The production function with regard to τ, i.e., the function which relates output per worker to the average length of the productive process – we shall henceforth call it the productivity function –, is the same in all branches of production. Fundamentally, this amounts to assuming that only one commodity is being produced.

6. The value of the subsistence fund is given.

7. The production process is assumed to be an "even flow" process as defined earlier.

On these assumptions the problem consists in determining four unknowns: the amount of product, the interest rate, the wage rate, and the period of production.

The "interest rate" with which Böhm-Bawerk is concerned is not the market rate of interest, but the internal rate of return (*ursprünglicher Zins*), i.e., the average rate of return earned in the process of production by the capital tied up in it. In equilibrium the market rate of interest simply reflects this internal rate of return; the latter is the source of the interest payments which have to be made at the market rate to the creditor, if an enterprise is financed by credit, but otherwise remain in the hands of the entrepreneur.

Böhm-Bawerk solves the problem by assuming a subsistence fund of given amount and trying out different wage rates until he finds a rate which brings the system into equilibrium. Here we shall make use of a

[7] In the arithmetical examples used by Böhm-Bawerk the rate of increase of output decreases from the start (see *Capital and Interest*, Vol. II, p. 356), but in his general formulation of the law he claims that the rate of increase begins to decrease only after a certain point (*op. cit.*, Vol. II, p. 84ff.).

diagrammatic exposition. Let us begin, as did Böhm-Bawerk, with the case of a single entrepreneur for whom the wage rate may at first be regarded as given. The entrepreneur has at his disposal a certain share in the subsistence fund; on the assumption that all entrepreneurs have the same share in the fund, the money value of his "capital" can be obtained by dividing the total value of the fund by the number of entrepreneurs.

In the case of the "even flow" period of production, which is assumed in Böhm-Bawerk's exposition, the services of the workers engaged by the entrepreneur are, on the *average*, removed from the moment at which they ripen into consumer goods by half the length of the absolute period of production – that is, by the full length of the average period of production. Let this average period of production be denoted by the Greek letter τ, to distinguish it from the absolute period of production t. The output of an average worker rises, as τ is being increased, first at an increasing, and then, from a certain point on, at a decreasing rate of increase. The curve $f(\tau)$ in Figure 2 represents this product of one worker as a function of τ. Let the wage rate, assumed to be given to the entrepreneur, be OL on the y-axis. From the point L we draw a system of interest curves. With simple interest, assumed by Böhm-Bawerk in his calculations, these curves take the form of straight lines. The distance of any point on such a line from the x-axis represents the capital originally invested – here equal to the wage rate – plus the interest accrued up to the corresponding point of time. The steeper lines, of course, represent higher rates of interest than those with a smaller slope. The entrepreneur who is endeavouring to maximize his rate of return will choose an average period of production which, in our case, is represented by OM. Here he reaches the highest interest line within his grasp, the line d_2.

The wage OL is paid by the entrepreneur in each unit period. Once the process of production is in full swing, the amount of capital per worker that is tied up in the process of production is represented by the area $OMCL$. The product emerging in each unit period is MP. Of this, MC is equal to the wage paid to the worker and PC remains as interest in the sense of an (absolute) return per unit period.

The point P is characterized by the fact that the slope of the productivity curve $f(\tau)$ (measured by the slope of the tangent to this curve at point P) and the slope of the interest line (here identical with that tangent) are equal. The slope of the interest line measures the internal return per unit period. The slope of the productivity curve measures the increase of output which occurs when the average period of production is slightly lengthened; in other words, it represents the marginal product that results from a lengthening of the average period of production. Under the assumption of an "even flow" period of production, such a lengthening implies that the amount of interest-bearing capital tied up in production is proportionally increased. For the individual entrepreneur this additional capital required per unit period is equal to the wage. The slope of the productivity curve represents the return on this additional capital, and the optimum average period of production is characterized by the condition that the "interest" (in the Böhm-Bawerkian sense) be equal to the marginal return on capital, or to put it differently, that the average internal return (the interest) yielded by the production process be equal to the marginal internal return obtained by the last lengthening of this process. The "interest", or the marginal and average returns discussed here are absolute amounts per unit period, not percentage rates. The *rate* of interest (the average internal rate of return as a percentage rate on capital per unit of time) is represented in Figure 2 by $(PC/LC)/OL$, that is, by the slope of the interest line LP divided by the wage rate OL, or by the total amount of interest PC which, in the case of the "even flow" period of production, is accruing continuously, divided by the amount of capital $LC \cdot OL$ tied up in the process. The same expression

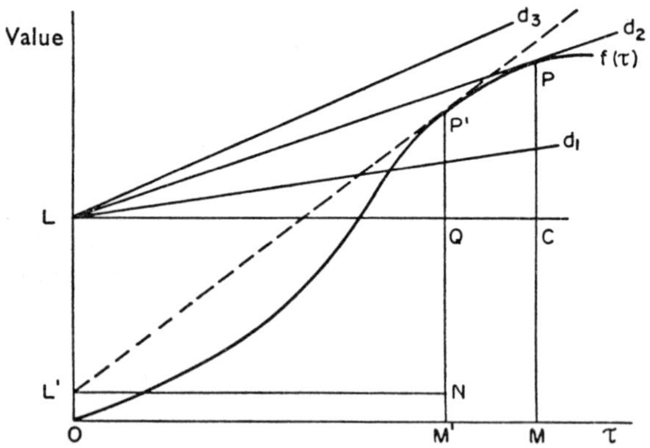

Fig. 2.

represents also the percentage rate of return on the additional capital which had to be applied to make possible the last increase in the average production period, and thereby the last increase in output. This latter percentage rate we shall call the marginal internal rate of return or the marginal product of capital (dp/dK). The maximization of the *average* rate of return on capital (Böhm-Bawerk's rate of interest) thus requires that this rate be equal to the *marginal* product of capital. The optimum period of production being determined, the entrepreneur will then engage as many workers as his capital permits.

We may also make use of Figure 2 in order to determine the equilibrium of the system as a whole. OL now represents the total sum of wages paid in each unit period by all entrepreneurs together, who are assumed to be working under completely identical conditions. The $f(\tau)$-curve represents the total product of all workers as a function of the average period of production. In the case of an "even flow" production process, the total amount of capital tied up in production at any given point of time is $OMCL$ for the optimum period of production. Two possibilities now arise. Firstly, at the given wage rate the subsistence fund may be insufficient to employ all the workers throughout the production period chosen. Then the wage rate will fall, and the average period of production will be shortened until all workers can be employed. (See Figure 2 which shows that if the wage bill per unit of time is reduced to OL', the optimum production period will be shortened to OM'.) Or, secondly, the wage rate may be too low, the production period too short, and the subsistence fund may not be fully absorbed. In this case entrepreneurs will compete for labour until a point is reached at which, as the result of the rise in wages and the extension of the period of production, the subsistence fund is absorbed.

The conditions for equilibrium are, therefore, as follows:

1. The product of a worker must equal his wage plus the amount of interest accruing during the average period of production.
2. The marginal product due to a lengthening of the average period of production must equal the interest earned per unit of time.
3. All workers must be employed and the subsistence fund must be equal to the total sum of wages paid out during the average period of production.

These three conditions, together with the productivity function $f(\tau)$

are sufficient to determine the four unknowns: the output, the wage rate, the interest rate, and the length of the period of production.[8]

Wicksell already emphasized that the second of these conditions cannot be replaced by the formula that the interest rate must be equal to the marginal product of the average period of production divided by the capital which makes the extension of the period possible[9]; in other words, we cannot say that in equilibrium the interest rate must be equal to the marginal product of capital. This formula is correct only with regard to the individual entrepreneur, for whom the wage rate is given. In considering the system as a whole, account must be taken of the fact that an increase in the capital stock (subsistence fund) will be partially absorbed by an increase in wages; the additional capital will not be absorbed exclusively by a lenthening of the production period.

Let us assume an increase in the capital stock which leads to a rise in wages and to a lengthening of the period of production. In Figure 2 the wage bill per unit period now is represented by OL instead of OL'. If we assume a small lengthening of the average period of production, then only an amount OL of capital is tied up by this change in the production period alone. We may say that the rate of interest is equal to the marginal product of the average period of production divided by that amount of capital which is absorbed solely by the lengthening of the process of production. However, the total amount of capital necessary for this lengthening of the production process is greater than OL, since the higher wage rate has to be paid not only for the time span added to the period of production, but throughout the entire period. To be more specific: the amount of capital tied up at any moment of time in an "even flow" process of production is represented by $OL'NM'$ in Figure 2 if the average period of production is OM' and the wage bill per unit period OL', and by $OLCM$ if the average period of production is OM and the wage bill OL. But only $M'MCQ$ has been absorbed at the higher wage rate by the lengthening of the period of production, while the remainder has been absorbed by the increase in wages. Hence it is obvious that the amount of capital could not constitute a correct index for the average length of

[8] See Mathematical Appendix, Section 1.

[9] Knut Wicksell, *Value, Capital and Rent*, trans. S. H. Frowein (New York, 1954), p. 136ff; cf. also Oskar Lange, 'The Place of Interest in the Theory of Production', *Review of Economic Studies*, **3** (1935–6) 183ff.

the production period, and that the interest rate is higher than the marginal product of capital.

We have arrived at this point without mentioning even once the famous higher valuation of present goods relative to future goods. It was possible to do this because we took the subsistence fund as given. This assumption implies that the overvaluation of present over future goods (Böhm-Bawerk's *agio* of present over future goods, expressed as a percentage rate), which for each owner of capital must "at the margin" be equal to the interest rate, is such that neither capital is used up nor saving takes place. If the marginal *agio* falls below the interest rate, saving will take place, wages will rise, the interest rate will fall, and the period of production will be lengthened until equilibrium is restored. In the new equilibrium the interest rate will once again reflect the *agio* of present over future goods "at the margin" for all suppliers of capital. It is here then, in determining the size of the subsistence fund, that there is the logical place in the analysis for the first two reasons for valuing present goods more highly than future goods.[10] We do not, however, intend to analyse here the reasons for saving. It is enough to point out that, according to Böhm-Bawerk, saving is unlikely to bring about the accumulation of so large a subsistence fund that the average period of production will be stretched beyond the point at which the output per worker ceases to rise. Therefore, the rate of interest will always be positive.

The foregoing exposition conveys the essence of Böhm-Bawerk's theory of interest. A few additional points should be mentioned which Böhm-Bawerk himself made in order to bring his theory closer to reality:

1. A demand for consumption loans will raise the interest rate above what it would otherwise be. Part of the subsistence fund will be split off for this purpose, so that the fund available for wage payments will be smaller. The period of production will be shorter, the wage rate lower, and the interest rate higher.

2. The same effect is ascribed by Böhm-Bawerk to the fact, hitherto disregarded, that the suppliers of the services of land also have to be paid out of the subsistence fund. However, he does not explain in detail how this effect comes about. In order to do so, it would be necessary to analyse

[10] The third reason, namely the superiority of present goods due to technical causes, has already been taken into account as it is the result of the greater productivity of more roundabout methods of production.

the determinants of the wage rate in relation to the price of land services.

3. Böhm-Bawerk further drops the assumption that all labour is homogeneous and that wage rates are the same in all kinds of employment. Since skilled labour receives higher wages than unskilled labour, taking account of skill differences has the same effect as assuming an increase in the quantity of unskilled labour: the rate of interest will be higher and the average (social) period of production for a given subsistence fund shorter.

4. Finally, Böhm-Bawerk abandons the assumption that all productivity curves have the same shape, i.e., that the relative increase in output resulting from an extension of the period of production is the same in all branches of activity. According to him this change in the assumptions does not affect his theory of interest. Its only consequence is that different industries will have different average periods of production. But for each industry the marginal product of the roundabout process will still be equal to the interest.

III. Critique

The critique of any theory can begin with three questions:

1. Are the premises sufficiently complete to make the theory realistic?
2. Are the premises acceptable?
3. Do the conclusions follow logically from the premises?

It is clear that Böhm-Bawerk had in mind a very simplified world. He theorizes in terms of only one original factor of production, and he neglects durable goods, the most important form of capital. He assumes identical productivity functions for all branches of industry, which amounts to assuming that only one kind of good is being produced. One has further to assume that this good is at the same time the unit of account, so that the productivity function which Böhm-Bawerk expresses in value terms is identical with the productivity function in physical units. If Böhm-Bawerk had in fact assumed different goods, he would not have been able simply to disregard the demand side. His problem would then have been to determine the relative prices of the goods. Even if the physical product of labour, as a function of time, increased in the same proportion in all industries, it could not do so in value terms. It is due exactly to this neglect of relative prices that Böhm-Bawerk's later introduction of differences in the value-productivity functions, of differences in wage rates, and of the services of land is so inadequate. But we should not blame Böhm-Bawerk for his simplified assumptions. It is, after all, the rule in the development of science that new theories are first established on the basis of greatly simplified premises, and that the successors of the originator fill in the gaps later. The real shortcomings of Böhm-Bawerk's theory are in some other premises which he adopts. Of these, we need to discuss only two: the concept of the period of production and the assumption of a subsistence fund of a given total value.

Knight[11] has repeatedly objected to the concept of the production period as used by Böhm-Bawerk, arguing that a production process has no determinable starting point. However far back into the past one were to trace the genesis of a product, one would never reach a stage of production at which only original factors of production are applied. Or, looking forward, all future consumption goods will be produced with the aid of already existing capital goods, never with original factors of production alone. Böhm-Bawerk might reply that he had never postulated a process of production without capital. At any given moment, he could say, a subsistence fund consisting of circulating capital is in existence, and current labour will be combined with this circulating capital. Even so, it must be admitted that at the very first stage of the process of production workers must have produced "raw materials" without the aid of capital goods, by the labour of their bare hands alone. It is evident that Knight's objection is really directed at Böhm-Bawerk's neglect of durable capital goods and the consequent lack of realism of his premises. This is a point we have already dealt with. Secondly, it has been objected[12] that some productive services never mature into consumption goods, since the output which they produce is transferred back to an earlier stage before it ever reaches the last stage of the production process. A case in point is

[11] See Chapter 8.

[12] See, for instance, Burchardt, 'Die Schemata des stationären Kreislaufs bei Böhm-Bawerk und Marx', *Weltwirtschaftliches Archiv*, **34** (1931) 525–564 and **35** (1932) 116–176. This and the foregoing point has been examined most exhaustively by W. Eucken in his 'Vom Hauptproblem der Kapitaltheorie', *Jahrbücher für Nationalökonomie und Statistik*, **145** (1937) 533–564, and in 'Der Wirtschaftsprozess als zeitlicher Hergang', *Jahrbücher für Nationalökonomie und Statistik*, **152** (1940) 113–152. Both papers have since been reprinted in the second edition of his *Kapitaltheoretische Untersuchungen* (Tübingen and Zürich, 1954).

wheat not baked into bread but used as seed from which another harvest of wheat is obtained. Of this harvest, a portion is, in turn, used as seed, and so on. Another example may be machine tools which are used for producing other machine tools, some of which in turn are used for making yet more machine tools. The most that can be said against this argument is that the fraction which, for this reason, never matures into consumption goods is so minute that it can be disregarded. It remains, nevertheless, true that there are such cases of productive inputs which never ripen out. A further difficulty arises as soon as durable goods are taken into account. It is really impossible to say how many units of the original inputs which went into the production of a durable good – as, for example, a house – mature during each unit period of its lifetime into consumption goods, i.e. into the service of the house. This is a point to which we shall have to return repeatedly.

Yet, even if we were willing to accept Böhm-Bawerk's simplified premises, we would still get into difficulties with the concept of the *average* period of production. In Figure 2 we measured the average period, τ, along the x-axis and output as a function of τ along the y-axis. The average production period is calculated, as was stressed earlier, as a weighted arithmetic average. This method of measuring the average period of production is justified by the fact that throughout his theory Böhm-Bawerk works with simple interest. It can easily be shown that his method of calculation rests on the assumption that productive inputs yield only simple interest. If a units of productive inputs are applied in the first, and another a units in the second stage of a production process having a total length of 2 unit periods (stages), and if the inputs yield only simple interest, then one may use the formula $a(1+2i)+a(1+i)= 2a(1+\tau i)$, involving the rate of interest i, to find the unknown average period of production τ. If we solve the equation for τ, we obtain an average production period of 1.5 unit periods. Böhm-Bawerk gets the same result from his formula $[(a\cdot 2)+(a\cdot 1)]/2a$. However, since the invested productive inputs will rise in value at compound interest, we must calculate the average production period on the basis of the compound interest formula. But once we do this, our equation will change to:

$$a(1+i)^2 + a(1+i) = 2a(1+i)^{\tau}$$

and if we solve this for τ, the resulting expression for the average production period will still contain the rate of interest:

$$\tau = \frac{\log(2 + 3i + i^2) - \log 2}{\log(1 + i)}.$$

Thus the length of the average production period can be seen to be dependent on the interest rate, if the average time distance between inputs and the appearance of a finished consumption good is calculated with the aid of the compound rather than the simple interest formula. But the interest rate itself is what we want to determine, and in Böhm-Bawerk's theory it is determined with the aid, among other things, of the function which relates output to the average production period.

The second weak point in the theory is the role assigned to the subsistence fund. It is treated by Böhm-Bawerk as having a given total value – given, as it were, out of the blue. The value of the fund is taken as a datum, just like the number of workers: One of the conditions for equilibrium, for instance, is that both the subsistence fund and labour are to be fully "employed".

Two objections can be raised against this manner of bringing the subsistence fund into the theory. In the first place, once we drop the assumption of a one-commodity economy, the subsistence fund must be expressed in value terms, as was indeed done by Böhm-Bawerk. The value of the fund, however, cannot be regarded as a datum, since it can be obtained only by discounting the flow of future returns; consequently it is a function of both the rate of interest and the length of the period of production. Thus the value of the subsistence fund is one of the unknowns, and Böhm-Bawerk's system lacks the additional equation which is necessary to determine it.[13]

The second objection to Böhm-Bawerk's way of utilizing the subsistence fund is connected with its time structure. He apparently assumes that, from the beginning, the existing fund possesses the time structure required for the period of production that emerges in equilibrium, an implicit assumption that remains hidden if a definite and arbitrary value of the subsistence fund is taken as the point of departure for the argument. Once this hidden assumption has been brought to light, it becomes evident that the "datum", subsistence fund, is not at all of the same nature as the

[13] See Mathematical Appendix, Section 1.

datum labour. The subsistence fund could be treated in the same manner as labour only if it were brought into the argument as a collection of real capital goods which, in the case of durable goods, are capable of yielding certain services, just as labour yields services, or, in the case of raw materials, can be applied to a variety of purposes. In short, there is no justification for introducing into the system as a datum a value of the subsistence fund which is somehow determined externally, nor is there justification in attributing to the subsistence fund in advance that time structure which it must have to satisfy the requirements of the equilibrium situation that is itself to be determined with the help of the fund. Hence Böhm-Bawerk's theory shows grave deficiencies. His system contains an insufficient number of equations and therefore cannot determine all of the unknowns.

CHAPTER 2

KNUT WICKSELL

Böhm-Bawerk's theory would have been in need of improvement in many respects even if no objections of a logical nature had to be raised against it. In the first place, it had to be brought closer to reality by dropping the restrictive assumptions that only one kind of good is being produced and that only one factor of production is being used. This expansion of the theory was contributed by Wicksell in his first work dealing with the problem of capital.[1] However, Wicksell held on to the assumption that only working capital is used in the production process. He also continued to calculate in terms of simple interest and to employ the concept of the average period of production. Let us now consider Wicksell's first contribution to the theory of interest.

I. Wicksell's Contribution in "Value, Capital and Rent"

Wicksell, too, begins his treatment of the problem by assuming first that only one commodity is being produced; only at a later stage of the analysis does he introduce several commodities. We shall follow the same procedure here. The premises which he adopts are those of Böhm-Bawerk. However, we have to replace the second premise listed above[2] by the following assumptions:

1. Labour and land are the only productive factors. All labour is homogeneous, and land has everywhere the same quality.
2. All workers are provided with the same amount of land.
3. The greater the amount of land with which a worker is equipped, the larger will be his product. But, at least after a certain point, his product will increase at a decreasing rate. This assumption is, of course, nothing other than the law of diminishing marginal returns.

[1] Knut Wicksell, *Value, Capital and Rent*, trans. S. H. Frowein (New York, 1954).
[2] See p. 12 *supra*.

4. Every input of labour services is accompanied by a corresponding input of land services. Hence every time wages are paid, a corresponding rent is also paid.

5. Wicksell defines the concept of land so as to include "rent-goods", that is, durable goods "which last 50, 100 or more years"[3], such as "streets, railways, buildings, etc".[4] They are included in the definition because the original cost of such goods has no influence on, for instance, the rent payable for a building or the freight charges of a railroad. Furthermore, the yield in the very distant future of such goods has practically no influence on their present capital value or profitability. Therefore they can be treated in the same way as land.

Once again we begin with the individual entrepreneur equipped with a share in the subsistence fund. For him the wage and the land rent are given. His problem is how much land to combine with each worker, and how long an average period of production to choose. Let us first assume that he has already solved the problem of combining labour with land. Then his only remaining problem is that of choosing the average period of production of the services rendered by these two productive factors. From Böhm-Bawerk's theory we know that the average internal return per unit of time (his "original" interest) will reach a maximum when it is equal to the marginal product due to a lengthening of the average period of production, or when the average rate of return on capital (the *rate* of interest) is equal to the marginal rate of return or the marginal product of capital. This result is valid here also. However, it is to be remembered that the capital investment per worker no longer consists only of the wage but is made up of the wage plus the rent for the land with which the worker is equipped. If we denote the wage by w, the rent per unit of land by r, and the amount of land combined with each unit of labour by h, the investment to be made per worker will be $w+rh$ instead of only w as with Böhm-Bawerk.

Let us now make the contrary assumption that it is the average period of production which is given, and that the entrepreneur has to decide how many units of land he wants to combine with one unit of labour. A line of argument analogous to the above leads to the conclusion that the entrepreneur will proceed to the point at which the rate of return earned

[3] Wicksell, *Value, Capital and Rent*, p. 118.
[4] Wicksell, *Value, Capital and Rent*, p. 119.

on the last unit of capital invested in land services becomes equal to the average rate of return on the total investment per worker. This conclusion is *not* identical with the one usually drawn, namely, that he will proceed to the point where the marginal product of land becomes equal to the rent of the last unit of land employed. This latter point lies beyond the one given by Wicksell's solution. If the entrepreneur were to go as far as that, he would indeed increase his total absolute net income, but the *rate* of return per unit of capital would diminish as soon as he had passed the point indicated by Wicksell. Putting this in another way, he would increase total net income even more if he stopped at Wicksell's point and used his remaining capital not for the purpose of combining more land with each unit of labour, but rather to engage additional labour and land in the Wicksellian optimum combination. The statement, that the entrepreneur will continue to combine land with each unit of labour until the (marginal) rate of return on the last unit of capital invested in land services is equal to the average rate of return on the total capital invested per worker, implies that the rent paid for a unit of land is equal to the marginal product of land discounted at the internal rate of return.

Thus we reach the conclusion that the entrepreneur will maximize his internal rate of return (the "original" rate of interest) if he selects a period of production such that this rate is equal to the marginal rate of return on the capital invested in slightly lengthening the average period of production; and if, in addition, he combines land with a worker in such a way that the marginal rate of return yielded by the last unit of capital invested in land services is equal to the average rate of return on the total capital invested per worker. The optimum combination of labour and land will then be repeated as often as the constraints of the optimum period of production and the given amount of capital at the entrepreneur's disposal will allow.

Considering the economy as a whole, neither wage nor rent are given. But, just as in Böhm-Bawerk's theory, if, at an arbitrarily assumed wage and rent, some land or labour cannot find employment, competition will cause rent and wage to fall and the average period of production to shorten until all land and all labour are fully employed. The reverse will happen if wage and rent are so low that not all of the subsistence fund is absorbed. We can characterize the equilibrium conditions of the system more precisely by a set of equations which determine the six unknowns:

the output, the wage rate, the rent, the interest rate, the amount of land to be combined with each unit of labour and the average period of production.

1. First of all, we have the productivity function which states that the output of a worker depends on the length of the average period of production and on the amount of land with which he is equipped.

2. The value of the product obtained from each worker equipped with land must be equal to the capital-sum invested in that combination of labour and land services plus the interest accrued during the average production period.

3. The marginal product of the average period of production must be equal to the interest per unit of time.

4. The rent must be equal to the discounted marginal product of land.

5. The amount of land used per unit of labour must be equal to the proportion of available land to available labour, since all land and all labour has to be employed in equilibrium and since all entrepreneurs are subject to exactly the same conditions of production.

6. The whole of the subsistence fund has to be absorbed during the average period of production by payment of wages and rents.

This exposition is basically a verbal statement of Wicksell's mathematical solution of the problem.[5] The reader may perhaps be struck by the fact that marginal analysis is used in the cases of land and of the period of production, but apparently not in the case of labour. But in equilibrium it is, of course, also true that the wage rate must be equal to the discounted marginal product of labour. This would have been evident at once if we had initially asked how much labour, how much land, and which average period of production would be used by an entrepreneur who had at his disposal a given share in the subsistence fund. Obviously, the answer to this question is that he would tend to proceed to a point where, in the first place, the marginal product of land, discounted by the internal rate of return, would equal the rent (which for any single entrepreneur is given), where, in the second place, the marginal product of labour, also discounted by the internal rate of return, would equal the given wage rate, and where, finally, the marginal internal rate of return on capital would equal the average internal rate of return. The require-

[5] See Mathematical Appendix, Section 2.

ment that the wage rate be equal to the discounted marginal product of labour then replaces the second of the conditions set forth earlier.

Let us now introduce a second commodity P_2 and at the same time assume that the first commodity P_1 serves as the unit of account. The productivity function of the second commodity is different from that of the first; and the output of a worker who, equipped with land, produces P_2 has to be expressed in value terms. The price of commodity P_2 is thus a new unknown in the problem. Furthermore, the number of unknowns increases because, apart from interest rate, wage and rent which must be identical for both branches of production, there has to be determined for *each of the two* industries individually: the amount of land per unit of labour, the average period of production, the output, and the total amount of labour, land and capital. But the determination of these unknowns does not present any difficulties. To begin with, the above 6 equations can be set up for each of the two industries. Then we add the constraint that the amount of land, labour and capital used in both lines of production together must be equal to the total amount of these three agents available – whereby the capital in the two industries must be expressed in terms of a common denominator. Such a common denominator presupposes the knowledge of the price of P_2. Thus the really new problem is the determination of the exchange relation between the two commodities. For this purpose we have to introduce the condition that in equilibrium the demand for P_2 must be equal to the supply of P_2.[6] No basically new problems will arise if the number of commodities is increased to more than two.[7]

II. Critique

Wicksell's first contribution to the theory of interest, as compared to the Böhm-Bawerk model, considerably increased the number of variables taken into account. He remedied some of Böhm-Bawerk's sins of omission by developing a general equilibrium system – in the style of Walras – containing more than one factor of production and more than one commodity, and, in contrast to Walras, he took into account the time factor.

[6] Of course, demand and supply must be in equilibrium for P_1 also. However, this condition need not be separately mentioned as it follows automatically from the others.
[7] See Mathematical Appendix, Section 2.

It is also to Wicksell's credit that his theory cannot be charged with implying the existence of workers who work without equipment of any kind, for by including "rent-goods" in his concept of land he has made it possible for us (whether or not he so intended) to think of labour even at the very first stage of production as being equipped with capital goods. Yet, he still remains exposed to the two main objections which had to be raised against Böhm-Bawerk.

In the first place, Wicksell here still calculates with simple interest; he is thus in the position of equating the average length of an "even flow" period of production with one-half of the absolute period of production. If compound interest were used in the calculation, this would not be possible, as we already know and as Wicksell himself admits later on. Many a reader might wish to raise a further objection against Wicksell's use of the average period of production. If two factors of production are used simultaneously, the average period of production can obviously be calculated only if we know the values of these two factors, since otherwise we would have no common expression for both. However, as the average period of production (together with other data) is itself used to determine these values, we seem to be turning in a circle – more precisely, to be lacking one equation. But at least in the case of an "even flow" process of production, assumed in Wicksell's theory, this would not be a valid objection. If, for instance, a combination of two units of labour and five units of land services is used, the unit of labour having a value of 1 and that of land services a value of 2, then in the case of an "even flow" production process the average period of production will be calculated from the formula:

$$\tau = \frac{12 + (2 \times 12) + \cdots + (t \times 12)}{12t} = \tfrac{1}{2}t + \tfrac{1}{2}.$$

We can again disregard the half-unit of time if we take the time unit small enough. Thus τ will be $\frac{1}{2}t$, whatever the level of wages and rent; and since t – the absolute period of production – is an altogether unambiguous concept in the present context, Wicksell is entitled to work with the notion of an average period of production. But as soon as the two inputs are applied in different ratios at different stages of the production process, as is always the case in the real world, the average calculated according to Böhm-Bawerk's method will no longer be equal to exactly one-half of the absolute period of production; it will depend on the relative values of the two factors. Then it is no longer possible to apply the concept of the average period of production in the theory of interest.

The objections which had to be raised against Böhm-Bawerk's use of the subsistence fund also remain. Wicksell, too, assumes the value of this fund to be a given magnitude, although it can in fact be calculated only once the interest rate is known. The composition of the fund or its time structure, in Wicksell's theory as well as in Böhm-Bawerk's, has *a priori* that form which will ultimately be required by the as yet undetermined equilibrium.

III. Wicksell's Contribution in "Lectures on Political Economy"

If Wicksell's exposition of his interest theory in the *Lectures on Political Economy* is compared with his earlier publications, it will be seen that during his work on the problem of capital he had become more and more aware of the deficiencies in Böhm-Bawerk's theory. It is no exaggeration to say that he perceived them all, although he was not able to overcome them all.

When he wrote his 'Lectures' Wicksell had realized that the average period of production becomes a function of the interest rate once the formula for compound interest is used to calculate the average time distance between the inputs and the final product.[8] It is undoubtedly due to this realization that he based his theory on a case in which the absolute period of production can be used: a production process in which all productive inputs are made simultaneously and the consumption goods become available at the same point of time. As an example he takes wine which is stored at one point of time and ready for consumption at a later point. Wicksell constructs an ingenious model which allows him to concentrate on what seems to him important in the theory of capital and interest without having to determine relative prices. He imagines an economy which has only one industry – that of cultivating vineyards and storing the wine after the harvest. It is assumed that the production of the wine requires no capital; the economy's capital thus consists exclusively of stored wine. Further, the economic process is completely continuous:

[8] Wicksell, *Lectures on Political Economy*, trans. E. Classen (2 vols; London, 1934–1936), Vol. 1: *General Theory*, p. 184.

every year wine is planted, harvested, and allowed to mature so that at any point of time the society's capital consists of several vintages, i.e., of wines which had been stored in different years. The prices of the different vintages are determined in the world market and increase with the age of the wine. From the individual producer's point of view the wage rate is fixed, and wage payments are the only kind of productive expenditure incurred since the land is assumed to be a free good. Consequently, the only problem which confronts the producer is that of determining the optimum length of storage. We know already the answer to this problem: the period which maximizes his average rate of return on capital per unit of time (the rate of interest) is determined by the condition that this rate of return must be equal to the marginal rate of return on that amount of capital which is necessary to prolong the storage of the wine by one unit period. As long as this marginal rate of return is greater than the average rate, any lengthening of the period must pull up the average rate of return until the two rates are equal. However, since we are now calculating at compound interest, the amount of capital tied up by a lengthening of the storage period will no longer be the wage bill alone but, rather, that sum plus compound interest, since the interest accrual becomes here – in contrast to the simple interest case – part of interest bearing capital. The producer will now proceed up to the point at which the increment in the value of output due to the last lengthening of the storage period divided by the total value of output is equal to the rate of interest. This solution is illustrated by Figure 3, which differs from Figure 2 only in that it is based on compound interest and shows the absolute period of production on the x-axis. In this new diagram the curve $W(t)$ shows the value of the wine produced by one worker. The curve begins below the point V which represents the cost of the grape juice and thus the wage rate; the value of grape juice, determined on the world market, is less than its cost. Starting from V we draw a system of compound interest curves d_1, d_2, d_3, of which the higher curves reflect higher rates of interest than the lower ones. Among these interest curves there is one, d_2, which is tangential to the $W(t)$–curve at L. The optimum period of storage is given by OM; with this storage time the rate of return is at a maximum because d_2 is the highest of the interest curves which can be reached by the $W(t)$–curve. For any point on curve d_2 the rate of interest is equal to the absolute rate of increase of the curve at that point (as measured by the slope of

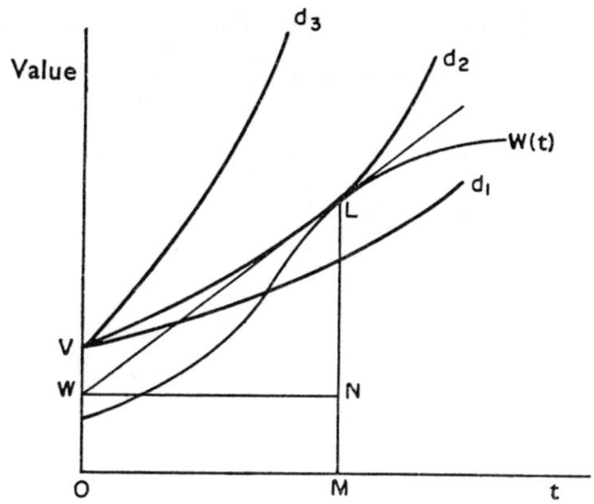

Fig. 3.

the tangent at that point) divided by the ordinate of the point. Thus at the point L the rate of interest is equal to $(LN/WN)/ML$. This expression also represents the marginal value product of the period of production divided by the total value product, or the marginal product of capital. Equality between the interest rate (average internal rate of return) and the marginal product of capital (marginal internal rate of return) is thus the condition for the optimum period of production.

The producer, who in our illustration chooses the storage period OM, will, if conditions do not change, continue to do so in the next and later years. He has at his disposal a certain capital, consisting of wines of different ages, which must suffice to cover the wages of workers producing grape juice for the period OM – that is to say, until this year's harvest of grape juice can be sold in the form of matured wine. Given the wage rate and the optimum period of production, he can with this capital engage a certain number of workers. The same applies to all other entrepreneurs. If the *aggregate capital* is enough to keep all workers employed at the given rate of wages, we have determined the optimum period of production, the interest rate, the wage rate and the value of the product for the equilibrium of the system as a whole. It must, however, again be stressed that the total capital necessary to increase output is larger than that capital tied up in the extension of the storage period since a certain amount of the additional capital will be absorbed by wage increases.

Wicksell goes one step further by assuming that two kinds of productive inputs are used: services of labour and of land. One kind is applied at the start of production, and the other at a later date not technologically fixed. The output then depends on the amounts of these two productive inputs and on the length of their investment periods. In order to maximize the rate of return on his capital, the individual entrepreneur has to solve the problem of deciding how much of the two inputs he will apply and what investment period to give each of them. His objective is attained if the wage rate is equal to the marginal product of labour discounted at the internal rate of return and the rent equal to the marginal product of land, likewise discounted; if, in addition, the average rate of return on capital invested per worker is equal to the increment in his product due to the lengthening of the investment period divided by his total product, and if the analogous condition is fulfilled with regard to land. It may happen, however, that the amount of capital is not sufficient to satisfy these conditions or, contrariwise, that if they are satisfied part of the capital remains unemployed. But competition will finally bring about full employment of labour and land while the whole of the capital is being absorbed by payments to the two productive inputs and the interest accumulated during their investment periods. The four marginal conditions and the constraints requiring full employment of all workers and all land and full absorption of the subsistence fund, together with the productivity function, suffice for the determination of wage rate, rent, investment period for the services of both labour and land, interest rate and output.[9]

IV. Critique

In his later work Wicksell took an important step forward. When he recognized that the average period of production, if calculated at compound interest, depends itself upon the rate of interest, he finally abandoned this concept and began to work in terms of the investment periods of individual inputs. This is particularly evident in the case just discussed in which two different factors of production are used at different dates, for here he is working in terms of t_1 and t_2, that is to say, with the absolute investment periods of each of the productive factors. However,

[9] See Mathematical Appendix, Section 3.

Wicksell sacrificed the concept of the average period of production very unwillingly since he realized that thereby the theory lost its simplicity. When there are only two factors of production, it is still relatively easy to work with the absolute investment periods. In reality, of course, a great variety of factors are usually applied during the period of production, with a great variety of investment periods, of which some are technologically fixed and others not. Under these conditions the determination of the interest rate becomes exceedingly complicated, and there can be no doubt that it would be greatly simplified if it were possible to work with an average period. According to Wicksell we can do this without gross error only when the investment periods of the productive inputs are so short that the results of calculating with simple and compound interest do not greatly differ.[10]

Wicksell, then, gave up using the average period of production in the cases he analysed and utilized instead the individual investment periods of productive inputs. In this way he overcame one of the objections to which his predecessor, Böhm-Bawerk, had laid himself open. He could not, however, overcome the difficulty connected with the subsistence fund, although he had perceived it clearly. In the discussion of the wine economy with its two different productive inputs, we find the following sentence concerning the subsistence-fund equation needed to determine the unknowns:" ...a further equation is required, which may be obtained either by supposing t or τ (t_1 and t_2 in our notation) ... to be given, or else by some supposition as to the money value of the social capital ...".[11] If t_1 and t_2 are known, it is of course possible to calculate the value of the subsistence fund. But the investment periods are among the unknowns of the problem; hence we cannot take them as data. One cannot escape the dilemma by assuming, instead, that the value of the fund be given, since this value, too, is an unknown. Accordingly, Wicksell, like Böhm-Bawerk, still lacks one equation.

The following passage shows still more clearly his doubt as to whether he is justified in assuming *a priori* a subsistence fund of the very value and time composition required by the equilibrium situation:

"In equilibrium, the capital employed in production has already assumed a certain technical dimension and composition, as well as a certain

[10] Wicksell, *Lectures on Political Economy*, Vol. 1, p. 183f.
[11] Wicksell, *Lectures on Political Economy*, Vol. 1, p. 182.

exchange value (expressed in terms of one of the commodities). It can now be asserted that, so long as capital of this magnitude and composition, or even of this exchange value, is maintained and utilized from year to year, equilibrium cannot be disturbed if, from the beginning, the other conditions of stability are fulfilled. But it would certainly be meaningless – if not altogether inconceivable – to maintain that the amount of capital is already fixed *before* equilibrium between production and consumption has been achieved. Whether expressed in terms of one or the other, a change in the relative exchange value of two commodities would give rise to a change in the value of capital, unless its component parts simultaneously underwent a more or less considerable change. But even if we conceive capital genetically, as being a certain quantity of labour and land accumulated in different years, a change in the value of commodities would also alter the conditions of their production and thus necessitate a larger or smaller change in the composition of capital."[12]

What Wicksell, and before him Böhm-Bawerk, accomplished amounts to a demonstration of the *conditions* for equilibrium, but they did not completely succeed in determining this equilibrium.

Nevertheless, Wicksell made an important improvement in Böhm-Bawerk's theory when he started to calculate at compound interest and gave up the concept of the average period of production in favour of the investment periods of individual productive inputs. Yet, he still left durable production goods out of account, and even he could not overcome the difficulties posed by the subsistence fund. It was left to Åkerman to incorporate long-lived capital goods into the theory, and it was Hayek who finally drew the necessary conclusions from the recognition that the value of the subsistence fund cannot simply be taken as a datum.

Let us now turn to Åkerman's theory.

[12] Wicksell, *Lectures on Political Economy*, Vol. 1, p. 202.

CHAPTER 3

GUSTAF ÅKERMAN

Åkerman took a long step forward in the development of that branch of capital and interest theory with which we are here concerned by expounding his own theory in terms of durable goods, the most important form of capital goods. But since his book[1], which consists mainly of numerical calculations, is one of the most laborious in economic literature, it is no wonder that his contribution has attracted little attention and exerted hardly any influence. It is not easy to give an adequate account of the contents of a book of this character, but I do hope that the following treatment of Åkerman's work will make his method and conclusions understandable.

I. The Determination of the Length of Life of Durable Goods

A durable good can be made more or less durable. A longer "life" involves higher costs of construction but not necessarily a longer period of construction. Åkerman, in fact, bases his calculations on the assumption that the period of construction is one year, regardless of the durability of the capital good. If its length of life is to be increased, more labour must be applied in its construction, and the additional labour necessary to increase the length of life by another year becomes progressively more – at least from a certain point onward. Åkerman denotes by i_1 the amount of labour necessary to produce a machine which has a useful life of one year (M-1-capital). The notations i_2, i_3, etc., denote the amount of labour necessary to extend the length of life of the capital good by a second and third year, and so on. The corresponding costs are obtained by multiplying these expressions by the wage rate. If we assume, with Åkerman, that the wage rate w is equal to 1, then i_1, i_2, i_3, ... will directly represent the

[1] G. Åkerman, *Realkapital und Kapitalzins,* Nos. 1 and 2 (Stockholm, 1923–4).

marginal cost of increasing the length of life. The total cost Åkerman denotes by iw, which under the same assumption reduces to i. His calculations are based throughout on the figures listed in Table 1, which show the additional labour necessary to prolong the useful life of the capital good by one year at a time.

TABLE I

Length of Life	Additional labour required $i_1 \ldots i_n$
1	$i_1 = 1$
2	$i_2 = 0.667$
3	$i_3 = 0.556$
4	$i_4 = 0.513$
5	$i_5 = 0.500$
6	$i_6 = 0.513$
7	$i_7 = 0.556$
8	$i_8 = 0.667$
⋮	⋮
n	$i_n = \ldots\ldots$

The value m of the services rendered annually by the machine remains the same from year to year. This value is equal to the number of service units which the machine provides during the year multiplied by the value of the unit of service. But how is the quantity of services to be measured? Åkerman measures it with the aid of the amount of labour entering into the construction of M-1-capital, that is to say by i_1. The unit value of the services is denoted by b so that $i_1 b = m$ equals the total value of the annual services.

The problem now is to find the most profitable length of life for the machine, given:

(a) The technical conditions for increasing the length of life, as expressed in the series $i_1 \ldots i_n$.

(b) The wage rate w; the combination of (a) and (b) yields the cost function with respect to the length of life.

(c) The value of the annual services rendered by the machine ($m = i_1 b$).

If we assume for the moment that the length of life is given, we can calculate the internal rate of return from the value of the services and the cost of the machine. If, for instance, the machine lasts two years, we can calculate the internal rate of return from the formula:

$$iw = \frac{i_1 b}{1 + z} + \frac{i_1 b}{(1 + z)^2}$$

which sets the total cost equal to the present value of the services discounted with z, the internal rate of return.

Åkerman now puts $(1+z)=x$ and writes, after transforming the equation:

$$\frac{i_1 b}{iw}(x + 1) = x^2$$

or, more generally:

$$\frac{i_1 b}{iw}(x^{n-1} + \cdots + x^2 + x + 1) = x^n .$$

This latter equation he calls the equation of profitability.

With the aid of this formula we can calculate the internal rate of return for all possible lengths of life of the machine and can then choose the length of life which yields the highest rate of return.

From Åkerman's specific calculations we can construct Table II, in which i_1 is taken to be 3.66; i_2, i_3 etc., can then be found with the help of Table I. The total costs are entered in the second column. For M-3-capital, for instance, these are equal to $(i_1+i_2+i_3)\,w$. Åkerman puts the value of $m=i_1 b$ at 3.356.

In this arithmetical example the optimum length of life is four or five years. In general, if we know the cost function with respect to the length of life and also the value of the service provided by the capital good, we can calculate the optimum length of life with the aid of the profitability equation.

The optimum length of life is characterized by the fact that the value of the machine's services in the last year, discounted at the average rate of return, is equal to the cost of extending the length of life by that last year. (In Table II the cost of increasing the length of life from four to five years is 1.83, which is equal to $3.356/(1.129)^5$.) This result can easily be derived algebraically.[2] But as it is our object here to illustrate Åkerman's approach, we have followed his more laborious route.

[2] See Mathematical Appendix, Section 4.

TABLE II

Lifetime (Years)	Costs iw ($w = 1$)	Present value of annual services whose value $m = i_1 b = 3.356$	Internal rate of return z, obtained by setting col. 2 = col. 3 (per cent)
1	3.66	$\frac{3.356}{z+1}$	negative
2	6.10	$\frac{3.356}{z+1} + \frac{3.356}{(z+1)^2}$	6.8
3	8.13	$\frac{3.356}{z+1} + \cdots + \frac{3.356}{(z+1)^3}$	11.5
4	10.01	$\frac{3.356}{z+1} + \cdots + \frac{3.356}{(z+1)^4}$	12.9
5	11.84	$\frac{3.356}{z+1} + \cdots + \frac{3.356}{(z+1)^5}$	12.9
6	13.72	$\frac{3.356}{z+1} + \cdots + \frac{3.356}{(z+1)^6}$	12.0
⋮	⋮		⋮
t	$(i_1 + i_2 + \cdots + i_t)w$	$\frac{3.356}{z+1} + \cdots + \frac{3.356}{(z+1)^t}$	⋮

Åkerman's solution of the problem of the optimum lifetime of a durable good can be presented in a diagram, although he himself has not done this. In Figure 4 let us measure the length of life t on the x-axis, and the total value of the services provided by the machine (the revenue curve) as well as the total cost on the y-axis. The total revenue curve would be a straight line, if future revenues were not discounted, since each additional year of life contributes the same amount of revenue to the total. If, however, we discount the total revenue, as we must, then the revenue curve will increase at a decreasing rate. We can cover the quadrant with a system of such revenue curves, each based on a different rate of interest; the lower the curve, the higher the rate of interest used. The curves R_1, R_2, and R_3 are curves of this kind showing the present value of the total revenue at different rates of interest. The slope of each curve at any given point measures the present value of the marginal revenue resulting from a small increase in the length of life – this marginal revenue being discounted at the rate of interest on which that curve is based. *TC* is the total cost curve which, following Åkerman's assumptions, grows first at a decreasing, but after a certain point at an increasing rate. The highest rate of return is reached at the point where the total cost curve is tangential to a total revenue curve; this is the point P_0 which corresponds to an optimum length of life *OM*. The present value of the total revenue is also equal to the total cost at the points P_1 and P_2, but the length of life corresponding to these points will not be chosen because the curves R_1 and R_2 are based on lower rates of interest than the curve R_3. With the lengths of life corresponding to points P_1 or P_2, the internal rate of return would thus be lower than with a length of life of *OM*. Clearly, at P_0 the conditions are satisfied that, firstly, the present value of the revenue be equal to the cost and, secondly, that the present value of the services of the last "year" (measured by the slope of the revenue curve at P_0) be equal to the cost of this last "year" (measured by the slope of the total cost curve, which is equal at this point of tangency to the slope of the revenue curve).

In the determination of the optimum length of life we have until now assumed that both the value of the services provided by the machine and

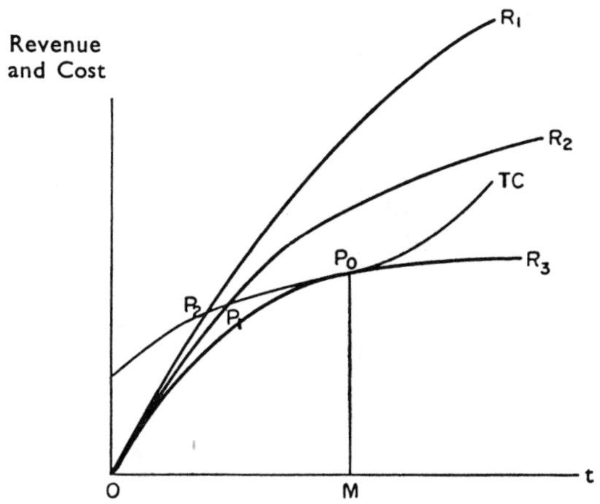

Fig. 4.

the function relating the cost of the machine to its length of life are given. The cost function is determined by the technical conditions of machine production and the wage rate – Åkerman's only cost factor – which is set at unity.

We may now group these factors somewhat differently. Our data now are (a) the technical conditions for extending the length of life of the machine, and (b) the relation between the value of a unit of machine services and the wage rate – that is, the ratio b/w. As soon as this ratio changes, the optimum length of life also changes. It is important to be clear about this interdependence, for otherwise the process by which Åkerman obtains an equilibrium for the system as a whole cannot be understood.

In order to show the dependence of the optimum length of life of a machine on the ratio b/w, Åkerman calculates what the ratio would be if the length of life were given and the internal rate of return were at its maximum. We know that under these conditions the present value of the services of the last year of the machine must be equal to the cost of "producing" this last year. We also know the profitability formula. With the aid of these two equations Åkerman obtains the result – which may at first seem surprising – that the length of life will be the *shorter* and the rate of return the higher, the *larger* the ratio b/w is.

Åkerman's method may be made clear with the help of an example. Suppose the length of life of a machine is two years. Our first equation, then, is:

$$i_2 w x^2 = i_1 b \tag{1}$$

which states that the additional cost $i_2 w$ necessary to prolong the life by a second (and last) year plus the interest accruing on this cost must be equal to the value $(i_1 b)$ of the services provided by the machine. The equation can be transformed to:

$$\frac{b}{w} = \frac{i_2}{i_1} x^2 \tag{1a}$$

Further, we have the general profitability equation:

$$x^2 = \frac{i_1 b}{i w}(x + 1) \tag{2}$$

From (1) and (2) we obtain:

$$x + 1 = \frac{i}{i_2} \tag{3}$$

From (3) we can calculate the rate of return, and from (1a) we then obtain the desired ratio b/w. The same method can be applied to any length of life of the machine, and these calculations show in fact that the larger the ratio b/w, the shorter is the length of life and the higher the rate of return.

This result can again be illustrated graphically. In Figure 5, two systems of cumulative discounted revenue curves analogous to those in Figure 4 are drawn. System I is based on a unit value b_1 for the services of the machine, and system II on a higher unit value b_2. The two curves of system II (II_1 and II_2) are calculated at the same rates of interest as the corresponding curves of system I (I_1 and I_2); e.g., curve II_2 implies the same interest rate as curve I_2. *TC* is the total cost curve. Let us now assume that b increases from b_1 to b_2, so that the ratio b/w becomes larger. We find that the optimum length of life shrinks from Ot_1 to Ot_2. The diagram also shows that the rate of return has been increased: curve II_2, to which the total cost curve is now tangent, is based on a higher rate of return than the old curve I_1.[3]

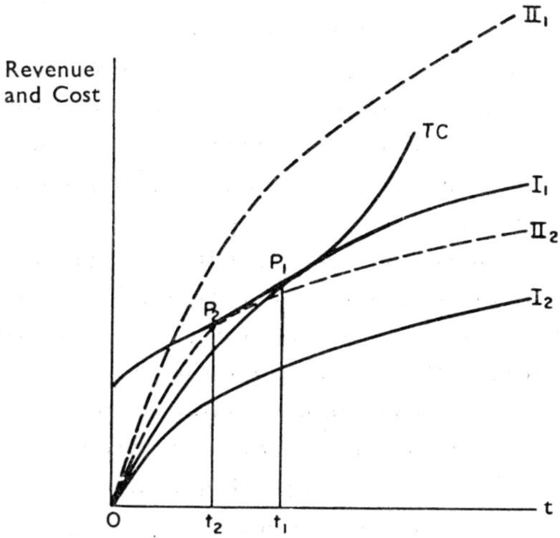

Fig. 5.

[3] See Mathematical Appendix, Section 4.

II. The General Equilibrium Analysis

We have determined the optimum length of life of a machine, assuming that the value of its services, the technical conditions for extending its life, and the wage rate were given. But in the system as a whole the wage rate and the value of the services provided by machines are not given; they have to be determined in a general equilibrium analysis. Åkerman carries out such an analysis arithmetically and offers his results – like Böhm-Bawerk – in tabular form.

Åkerman proceeds from the following assumptions and data:

1. The technical conditions for extending the length of life of the machine are those reflected in the *i*-series of Table I. These conditions can be expressed by saying that the amount of labour necessary to prolong the life is a function of the length of life n, or $f(n)$. The symbol i represents the total number of workers occupied in the machine industry. If only M-1-capital is being produced, $i = i_1$, i.e., all workers are engaged in producing machines with a length of life of one year. According to Table I, $i_2 = 0.667\ i_1$ additional workers are needed to prolong the lifetime of machines by a second year. If, therefore, M-2-capital is being produced by the i workers employed in the machine industry, i_1 workers will be engaged in producing, as it were, the first year of the lifetime of the machines, and i_2 in producing the second year. How large i_1 (and $i_2, i_3 \ldots$) will be in the system as a whole can be calculated with the aid of the figures in Table I only after i and the length of life of the machines have been determined by the system of equations giving the equilibrium solutions for all variables.

2. Once the machines have been built they co-operate with labour in the production of consumer goods. It is assumed that only one kind of consumer good is being produced which becomes available *at once* when the machine is set in operation. Åkerman thus disregards the problem of circulating capital in the production of consumer goods. Hence the output of such goods is a function of two factors only, vis. the services provided by the machines and the labour co-operating with machines; so $p = f(r, c)$, where p represents the annual output of consumption goods, r the quantity of machine services, and c the number of workers engaged in the production of consumer goods. We may recall that the annual total of services of a machine is measured by the amount of work necessary to

produce M-1-capital. If all workers engaged in the machine industry produce M-1-capital ($i = i_1$), the services r of the existing machines are also i_1. Suppose, however, the machines represent M-n-capital. Since in a stationary state the age-distribution of the machines is perfectly even, $1/n$ of the existing machines have to be replaced every year. These replacements render i_1 of services per year. The total of services of *all existing* machines, r, is therefore ni_1. According to Åkerman, the production function $p = f(r, c)$ is linear and homogeneous. This means that if r and c increase by a certain percentage, output will increase at the same percentage.

3. It is assumed that M-capital is constructed in one year – regardless of the length of life of the machine – while, as already stated, the production of consumer goods does not take up any time.

4. The given amount of capital (K) is invested entirely in machines.

5. The given number of workers (A) is divided into two parts, one producing machines and the other consumer goods. The number of workers employed in the machine industry, as we already know, is denoted by i, and the number in the consumer goods industry by c.

According to Åkerman it is possible to calculate from these data the seven unknowns, which are:

1. The wage rate, w.
2. The value of a unit of machine services, b.
3. The optimum length of life of the machines, n.
4. The rate of interest or internal rate of return, which we shall again designate by z. Åkerman himself uses x for the expression $(1+z)$.
5. The number c of workers engaged in the consumer goods industry.
6. The number i of workers engaged in the machine industry.
7. The output of consumer goods, p.

To determine these unknowns numerically is a formidable task. In the following exposition we shall simplify Åkerman's procedure as much as possible. Let us first assume, with Åkerman, that all the available capital is M-1-capital so that for the moment the length of life of the machines is given. We may then establish the following equations for the determination of the equilibrium.

First we have the production function:

$$p = f(r, c)$$

In his calculations Åkerman assumes that this function has the special form:

$$p = k\sqrt{cr} \tag{1}$$

where k represents a constant which in his calculations is taken equal to 200, so that:

$$p = 200\sqrt{cr} \tag{1a}$$

We can express r in terms of i. On the assumption that all capital is M-1-capital, r equals i_1; in the case of a one-year length of life of machines (M-1-capital), i_1 equals i, and thus r equals i.

We know further that in equilibrium the marginal product of labour is equal to the wage rate and the marginal product of machine services is equal to the value of a unit of such service. These marginal products we can obtain by partially differentiating the production function with respect to c and r. Thus we have for the wage rate:

$$w = \frac{k}{2}\sqrt{\frac{r}{c}} = \frac{k}{2}\sqrt{\frac{i}{c}} \tag{2}$$

$$w = 100\sqrt{\frac{i}{c}} \tag{2a}$$

and for the value of a unit of machine service:

$$b = \frac{k}{2}\sqrt{\frac{c}{r}} = \frac{k}{2}\sqrt{\frac{c}{i}} \tag{3}$$

$$b = 100\sqrt{\frac{c}{i}}. \tag{3a}$$

We also know that the value of the capital equals the number of workers employed in its construction multiplied by the wage rate, i.e.:

$$K = iw \qquad (4)^4$$

[4] This equation actually implies that the construction of the machine takes no time at all – in contrast to Åkerman's explicit assumption that construction takes one year. On the latter assumption an expression for the interest accrued during the construction period should have appeared on the right-hand side of the equation. Åkerman neglects this, proceeding on the premise that the average construction time of a machine is half

As Åkerman puts the value of the capital stock at 333.3, we have:

$$333.3 = iw \tag{4a}$$

Further, the number of workers employed respectively in the machine industry and the consumer goods industry must add up to the total number of workers, thus:

$$A = i + c \tag{5}$$

As A is assumed to be 100, we have:

$$100 = i + c \tag{5a}$$

Finally, the value of a unit of machine services must be equal to the wage rate plus the interest accrued during one year since, by definition, such a unit is equal in the case of M-1-capital to the product of one worker. Hence we have:

$$wx = b \tag{6}$$

where $x = (1 + z)$.

These equations suffice to determine the six unknowns, which are: the value of the unit of machine services, the wage rate, the rate of interest, the number of workers in each of the two industries, and the output of consumer goods.

The numerical values in the above equations give the following results:

Wage rate = 33.3
Value of the unit of machine service = 300
Interest rate = 800%
Social product = 6,000
Number of workers producing machines = 10
Number of workers producing consumer goods = 90

These are the figures inserted in Table III, *infra*, for the state of equilibrium designated by Ia.

Up to now we have simply assumed that all capital is M-1-capital. In

a year, and that on the average the services of the machine have to be "waited" for half a year. Thus the centres of gravity, so to speak, of the construction period and of the "maturing period" are separated by only one year; hence no great error is involved in assessing the construction costs as equal to the number of workers multiplied by the wage rate, and in then equating the value of the services during one year to the cost plus the interest accrued for *one year* (equation (6)).

fact, however, the life of the machines is one of the unknowns. Åkerman, of course, was aware of this, and from the mass of his numerical calculations the following general argument can be deduced: If we increase the amount of capital we obtain different values for the wage rate, the price of machine services, etc. We know from our discussion of the factors which govern the length of life of a machine that its durability depends on the ratio between the value of the machine services b and the wage rate w in such a way that lengthening the life becomes profitable when b diminishes relative to w. Now, an increase in the capital stock brings about just such a change in the ratio b/w since, according to marginal productivity theory, b will fall when the capital stock is increased while w will rise. It follows that sooner or later a point must be reached at which the capital becomes M-2-capital, still later M-3-capital, and so on. This possibility of increasing the durability of the capital stock has the effect of a valve through which additional amounts of capital can find an outlet so that the interest rate does not fall as rapidly as it would if the process of production could only be broadened and not also be deepened. We now have to discuss three complications which arise once the machines have a length of life in excess of one year.

1. Let us start with M-2-capital. We know that an extension of the durability of a machine to two years will take place only if the amount of capital has grown enough to bring about a ratio of b to w which makes it profitable to employ M-2-capital.[5] If we wish to calculate for this case the wage rate, the unit value of the machine services, etc., we can no longer use our simple capital equation (4) in which the total value of capital is put equal to the number of workers engaged in machine production multiplied by their wage rate. We must now take account of the fact that each year only a *portion* of the capital "matures" in the form of consumer goods. This portion must be large enough to replace those machines which are scrapped each year because of their age, or, to put it differently, it must be large enough to pay the workers engaged in the production of replacement machines. It is *this portion* which is equal to

[5] With Åkerman's concrete assumptions, this happens when $b/w = 1.5$. Åkerman adopts this figure as the starting point for his calculations, working "backwards" to arrive at the amount of capital necessary to satisfy this condition. From the economic point of view the datum is, of course, the amount of capital, and b/w is the quantity to be determined.

iw, but the *total* capital stock is greater, and our problem is to determine how much greater. Åkerman applies in his calculations what he calls the "practical" method of depreciation, according to which an equal amount is written off each year. With this assumption we can work out the total value of the capital. All workers employed in machine production produce M-2-capital, for which the construction period is one year. The value of the machines produced each year is iw. In addition each year machines are in existence which had been produced in the previous year and whose book value is $iw/2$. The total value of the capital stock therefore is $K = 1.5iw$. This, then, is our new capital equation (4). For M-3-capital the equation would be $K = 2iw$, and so on.

2. If the capital lasts for more than one year, it is no longer true that $r = i_1 = i$ as was the case for M-1-capital. We recall that for M-n-capital with an even age-distribution the total of services rendered by all existing machines, r, was equal to ni_1. For M-2-capital this means that $r = 2i_1$. According to Table I, $i = i_1 + 0.667i_1$, or $i_1 = i/1.667$. Hence the services of M-2-capital are $r = 1.2i$ per year.

3. Further, we must replace the profitability equation for one year by the corresponding equation for two years, so that equation (6) becomes $[i_1 b(x+1)]/iw = x^2$.

With the aid of these equations we can determine the unknowns on the assumption of M-2-capital. The figures in Table III below have been calculated in this manner. The table represents a condensation of four tables given by Åkerman, from which only the important figures are reproduced here. The figures which reflect the function $f(n)$, showing how much additional labour is required in the construction of machines in order to increase their lengths of life, have already been given in Table I and are not repeated. In column 1 of the present table the equilibrium situations reached with different quantities of capital have been identified by combinations of Roman numerals and small letters; all equilibria designated with I (Ia, Ib, etc.) refer to situations in which the optimum length of life of the capital stock is one year, and those marked II, III, etc. to optimum lengths of life of two, three, etc. years. The critical ratio b/w can be taken from columns 4 and 5. The number of workers engaged in producing consumer goods, which can be obtained by subtracting the number engaged in producing machines from the total number of workers, is not separately shown in the table.

TABLE III

Equilibrium system	Value of capital stock (K)	Optimum years of life (n)	Wage rate (w)	Value of machine service unit (b)	Rate of interest (z)	Number of workers in machine production (i)	Social product (p)
Ia	333	1	33.33	300	800	10	6,000
Ib	1,000	1	50	200	300	20	8,000
Ic	2,700	1	75	133.5	$73\frac{3}{4}$	36	9,600
Id	2,975	1	78.28	127.8	$63\frac{1}{4}$	38	9,708
Ie	3,266	1	81.65	122.5	50	40	9,798
IIa	4,380	2	81.65	122.5	50	35.7	10,500
IIIa	6,790	3	90.3	110.8	$30\frac{1}{4}$	37.6	11,260
IVa	9,750	4	98.2	101.8	$19\frac{1}{4}$	39.7	11,860
Va	13,000	5	104.5	95.8	$12\frac{7}{8}$	41.4	12,260
VIa	17,100	6	111.5	89.8	$7\frac{3}{4}$	43.7	12,560
VIIa	22,300	7	119.5	83.7	$3\frac{3}{8}$	46.7	12,720
VIIb	25,500	7	127.5	78.5	0	50.0	12,750
VIIIa	31,200	8	132.7	75.4	-2	52.2	12,660

From his calculations Åkerman draws various conclusions, the most important of which are the following.

1. In systems Ia–Id the capital stock is increasing, but not enough to bring about a ratio b/w such as would force an increase in the length of life to two years. The increase of the capital stock thus takes the form of "broadening" the capital structure, not of "deepening" it. This is obviously due to the assumption that the durability of machines can be extended only by whole years.[6] If continuous changes were possible, changes in depth would result in this phase also. The degree to which an increase in the capital leads to a change either in the "breadth" or in the "depth" of the capital structure depends on the effect of the change in the ratio b/w on the length of life of the machines, and this effect in turn depends on the form of the function $f(n)$.

[6] The system Ie is characterized by the fact that individual entrepreneurs will be just as likely to choose machines lasting two years as machines lasting one year. However, if all of them were to choose machines with a length of life of two years, the capital would be insufficient and a relationship b/w would arise such as to enforce a return to M-1-capital.

2. The table shows that an increase in capital is accompanied by an increase in the wage rate. In systems Ia–Id wages grow faster than in systems IIa–VIIa, which means that the possibility of lengthening the life of the machines retards the increase in wage rates which occurs as a consequence of the increase of the capital stock.

3. We have already seen in our discussion of Böhm-Bawerk's theory that the interest rate is not equal to the marginal product of capital if this is taken to mean the increase in output divided by the increase in capital. This is due to the fact that part of the increase in capital will be absorbed by higher wages. Åkerman, who recognized this, maintains, however, that the interest rate is equal to the marginal product of capital provided the latter is measured in units of "labour maintenance". However, it is not worth-while to discuss this point at length.

4. According to Table III the interest rate falls to zero when the life of the machine reaches 7 years, and it becomes negative at higher lengths of life. The reason is obvious. It can be seen from Table I that from the sixth year on the marginal cost of increasing the length of life begins to rise, while the average cost reaches a minimum at 7 years. The point at which the average costs are at a minimum corresponds, in Böhm-Bawerk's theory, to the point at which the product per worker is at a maximum. We know that the interest rate becomes zero when the point is reached at which a lengthening of the period of production ceases to increase the output. For analogous reasons the interest rate becomes zero when in the case of durable goods the average costs reach their minimum.

III. Methods of Depreciation and the Average Period of Production

So far we have omitted to give an account of Åkerman's discussion of a number of special points which constantly interrupt his main line of thought. Two of these are of interest for the theory of capital; one concerns the problem of the depreciation method and the other the problem of the average period of production.

Åkerman adopts in his calculations the "practical" method of depreciation, according to which an equal amount is written off each year. If this method is used, an M-4-capital structure in which a machine with a value of 10 has just been installed, a second is one year old, and so on, has a capital value of 25 (i.e. the sum of 10+7.5+5+2.5).

Such a depreciation method is evidently "arbitrary" in the sense that it cannot be justified on economic grounds. Åkerman uses it only because it simplifies his calculations. He regards as theoretically "correct" another system based on his notion that it is possible to find out how large a share of the labour applied in the construction of the machines "matures" annually in the form of machine services. This he calls the "abstract" method of depreciation. An example may serve to explain it. Let us assume the rate of interest is 15% and the value of the annual services of the machine is 3.50. Then Åkerman regards the services obtained from the machine during the first year as the result of an amount of labour i_1 which, multiplied by the wage rate, grows to the value 3.50 after one year; correspondingly the services yielded by the machine in the second year as the result of $i_2 w$, and so on. If we now take the wage rate to be equal to 1, we obtain the following equations:

$$i_1(1.15) = 3.50$$
$$i_2(1.15)^2 = 3.50 \quad \text{etc.}$$

whence we obtain

$$\begin{aligned} i_1 &= 3.05 \\ i_2 &= 2.65 \\ i_3 &= 2.30 \\ i_4 &= 2.00. \end{aligned}$$

This series adds up to 10 which is sufficient to replace one machine every year. We are also in a position to calculate the capital value of the machines at any point in time; the "abstract" system yields, in the above case of four machines with a lifetime of four years, a book value of 23.25, as against 25 obtained when the "practical" method is used.

A third method, which Åkerman calls the "theoretical" method of depreciation, proceeds from the postulate that the rate of return on the book value of the capital shall remain the same each year. This object is achieved by calculating the amortization quotas i_1, i_2, etc. for the first year from the formula:

$$\frac{3.50 - i_1}{10} = \frac{15}{100}; \quad i_1 = 2$$

and for the second year from the formula:

$$\frac{3.50 - i_2}{8} = \frac{15}{100}; \quad i_2 = 2.30$$

For the third and fourth years we obtain in this way $i_3 = 2.65$ and $i_4 = 3.05$. The total book value of the capital is here 26.75. A comparison with the second depreciation method shows that there the write-offs follow one another in exactly the reverse sequence: what here is written off in the fourth year was in the second system written off in the first year.

No economic justification can be claimed for any of these methods. It is impossible to know how many of the productive inputs which were applied in the construction of the machines mature in particular years. Åkerman, who holds the second method to be correct, can in no way prove that the labour services applied in the construction of the machines really mature in the order implied by this method. He has simply made an *assumption*, which is neither more nor less justified than the corresponding assumptions underlying the first or third depreciation method. Wicksell was perfectly right in remarking that "the annual uses successively following one another constitute a kind of joint-supply (to adopt Marshall's terminology), and fundamentally it is just as absurd to ask how much labour is invested in either one or the other annual use as to try to find out what part of a pasture goes into wool and what part into mutton".[7]

The arbitrariness of the depreciation method – and the fact that the total value of the capital differs according to which method is adopted – will play a decisive role in the critique of Åkerman's theory.

We have already noticed in the discussion of Wicksell's theory that even in the case of variable capital the average period of production depends on the rate of interest once we calculate at compound interest. Åkerman now shows, (1), that in the case of durable goods the average period of production – in the sense of a period of waiting for the services of the machines – depends on the depreciation method adopted and, (2), that even with simple interest the average period of production depends on the rate of interest, if we adopt the second or the third method of depreciation, although not if we adopt the first method. Both these points

[7] Wicksell, *Lectures on Political Economy*, Vol. 1, p. 260.

can be covered by the same example in which we shall compare only the "practical" and the "theoretical" system. Assuming M-4-capital, as above, the average time of waiting is calculated as follows if the "practical" depreciation system is used (assuming that the first write-off takes place at the beginning of the first year):

$$\frac{(2.5 \times 4) + (2.5 \times 3) + (2.5 \times 2) + 2.5}{10} = \frac{25}{10} = 2.5 \text{ years}.$$

This is the formula used in Böhm-Bawerk's calculation of the average period of production in the case of variable capital. The average is independent of the interest rate since it was, by implication, calculated at simple interest. It will be seen that the same result is obtained if the full formula, involving the interest rate,

$$2.5(1 + 4z) + 2.5(1 + 3z) + 2.5(1 + 2z) + 2.5(1 + z) = 10(1 + tz)$$

is solved for t. If we adopt the "theoretical" system, the average works out as follows:

$$\frac{(2.00 \times 4) + (2.30 \times 3) + (2.65 \times 2) + 3.05}{10} = 2.325 \text{ years}.$$

Thus the average period of production changes according to the system of amortization adopted. Furthermore, if the second system is used the average evidently depends on the rate of interest even if we calculate at simple interest since the amortization quotas of the successive years are dependent on the rate of interest. If, for instance, in one case the rate of interest were to be 15%, in another 10%, then the average period of production in the first case would be 2.363 years and in the second case 2.5 years.

IV. Critique

Like Wicksell in his last work on the problem of capital, Åkerman made no use of the concept of the average period of production in his general equilibrium analysis; and he was also aware of the fact that the average period of production will, in the case of durable capital, depend on the rate of interest, even if we calculate with simple interest, unless the "practical" depreciation method is adopted. Since Åkerman abandoned the average period of production, one might at first sight expect that, like Wicksell, he would work in terms of the individual investment periods of the productive inputs. But, as already shown, there is no way of determining these in the case of long-lasting capital goods, Åkerman's view to the contrary not withstanding. To repeat, it is impossible to say how many of the productive inputs originally applied in the production of a machine remain "stored" in it once it has begun to render its services. But, as Åkerman's own treatment of the problem shows, it is not at all necessary to know the investment periods of the inputs that have gone into the construction of a machine. All that one needs to know in order to determine the length of life of, and the investment in, a machine is to what extent additional productive inputs can extend the lifetime of the machine. Undoubtedly, such an extension would not always be possible. Although Åkerman never considers the case of durable goods with a technically given lifetime, it would be easy to fit it into his theory.

The two conclusions – (1), that we do not need, and in fact cannot use, the concept of an average period of production and, (2), that for the determination of the length of life of capital goods we need to know only the functional relationship between the length of life and the quantity of productive inputs but not the investment period of the latter – are the significant results of Åkerman's work.

Yet, his solution is still subject to the other two objections raised against Böhm-Bawerk's theory: first, that he takes as a datum in his system the total value of the existing capital stock and, second, that in his general equilibrium analysis he assumes from the start that the capital has the time structure which will ultimately have to emerge in the equilibrium that is to be determined.

The correct way to calculate the value of durable goods is that of discounting the flow of their future returns. This makes it immediately obvious that the "datum" capital – in Böhm-Bawerk's case the subsistence fund – depends on the rate of interest, one of the unknowns in the problem. At first sight, however, Åkerman seems to be able to circumvent this difficulty by determining the value of durable goods from their cost – so that the rate of interest does not appear to enter into the calculation, at least if the construction time of the durable goods is disregarded. As we have already noticed, however, it is not known how much of the original cost remains "stored" in old machines still in operation. This problem Åkerman avoids by using a method of depreciation in which an equal portion of the value is written off each year, which amounts to the assumption that the machines wear out uniformly. But as was pointed out before, any other depreciation method would be equally justified. If Åkerman had used in his analysis the "abstract" system, which he mistakenly regards as the correct one, his annual depreciation charges would also have become dependent on the rate of interest. The same would have been true if he had adopted the third depreciation method described above. Since all three methods are equally justified, but since the three, as has been shown above, yield different values for the total capital stock in existence, it follows that the capital fund taken as a datum is a quite arbitrary quantity even if calculated on the basis of the cost of construction of the capital goods. But even if one holds the opinion that the first or "practical" system is for some unknown reason the "proper" one – which would be a way around the difficulty since the capital value would then no longer be dependent on the interest rate – it would still not be permissible to take the capital value as a datum, as it would still be dependent on the level of wages; and the wage rate, like the rate of interest, is itself a result of the equilibrium which the value of capital is supposed to help determine. In short, Åkerman's system lacks an equation with which to calculate the value of the capital.

Wicksell undertook to formulate Åkerman's results mathematically.[8] It is not necessary to reproduce this work here in detail.[9] It will be enough to say that Wicksell's treatment of the matter brings out very clearly the difficulty involved in taking capital as a datum. Wicksell's unknowns are: (1) the social product, (2) the wage rate, (3) the value of a unit of machine service, (4) the value of the capital, (5) the rate of interest, and (6) the length of life of the machines. He takes the lifetime of the machine, t, as the independent variable and determines the remaining five unknowns through a system of five equations in t. But, from the point of view of the system as a whole, the length of life, t, is not given. Usually it is capital which is taken as a datum; in either case, of course, it remains true that we lack one equation. Wicksell arrives at a solution only by taking one of the unknowns as known.

We need not discuss at length the second of the weaknesses in Åkerman's

[8] Wicksell, *Lectures on Political Economy*, Vol. 1, pp. 274ff.

[9] Parts of it are used in the Mathematical Appendix, Section 4.

theory. The equilibrium systems shown in Table III presuppose that the existing capital already has the right composition; e.g., that it already is M-2-capital if the equilibrium analysis results in a length of life of two years. They also presuppose, of course, that capital has the right age-composition; e.g., in the case of M-2-capital, that half of the machines are new and the other half one year old – or, in the case of M-3-capital, that one third are new, one third one year old and the last third two years old. Like the assumption of a given capital value, this amounts to making a datum out of one of the conditions necessary for the equilibrium. Hayek, to whom we shall now turn, recognized these fundamental weaknesses of the theory. Let us see how he dealt with them.

CHAPTER 4

FRIEDRICH A. VON HAYEK

Hayek belongs only in part to the school of thought dealt with in this section. There can be no doubt that the roots of his theory of capital[1] reach deeply into the ground which nourished also the theories of Böhm-Bawerk and Wicksell. For him, too, the theory of capital and interest is indissolubly tied up with the problem of the time structure of production. But his recognition of the fundamental weaknesses of the theories of his predecessors led him to conclusions which diverge considerably from theirs. In particular, as will be seen, his point of view is not a static one in the sense in which this is true of his predecessors.

I. Exposition

In Hayek's view the theories of his predecessors describe only the conditions under which a stationary equilibrium might exist; but being restricted to equilibrium conditions, the theories by-pass all the more important problems of capital. As he sees it: "The main problems are to explain what types of instruments will be produced under given conditions, and what will be the consequences of producing particular instruments. And these problems will of course be non-existent if we assume from the beginning that the same stock of instruments will be constantly reproduced. The impossibility of treating the problems of capital adequately within the framework of a stationary equilibrium becomes, of course, even more obvious as soon as we include, as we must, the problems relating to what are usually described as 'saving' and (new) 'investment', since these are activities which imply by definition that the persons under-

[1] Friedrich A. Hayek, *The Pure Theory of Capital* (London, 1941). This is an exceptionally difficult book, and it is quite possible that our interpretation of it does not everywhere agree with what Hayek wanted to express. Anyone who has seriously tried to work his way through Hayek's book will surely understand our point.

taking them want to alter their future position, and consequently will do in the future something different from what they are doing in the present."[2]

Hayek, therefore, develops a concept of equilibrium which has nothing to do with the stationary economy. An equilibrium, in his sense of the word, exists when, in any given situation with a given structure of real capital, the plans of entrepreneurs and those of consumers are so adjusted that their execution does not lead to any disappointment, so that every entrepreneur is able to sell the output which he planned to sell at the prices which he expected. "In any given situation there will be one (and in most instances only one) way in which the plans of the various entrepreneurs can be made to harmonize with one another and with the preferences of the consumers. The use of the equilibrium method here then means constructing an imaginary state in which the plans of the different people (entrepreneurs and consumers generally) are so adjusted to one another that each individual will be able to sell or buy exactly those quantities of commodities which he has been planning to sell or buy."[3] An imaginary situation of this kind is not easy to analyse, and many economists have taken refuge in the concept of a centrally planned economy where the variables can be made to harmonize by a *single* will, as is the case either in a Robinson Crusoe economy or in a modern economy which is directed by a dictator. Throughout a large part of his book Hayek adopts this latter approach.

Hayek – whose main attention, as already stressed, is directed to the theory of capital – analyses in detail the functional relationships existing between the input of productive services and the resulting output. He endeavours to classify them with the help of his concepts of the "input function" and the "output function" and, with these concepts, to describe the time structure of production. As we are here concerned with the theory of interest, it does not seem necessary to consider in detail these difficult concepts.[4] We shall, therefore, turn at once to those sections of Hayek's work which are important for the theory of interest.

[2] Hayek, *Pure Theory*, pp. 15–16.

[3] Hayek, *Pure Theory*, p. 26.

[4] The revived concern with the theory of capital during the thirties led to some detailed studies on the concept of the "period of production" which cannot be dealt with in the present book. The reader may be referred to: C. H. P. Gifford, 'The Concept of the Length of the Period of Production', *Economic Journal*, **43** (1933) 611–618;

Hayek's criticism of his predecessors is directed mainly to the two weak points which have already been brought out in our discussion. On the one hand, it is not possible to take the value of the subsistence fund as a datum. "This stock of non-permanent resources, in the form in which it exists as a datum" – he writes – "is not some definite quantity of capital; for it can be expressed as a single magnitude only after the relative values of the items of which it is composed have been determined. And these values are clearly a resultant of the same equilibrating forces as determine the investment periods. The initial datum from which we have to start is simply an enumeration of all the items of which this stock of non-permanent resources is composed, and of all their technical attributes ... The quantity of capital as a value magnitude, no less than the different investment periods, are not data, but are among the unknowns which have to be determined."[5]

Nor, on the other hand, is it possible to use the concept of an average period of production. "All attempts to reduce the complex structure of waiting periods, which is described by the input functions *and* the output functions, to a single aggregate or average investment period ... are bound to fail, because the different waiting periods cannot be reduced to a common denominator in purely technical terms."[6]

Thus Hayek replaces the datum "capital" by the given stock of capital goods which happen to be available as the result of what might be called historical accident and works, to the extent that this is possible, with the investment periods of the individual productive inputs. He imagines an economic dictator with full knowledge of all income streams which the given stock of real capital goods and the currently available productive

---

C. H. P. Gifford, 'The Period of Production under Continuous Input and Point Output in an Unprogressive Community', *Econometrica*, **3** (1935) 199–212; K. E. Boulding, 'Time and Investment', *Economica*, New Series, **3** (1936) 196–220; J. Marschak, 'A Note on the Period of Production', *Economic Journal*, **44** (1934) 146–151; J. M. Fleming, 'The Period of Production and Derived Concepts', *Review of Economic Studies*, **3** (1935–1936) 1–17; H. T. N. Gaitskell, 'Notes on the Period of Production', *Zeitschrift für Nationalökonomie*, **7** (1936) 577–595, and **9** (1939) 215–244; J. R. Hicks, *Value and Capital* (2nd ed., Oxford, 1946), ch. XVII.

[5] Hayek, *Pure Theory*, pp. 191–192. Hayek uses the expression "non-permanent resources" to describe his concept of capital goods. Roughly speaking, this covers all capital goods, whether durable or not, including extractable resources still underground but excluding land and those very long-lived goods which Wicksell calls "rent-goods".

[6] Hayek, *Pure Theory*, p. 141–142.

inputs can be made to yield. The dictator sets himself the task of producing an income stream which is to remain constant and is also to be at a maximum; moreover, this maximum stream of income is to be attained *immediately*. By a constant income stream Hayek understands a flow of consumption goods of such composition as is required to keep it period after period on the same indifference curve or, more exactly, since we are dealing with many kinds of consumption goods, on the same n-dimensional indifference surface. This indifference system reflects the needs of the economic community as seen by the dictator. According to Hayek, it is neither necessary nor even possible that the composition of the consumption goods should remain the same; in the course of time some of them will need to be replaced by others so that the composition of the flow of goods is continually changing. Obviously this does not prevent the different combinations from always remaining on the same indifference surface. "At successive points of time additional quantities of some commodities (or perhaps commodities which were known but not produced previously) can be substituted for some of the commodities available at earlier moments, but they must always be in such quantities that the additions just compensate for the deductions without making the total in any way more or less attractive."[7] Accordingly, the assumption of a constant income stream does not imply a stationary economy: the dictator's plan must envisage from the very start an endless succession of changes. "These changes would, it is true, rapidly decrease in magnitude as time went on, and would after a while become insignificant, but in principle they would continue in some small degree for ever."[8] Thus our economy is in a state of continual change, ever striving towards a stationary state but in principle never reaching it. It is precisely for this reason that Hayek developed the new equilibrium concept explained above. The dictator's plan envisages that the production of commodities (and of capital goods) is "harmonized", and in this sense "equilibrium" will exist; but this equilibrium is not that of a stationary state, a state towards which the economy tends but which, in principle, it never reaches.

This notion of Hayek requires some further comment. The dictator, it is assumed, achieves *immediately* the new maximum income stream which is to be kept constant. Why should he, in the course of time, replace by

[7] Hayek, *Pure Theory*, p. 159.
[8] Hayek, *Pure Theory*, p. 167.

other goods some of the consumption goods initially produced, if this does not increase the flow of income? Would it not be reasonable – would it not indeed be necessary – to assume that the composition of the consumption goods, once chosen, would permanently be reproduced? This assumption, moreover, would have considerably facilitated the whole analysis, since the relative values of the consumption goods would not continually be changing with the passage of time.

Hayek's reason for maintaining that the composition of the stream of goods will be continually changing is that "we start out with an assortment of non-permanent resources, which is the result of a particular historical development, and which will consist in large part of items which it is either impossible or else unprofitable to reproduce".[9] A simplified example may help to clarify this point.

Let us assume that coal, instead of being used for heating a house, is used in a blast furnace and that this roundabout application leads, say, five years later to a product which has greater utility (greater value) than the coal would have yielded in heating a house. This new method of utilizing the coal means, on the one hand, an increase in the flow of income from the sixth year onwards, which will be maintained since the coal will be applied in this roundabout manner every year from now on. It also implies, however, a drop in the consumption for five years, as the heating of the house cannot be continued. Since the maximum level of the income stream must be attained immediately, this gap will have to be filled. It will therefore be necessary to draw sufficient productive services out of the remainder of the system – services which hitherto had been used in the production of real capital goods that would have been completed and ready to yield their services at the end of the five year period – and to apply these immediately in the production of consumer goods. These productive services for which the investment period has now been shortened will yield a smaller product in this shorter period of production; it will, nevertheless, be advantageous to redirect them on condition that the increased product yielded after five years by the new way of using the coal will be greater than the loss caused after five years by the reallocation of the necessary amount of productive services from the longer to the shorter production period.

[9] Hayek, *Pure Theory*, p. 166.

In the real world the immediate attainment of a maximum income stream, to be maintained at a constant level, would of course necessitate extraordinarily complicated adjustments. But the general rule is, according to Hayek, relatively simple to state. It is at this point that, for the first time, we come up against the problem of interest. The rule as formulated by Hayek is that, "whenever the rate of increase of the product which can be obtained by lengthening the investment periods of some units of input is greater than the rate of decrease of the product caused by shortening the investment periods of other units of input by the same interval of time, it will be advantageous to make the corresponding changes ... Hence the condition for maximising the total income stream which we have been seeking is that this rate of increase of the product due to an extension of the investment period by a given interval shall be the same for all investments."[10] We shall have to return to this passage later on.

As soon as Hayek turns to the details of the problem of investment and considers the various cases of relationships between productive inputs and the resulting product, he, too, does not disdain to use – at least temporarily – the auxiliary assumption of a stationary state. He first takes the "point input – point output" case in which the resources are applied at one point in time and the product becomes available at a later point (the case of trees, or that of wine), the length of the investment period being variable. From this he goes on to the "continuous input – point output" case in which the resources are applied continuously but the product matures at a single point in time, while the investment period of each input can be separately varied so that it becomes possible to isolate the product of individual inputs. For these cases the rule must hold that in a *stationary* economy the internal rate of return must be the same on all inputs and equal to the rate of interest ruling in the system. As long as this condition is not satisfied for a particular production process it will be advantageous to adjust the investment periods of the inputs and the volume of output until the equality is obtained.

Hayek considers three further cases. First, a case of "continuous input – point output" in which, by contrast to the one discussed above, the investment period for the individual inputs cannot be altered because it

[10] Hayek, *Pure Theory*, p. 165.

is technologically fixed. Here we cannot isolate the product resulting from individual inputs. The equilibrium condition requires that the value of the product should exceed the value of the inputs by an amount calculable from the investment periods of the inputs and the rate of interest ruling in the economy. The equilibrium is attained by extending the production of such goods until a point is reached where the consequent fall in the value of the product and rise in the value of the inputs make the internal rate of return on the inputs equal to the rate which prevails in the system as a whole. An analogous solution is found in the case of "point input – continuous output with invariable investment period", that is, in the case of a durable good which (ideally) is produced instantaneously at a certain point of time and yields services over a lifetime which, for technical reasons, is of invariable length. The value of the services obtained from the good, discounted at the prevailing rate of interest, must in equilibrium equal the cost of the good; this equilibrium also is attained by adjusting the volume of production. The last case is the one already known from Åkerman: the case of a durable good whose lifetime can be extended by greater investment outlays. Here, again, equilibrium is reached when the value of the productive services discounted at the prevailing rate of interest becomes equal to the cost of the good. At the same time, the condition must be satisfied that the discounted value of the "last" unit of service must be equal to the additional costs which enabled the good to render this last unit of service. The output and the length of life of the durable good will be adjusted until these conditions are satisfied.

Hayek has thus up to this point shown that for all these different investment cases the rate of interest, in the sense of an internal rate of return, must in stationary equilibrium be uniform and equal to the interest rate prevailing in the system. But no answer has so far been given to the question, what in fact determines the level of this rate of return or rate of interest.

Hayek's predecessors answered this question with the aid of the subsistence fund. Hayek rightly rejects this answer; moreover, it is not his intention to explain interest in the stationary state which according to him is in principle never reached.

As we know, Hayek replaces the subsistence fund by the assumption of a "fortuitously" given structure of real capital, and the assumption of a stationary equilibrium by the assumption that the dictator keeps the flow of income constant. Does he in fact succeed in determining the level of interest with the aid of these two assumptions? In so far as any answer to this is implicit in his book, it has to be pieced together from various references since the problem is nowhere treated comprehensively, and the answer which emerges is not very clear.

The general idea underlying Hayek's solution seems to be that the rate of interest is determined by (a) the functional relationships between the output and the investment periods of the inputs, (b) the given amount of real capital and (c) the assumption that the flow of income is to be maximized while being kept at a constant level. The latter assumption imposes constraints with regard to the length of the periods for which the inputs can be invested. "The factor which limits the possible extensions of the investment periods is that as one unit of input is invested for a longer period, the output stream at the earlier date is reduced and the value of the products maturing at this earlier date is consequently raised. This means that the value of the marginal products of units of input invested for that earlier date increases, with the result that it becomes profitable to invest more for that date ... Therefore the condition that all input must be invested in such a way that the ratio between the marginal rate of increase of the product and the size of the whole product is the same for all units of input, also determines the period for which each of the units of input has to be invested."[11]

These propositions – which restate the rule already given for maximizing the flow of income – must apparently not be taken to mean that "the ratio between the marginal rate of increase of the product and the size of the whole product" which must be the same for all units of input must also be the same for all successive dates in the future. According to Hayek, that would be true only for the stationary state. All he really means is that these internal rates of return must be equal for processes which mature at the same moment of time. "For all processes maturing at the same time the ratio between the rate of increase of the product and the size of the product itself will have to be the same. This does not mean that these ratios must also be equal for processes terminating at different moments. That is true only under stationary conditions."[12] But this means nothing other than that the rate of interest changes over time and

[11] Hayek, *Pure Theory*, pp. 190–191.
[12] Hayek, *Pure Theory*, p. 184.

will – or at least may – be different in successive (small) unit periods, even though the income stream is held constant. Hayek gives no further explanation for this conclusion.

According to Hayek, the rates of return for investment periods of different lengths are linked by a fixed rule, and it is here that he comes up against the problem of the structure of interest rates. When an investment yields 5% if limited to a single unit period, but 6% in a second unit period if it is repeated, then the yield of an investment over these two successive periods must be 11.3%. The average interest rate per unit period on the two year investment consequently is 5.5%. At first sight, this statement seems to contradict Hayek's rule that the internal rate of return must be the same for all processes which end at the same point in time. Apparently we must interpret this to the effect that the longer process in the first period yields 5%, but in the second period 6%.[13]

Thus we learn: (1), that the condition of a constant maximum income stream determines the investment periods of the productive inputs and thus the rate of increase of their product divided by this product (the rate of interest); (2), that this ratio must be equal for all investments in units of inputs throughout the system which mature at the same date, although not for those which mature at different points in time; (3), that a definite relationship must exist between the internal rates of return or rates of interest on investments for longer and shorter periods.

Hayek considers the determinants of the rate of interest at two other places in his book.

The assumption of a constant income stream is for him only a provisional tool of analysis. He later replaces it by the assumption that saving and investment are taking place in the economy, and we find in the relevant chapter of his book an exact answer – although valid only for a simplified model – to the question of what determines the rate of interest in the individual periods. But as the answer is basically not different from that given by Irving Fisher, we shall defer discussion of it, to avoid repetition, until we take up Fisher's theory. It should, however, be stressed at this point already that Hayek confines himself here to showing how the productivity of *new investments* together with the willingness to save – the latter a function of "time preference" – de-

[13] We shall return to this point in discussing Fisher's theory.

termine the rate of interest. In this part of his book Hayek thus belongs to those authors who let the rate of interest be determined in the market for new capital and hence assume a progressive economy. It is, therefore, only logical if we discuss Hayek's solution of the interest problem in a progressive economy in connection with one of the authors dealt with in the second part of this book.

Finally, Hayek also considers the problem of interest in a competitive economy. His analysis is quite unusual. He again starts from a given structure of real capital, the capital goods being distributed among individuals. He first assumes that the owners of finished consumer goods and of real capital goods capable of being converted into consumer goods during a single unit period will in fact consume those goods within one unit period. In this case those capital goods which cannot be converted into consumer goods during one unit period would be entirely without value. In the next stage of the analysis Hayek assumes that an increasing quantity of consumer goods will be "invested" instead of being consumed; that is to say, they will be exchanged for capital goods which will produce consumer goods in the more distant future. In consequence, a value will attach to these capital goods, which will rise the higher, the more consumer goods are being diverted to investment purposes. In equilibrium – which, however, is never quite reached – "the values of the future consumers' goods (in terms of present consumers' goods) must exceed their costs (in terms of present consumers' goods) by an amount which bears a uniform relationship ... to the time which will elapse before the future consumers' goods become available".[14] The return to be obtained from these "investments" is determined, therefore, by the price relationship between capital goods and consumer goods. This relationship, in turn, is determined by the demand, expressed in terms of present consumer goods, for future consumer goods which at present have the form of real capital.

II. Critique

Hayek correctly diagnosed the weaknesses of his predecessors' theories: namely, that they took the subsistence fund as a datum and ascribed to it *a priori* a composition which it could only obtain as a result of the

[14] Hayek, *Pure Theory*, p. 264.

process creating an equilibrium; furthermore, that some of them worked with the concept of an average period of production. He chose a different starting point, assuming a fortuitously given structure of real capital and abandoning the concept of an average production period. In these respects we must undoubtedly follow him. It is important to visualize once again where his reconsideration of the crucial problems led him. In the first place, he does not develop the theory for a stationary state. Secondly, he contemplates successive points in time or, better, successive unit periods between which the rate of interest changes. These unit periods are not independent of each other but are interrelated by the consequences resulting from the assumption of an income stream which remains constant throughout all of them. Hayek thereby approaches the theories of the group of authors which will be treated in the second part of this book.

Hayek's solution to the problem of the determinants of the rate of interest is given in three parts, which stand rather independently side by side.

The first solution – that which assumes a given structure of real capital, works with individual investment periods, and proceeds from the assumption that the dictator of the collective economy is endeavouring to secure a maximum constant income stream – does not seem to me satisfactory as it gives no sufficiently precise answer to the question, what exactly it is that determines the level of the successive interest rates per unit period. There is no doubt that these are determined "somehow" by the functions which express the dependence of the product on the investment periods of the inputs, together with the assumption of a given structure of real capital and of an income stream which must be maximized and kept at a constant level. But exactly how these factors, in combination, determine these interest rates did not become clear to us, at any rate, from Hayek's book.

It is a second deficiency that, wherever this problem is attacked, consideration is given only to very simple cases of investment in which Jevon's interest rate formula "rate of increase of the produce divided by the whole produce" can be applied. How other cases would fit into this framework – and, in particular, the case of durable goods for which there can be no question of the product maturing at a single instant – is not clear at all. This problem is considered only for the stationary economy, and even there it is merely shown that the internal rates of return must be the same for all investments, but not what determines the level of this rate of return. No doubt the ultimate source of the difficulty lies in the fact that the notion of an immediately attainable maximum income stream overtaxes our powers of perception. What kind of dispositions are to be made by the central planning office in order to achieve this end; what they imply for the investment periods of the productive inputs over different time spans; how the length of life and the quantity of durable goods should be selected under this assumption – all these are questions to which it is difficult, if not impossible, to give a precise answer. Starting from the assumption that a constant maximum income stream is to be reached at once, we shall hardly get much farther than to the rather general answers to be found in Hayek's work.

The critique of the second solution of the interest problem – which takes account of new investments and saving – will be deferred until we have considered Fisher's theory.

The third solution applicable to a competitive economy, which we merely outlined above, scarcely purports to supply a complete answer to the question of the level of the interest rate. Fundamentally it says little more than that the rate of interest falls with an increase in the demand for capital goods, and that in a state of equilibrium the rate of interest must be the same throughout the system. Here Hayek no longer refers to the productivity of inputs as a function of their investment periods which previously had played such a large role in his interest theory. In this part of his book, too, he fails to give a precise answer to the question as to how exactly the level of the interest rate is determined.

CHAPTER 5

CONCLUSIONS

The development of theories of interest for a stationary economy, which we traced in the preceding chapters, offers a good example of the evolution of scientific thought. Böhm-Bawerk had based his theory on greatly simplified premises: the only productive factor contained in his analysis was labour; he assumed an "even flow" process of production in which only one product was produced and only circulating capital existed; he worked with simple interest. Wicksell elaborated this theory by introducing more than one factor of production and more than one product, and by applying a general equilibrium analysis of the Walrasian type, improving, however, upon Walras by taking the time element into account. In his later contributions, Wicksell substituted compound interest for simple interest and also examined the case of productive inputs whose investment periods could be varied individually. But he, too, retained the assumption that only circulating capital existed. Åkerman took the next step by formulating his theory entirely for the case of long-lived durable goods. Hayek, finally, undertook a complete classification of the various types of investments and investigated these – at least for the case of a stationary economy – without, however, arriving at a clear-cut solution to the problem of the level of the interest rate. Thus the group of theories discussed in this part of the book has at least the merit of having defined the whole range of investment possibilities which a complete theory would need to cover. At the same time, the development of the theory demonstrated that certain concepts and ideas were untenable and had to be abandoned. This finally led to the realization that an interest theory for a stationary economy, such as the authors of this group – with the exception of Hayek – had been striving to formulate, was impossible to construct along the lines they had attempted to follow.

The first of the concepts which had to be given up was that of the average period of production. In Wicksell's later writings, the shortcomings of this notion had already been recognized; and Wicksell actually worked with the individual investment periods of productive inputs. Åkerman, too, made no further use of this concept. He found that the knowledge of the relation between the volume of inputs and the length of life of durable goods was all that was required for his analysis. Hayek shunned the concept of an average period of production as a matter of principle.

The second concept which created difficulties was that of capital or of a subsistence fund. All of the authors, with the exception of Hayek, worked with it; and all of them thereby exposed themselves to the objection that the subsistence fund, in the sense of a given value magnitude, cannot be taken as a datum but is itself one of the unknowns, so that the system of these writers lacked one equation for determining the equilibrium. In addition, it was tacitly assumed that the subsistence fund had *a priori* the composition that would eventually emerge in the equilibrium to be determined, which again is not an admissible procedure.

Hayek, therefore, quite rightly replaced the subsistence fund in value terms by the given structure of real capital goods. But once we take this step, we must abandon the idea of developing the theory of interest for a stationary state. Here again Hayek was right, for it is not to be expected that this fortuitously given structure of real capital will be maintained and reproduced. Given the wants, the quantity of available productive inputs and the state of technical knowledge some of the real capital goods existing at the start will not be replaced at all, whilst others will be produced in greater quantities than before. We therefore necessarily find ourselves in a changing economy. That being so, the natural procedure to follow – starting off from the given structure of real capital and from the other data – is to take a unit period of time and to analyse how the rate of interest in that unit period results from the interaction of these data. This involves proceeding, as all our authors have sought to do, by way of general equilibrium analysis; i.e., wages, prices, and interest rate must be determined simultaneously in the unit period. This equilibrium, however, is not a stationary or permanent one, but a temporary equilibrium valid only for the unit period under consideration.

This way of approaching the problem has the further advantage that we can dispense with the distinction between reinvestment and new investment. All cases of investment, whether they be reinvestment or new investment, will have to be handled with exactly the same analytical tools. In fact, if the given structure of real capital is taken as the point of departure, an economy in which only replacement investments are undertaken is quite inconceivable, since such a concept is clearly open to the objection that had to be raised against all the authors preceding Hayek, namely, an objection to the *a priori* postulate of that very structure of real capital which the ultimate equilibrium would require.

The idea that the theory of interest must be treated in the framework of general equilibrium analysis is not the only one which, albeit in modified form, has to be taken over from the type of interest theory here discussed. The most important characteristic of this type of theory is the analysis of the role of time in the process of production and investment. This analysis also must have its place in a complete theory of interest, since the entrepreneurs' investment plans on which their demand for capital depends, must incorporate not only their decisions on the "breadth" but also on the "depth" of the investments. As there are many types of relationships between the investment period of productive inputs and their output, all these cases should in principle find a place in a complete theory of interest. In the course of the development of the group of theories treated in this first part of the book, all these cases were brought to light. The cases are, in outline, the following:

1. The case of "point input–point output", as illustrated by the examples of trees and wine. Here it is possible to vary the length of the investment periods of the productive inputs. The problem is to determine these periods and, of course, at the same time to determine the breadth of investment. This is the case on which Wicksell based part of his exposition.

2. The case of "continuous input–point output" which, strictly speaking, needs to be divided into three subsidiary cases:

a) All coefficients are technologically given, including the time coefficients; in other words, the productive inputs have to be applied in a particular combination and in a particular sequence. The investment period of the inputs is not variable. The problem consists only in determining the breadth of investment.

b) The absolute period of production is technologically given while the proportions in which the inputs can be applied and the investment periods of the individual inputs are variable. Here the problem is that of choosing the combination of inputs and their investment periods, as well as the breadth of investment.

c) The absolute period of production is also variable. If the possibility of variation consists only in the ability to lengthen the absolute period of production by the uniform application of new inputs, we have the case on which Böhm-Bawerk based his theory. To put it more precisely, a production process which through uniform applications of inputs comes to an end at the point of time t_n can be extended to points t_{n+1}, t_{n+2}, etc., through further uniform applications of inputs. Here, therefore, the problem is to determine the breadth of the investment and the length of the absolute period of production; the latter simultaneously sets the length of the investment periods of the individual productive inputs.

3. The case of "point input–continuous output"; i.e., that of durable goods. To be quite correct this ought really to be described as a case of "continuous input–continuous output", since durable goods cannot be produced at a single point in time. It is, however, desirable to consider separately the production of these goods and their utilization. The former can be subsumed under one of the other heads, while for the utilization of the durable goods we do indeed have a "point input" at the moment of acquisition of the durable goods. Here are two subsidiary cases:

a) The useful life cannot be changed by way of additional expenditures; then only the breadth of the investment has to be determined.

b) The useful life can be lengthened by increasing the inputs: the case assumed by Åkerman; then not only the breadth of the investment, but also the length of life must be determined.

In neither of these two subsidiary cases is it possible to operate with the investment period of particular productive inputs, since it is impossible to know how many of the original inputs are used up in the services of the durable goods during any particular unit period. But the knowledge of this relationship is not necessary; in case (b) it is sufficient to operate "on the margin", and to this end we need to know only the relationship between additional applications of inputs and the increase in the useful life of the capital good.

The analysis of all these cases is necessary for solving the problem of interest even if the object is merely to determine the interest rate in a unit period since only by such analysis can we obtain the demand for capital by the investors. This is quite obvious in the case of the variable length of life of capital goods. How much capital the entrepreneur needs in a particular unit period depends, among other factors, on what length of life he chooses. But even in the case of "circulating" capital such an analysis is indispensable. The argument, for instance, that in the case of tree-planting the capital requirements in the current period depend only on the "breadth" of the planting and not on the duration of growth chosen is not tenable since it can be shown that breadth and depth of the investments can be determined only simultaneously.

It will become apparent that this approach to the interest problem, to which we were led by our examination of the theories of interest for a stationary state, moves us closer to the second group of interest theories which will now be examined.

PART TWO

INTEREST THEORIES FOR A PROGRESSIVE ECONOMY

In this part of the book we shall consider interest theories which do not take as their starting point a stationary economy, but assume a progressive economy with net investment and saving. The three representative theories here discussed are those of Léon Walras, Irving Fisher, and F. H. Knight.

CHAPTER 6

LÉON WALRAS

I. Exposition

Any attempt to expound Walras' theory of interest meets with the difficulty that he built it into his system of general equilibrium. Hence a complete exposition would require the presentation of the entire Walrasian system. Since Walras' equations have been frequently reproduced, both in simplified versions and in their full form, and as it is not our task to enter into a discussion of the entire system, it seems best to give merely an outline of Walras' general analysis, stressing those aspects which are important for his interest theory. We shall then isolate those parts which have a direct bearing upon the theory of interest, i.e., the equations which determine savings, the rate of interest, and the prices and quantities of capital goods.

According to Walras, all consumption goods are the result of the cooperation of productive services yielded by capital goods. There are three different categories of these capital goods: land, labour, and what Walras calls capital goods "proper" – by which he means produced durable capital goods. He assumes that production is timeless in the sense that these productive services furnish the consumer goods immediately. Thus he disregards circulating capital. Land, labour, and capital goods proper represent three very broad categories, and each of these has to be thought of as subdivided into as many parts as there are different kinds of land, labour, and capital goods. The quantity of services offered by each of these capital goods depends, in principle, on their prices as well as on the prices of all other goods and services. Besides the supply functions of these services we have as data the wants of the consumers, reflected in marginal utility functions from which the demand functions can be derived, and the technically fixed coefficients of production. Later in his analysis, Walras substitutes variable coefficients for fixed coefficients;

but as his capital theory is based on the hypothesis of fixed technological coefficients, we shall make the same assumption here.

In the first phase of his argument Walras neglects the depreciation of capital goods proper; i.e., he regards these as indestructible and treats them in the same way as land. On this assumption and on the assumption of free competition, Walras obtains a system of four groups of equations for the determination of equilibrium. The first group expresses the quantity of productive services offered as a function of all prices expressed in units of the good which has been chosen as the *numéraire*; the second group expresses the demand for consumption goods as a function of all prices; the third equates the quantity offered of productive services with the quantity demanded; and the fourth group equates the prices of consumer goods with their costs. These four groups of equations are sufficient to determine the four groups of unknowns, which are (1) the quantities of productive services actually used; (2) the prices of these services; (3) the quantities of the various consumer goods produced; and (4) their prices.

The following new unknowns appear, according to Walras[1], once the problem of interest is introduced: (1) the amount of savings; (2) the rate of interest; (3) the quantity of new capital goods produced; and (4) their prices.

It can be seen from this that Walras is not attempting to solve the interest problem for a stationary economy but, instead, assumes a progressive economy in which saving and investment take place. What he tries to analyse is the rate of interest for a given period in a progressive economy. To determine the new unknowns he establishes a corresponding number of equations which express: (1) saving as a function of the rate of interest and of the other prices; (2) the equality between the value of savings and the value of newly produced capital goods; (3) the equality between the costs of these capital goods and their prices; and (4) the equality between the discounted value of the services of capital goods and the prices of these capital goods.

It must now be our task to explain this solution in more detail. Let us

[1] Walras' theory of interest is to be found in Section V of his *Éléments d'économie politique pure* (4th ed., Lausanne-Paris, 1900). The references below are to the English translation, *Elements of Pure Economics*, trans. W. Jaffé (London, 1954), Part V, pp. 267–312.

begin with Walras' definition of an excess of the revenue of an individual over his expenditure. His revenue depends on the quantities and the prices of the productive services which he offers. Such services must, of course, include the services yielded by the already existing capital goods in his possession. If we now drop the assumption that the capital goods are indestructible, we must define the prices of the capital services as the gross prices, i.e., the prices before deduction of depreciation. In the case of an individual the excess of revenue over expenditure, which Walras denotes by e, can be zero; this means that the individual consumes his entire gross income, including the amortization quotas of the capital goods in his possession. The "excess" may also be negative – namely, if the individual sells capital goods and spends the cash he receives; but this cannot happen for the economy as a whole. Finally, e can be positive. If e is exactly equal to the depreciation charges, an individual is replacing his capital; if it is larger than these charges, he saves. Thus a positive e does not necessarily signify that saving takes place; it is quite compatible with the consumption of capital. Walras, however, concentrates on the case of the progressive economy; and, in what follows, we shall use the expression, S, as our notation for the excess of revenue over expenditure for the society as a whole, so that a positive value of S signifies net saving.

This saving provides the means for the purchase of a "good" whose price is the reciprocal of the rate of interest. This "good" Walras defines as the right to a perpetual flow of income equal to one accounting unit. We may call it a "perpetual rent" and could imagine that the right to this perpetual rent is certified in a bond.

Walras uses the notation E for this good. The price of E is

$$p_e = \frac{1}{i}$$

We may further imagine that each capital good represents a certain number of units of E which the buyer acquires by the act of purchasing the capital good. The capital goods are thus regarded as sources of a perpetual rent, which implies the assumption that they will always be automatically replaced. A capital good K which yields a certain service per unit period and which is continuously being renewed, so that it can be regarded as the source of a perpetual rent, has a price which is equal to the price of this service less the depreciation charge, divided by the rate of interest:

$$P_k = \frac{p_k - mP_k}{i}, \quad \text{or} \quad P_k = \frac{p_k}{i + m}$$

where P_k is the price of the capital good K, p_k the price of the service per unit period, m the depreciation quota expressed as a percentage of the value of the capital good, and i the rate of interest.[2] If we use π_k to denote the price of the service less the depreciation charge, we may write $P_k = (\pi_k/i)$. The capital good represents π_k units of the good E with the price $1/i$; hence its own price is π_k/i. An individual's demand for capital goods expressed in terms of demand for the good E is, like the demand for all goods, a function of all prices, so that

$$d_e = f_e(p_{t'} \ldots, p_{p'} \ldots, p_{k'} \ldots, p_b \ldots, p_e)$$

where $p_{t'}$ denotes the price of the land service $t'\ldots$; $p_{p'}$ the price of the labour service $p'\ldots$; $p_{k'}$ the price of the service of the capital good $K'\ldots$; p_b the price of the consumer good $b\ldots$, and $p_e = 1/i$ the price of the good E. The consumer good a serves as *numéraire*.

From this function which represents the demand of an individual for the good E, Walras obtains the aggregate demand for this good by adding up all individual demands.[3] From this aggregate demand for the good E we can obtain the aggregate sum of savings by multiplying the aggregate demand for E at each given price p_e with this price. The resulting expression represents the aggregate supply of savings:

$$S = D_e p_e = F_e(p_{t'} \ldots, p_{p'} \ldots, p_{k'} \ldots, p_b \ldots, p_e)\, p_e$$

or, since $p_e = 1/i$,

$$S = F_e(p_{t'} \ldots, p_{p'} \ldots, p_{k'} \ldots, p_b \ldots, i) \qquad (1)$$

[2] Walras introduces in addition to the depreciation charge also an insurance premium which we disregard as it is irrelevant for our present purpose.

[3] Walras (Elements pp. 274–76) describes the shape of this demand curve on the assumption that all prices except p_e remain constant, but his description is not intelligible to me. Jaffé has given an interpretation of the curve which is quite acceptable, but does not seem consistent with the corresponding paragraph in Walras' book; cf. W. Jaffé, 'Léon Walras' Theory of Capital Accumulation', in *Studies in Mathematical Economics and Econometrics, in Memory of Henry Schultz* (Chicago, 1942), p. 45. Fortunately, this matter is not important for Walras' theory of interest.

where S stands for savings. If we assume all prices except p_e (or i) to be fixed, this function can be shown graphically as a curve. Walras himself described it[4], and according to his description it has the shape of the curve depicted in Figure 6.

In examining this curve it must be borne in mind that the rate of interest *falls* as one proceeds upward from the origin along the vertical axis. Hence the point T shows that at a very low rate of interest no saving occurs; if the rate of interest rises, saving begins and it increases up to point S; at higher rates of interest, however, saving decreases again and tends to zero as the rate of interest approaches infinity. That saving drops off again when the rate of interest has reached a certain level becomes obvious when we consider that at a rate of interest equal to infinity practically nothing would be saved, since the saving of a single unit of money would be enough to secure an infinitely large perpetual income. But if at a very high rate of interest saving is minimal and the same is true at a very low rate of interest, then a point S must exist, corresponding to a positive rate of interest, before and after which saving is less than at S itself.

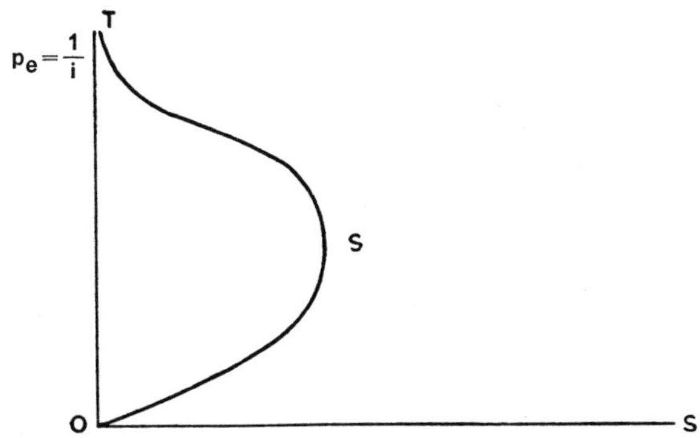

Fig. 6.

Savings are, in equilibrium, equal to the value of the newly produced durable goods. The total quantity demanded of new capital goods, multiplied by their prices, must be equal to savings, so that:

$$D_{k'}P_{k'} + D_{k''}P_{k''} + \cdots = S \tag{2}$$

where $D_{k'}$, $D_{k''}$ etc., represent the quantities demanded of newly produced capital goods K', K'' etc. and $P_{k'}$, $P_{k''}$ etc. their prices.

[4] Walras, *Elements*, p. 275.

But what determines the quantity itself of the capital goods to be newly produced? The equilibrium supply must satisfy the condition that the price of the capital goods has to be equal both to the discounted value of the net revenue they yield *and* to their costs, so that for K':

$$P_{k'} = \frac{\pi_{k'}}{i} \tag{3}$$

and

$$P_{k'} = k_{t'}p_{t'} + \cdots + k_{p'}p_{p'} + \cdots + k_{k'}p_{k'} + \cdots \tag{4}$$

That is to say, the price must be equal to the value of all the services which contribute to the production of the capital good ($k_{t'}$ =amount of services contributed by land of the type $K_{t'}$; $k_{p'}$ =amount of services contributed by labour of the type $K_{p'}$; and correspondingly for the capital good $K_{k'}$). The same applies to every type of capital good. Thus we have equations (1) and (2) together with the two groups of equations (3) and (4) to determine the unknowns: (1) the amount of saving; (2) the rate of interest; (3) the prices and (4) the quantities of new capital goods. It should be noted that we have stressed here only those equations which are important for the theory of interest. Walras later builds these equations into his general equilibrium system, combining them with the four groups of equations mentioned earlier which must, of course, be satisfied at the same time. Obviously the process of saving and investment affects all prices in the system. The whole structure of prices – both of productive services and of consumer goods – will be different from that which would have emerged in the absence of saving and investment.

Walras devotes an entire and very difficult chapter (his *25ème Leçon*) to a discussion of the process by which economic equilibrium establishes itself. In broad outline this process, in so far as it affects the markets which concern us, can be described as follows:

Let us assume that some interest rate i is called out at random in the market (*crié au hasard*) and that equally random quantities of capital goods are being produced. At this rate of interest every individual determines how much to save, and by adding up all the individual savings we can obtain the total saving in the economy at the given interest rate. The quantities produced of the capital goods, on the other hand, have a value which is calculated by capitalizing the flow of the net revenue obtainable from them. The net revenue is for the time being determined on the basis of a likewise "random" price of the productive services of the capital goods. Thus we obtain the value of the capital goods produced; but there is now no guarantee that this value is equal to the aggregate saving coming forth at the assumed rate of interest. If, for instance, saving is greater than the value of capital goods produced, the rate of interest will have to fall and the value of capital goods will have to rise. But if, at the resulting "equilibrium" in this market, the prices of capital goods exceed their costs, the "equilibrium" will not be stable. If the value of the capital goods, as calculated by capitalizing the flow of their net revenue, is higher than their costs, the production of these goods will be expanded. The costs of capital goods, however, are according to Walras a function of the quantities produced: the supply of productive services which can be utilized for the production of additional capital goods will increase only when their prices rise.[5] Thus the production of capital goods can be expanded only at rising costs, and the costs of these goods will approach the demand-price (i.e., the discounted value of their net revenue). This will, of course, in turn change the demand curve for funds in the capital market as well as the supply of savings. Ultimately prices and quantities of capital goods, interest rate, and saving will all "shake down" in such a way that the above four equations are satisfied.

II. Critique

Walras' theory of interest is clear and unambiguous. Unlike Böhm-Bawerk, Wicksell, and Åkerman, he seems to have enough equations to determine the rate of interest as well as the other variables of the system. Even so, his theory does not seem to us to satisfy fully the demands to be made on a theory of interest.

Walras' theory is what nowadays would be called a "loanable funds" theory, such as we shall come to discuss later, according to which the rate of interest is determined by supply and demand in the market for loanable funds. In contrast to modern theorists, Walras assumes that the loanable funds consist of savings only; he does not take account, e.g., of the additional funds obtainable from the banking system. On the other hand,

[5] Walras, *Elements*, p. 292.

he achieves more than these modern theorists in that he constructs his theory of interest within the framework of a general equilibrium theory, whereas they content themselves with a partial equilibrium analysis limited to the market for loanable funds.

Both he and they, however, neglect to analyse the investment process itself – an analysis which the theorists discussed earlier at least attempted. The problem of the investment periods of productive inputs and of the length of life of durable consumption and production goods – in short, the problem of the time structure of production – is completely disregarded by Walras. He simply assumes that the capital goods yield a net return. Thus he has fewer unknowns than the group of theorists treated in Part I and therefore has no need for the particular equation determining the period of production which Böhm-Bawerk and his successors lacked. The question as to how much will be invested receives only the general answer that investment will take place until the discounted value of the net revenues attributable to capital goods becomes equal to the cost of these goods. This lack of any real analysis of the investment process itself does not, indeed, make Walras' theory incorrect, but it does make it incomplete.

A second shortcoming of his theory seems to me due to the fact that he transfers the tools of static equilibrium analysis to the analysis of a progressive economy without making the necessary modifications. Thus, he assumes that the prices of the services of new capital goods, which must be capitalized to obtain the prices of the capital goods themselves, remain for ever at the level that establishes itself during the unit period in question. But in an economy which is growing as the result of net investments, relative prices must be changing from one period to the next, unless we make the impossible assumption (which Walras does not make) that all productive factors, including land, are increasing at a uniform rate. In an economy where only capital is increasing, the supposition that the prices of the services of capital goods will for ever remain the same is not justified. Static assumptions are simply not applicable to a dynamic economy.[6]

The inheritance from static analysis is shown also in the fact that all

[6] Nowadays one might seek to defend Walras by ascribing to the entrepreneurs "static price expectations" which in later periods would not be fulfilled. But this approach was far from Walras' mind.

capital goods are regarded as sources of a perpetual net income, although they are not considered to be indestructible and must therefore be amortized. The assumption that all amortization quotas are automatically reinvested might perhaps be justified for a stationary equilibrium, but not for a progressive economy. The continuous changes in the price structure, which necessarily occur, must bring it about that certain capital goods will no longer be able to earn even their own depreciation and will thus cease to be sources of a perpetual income.

Finally, the influence of the static approach may be seen in Walras' conclusion that in equilibrium the prices of the new capital goods must be equal to the prices of those which already exist. This statement is, in any case, somewhat obscure, in so far as existing capital goods which have already been in use for one, two, or more years simply cannot have the same price as new ones. What Walras means, obviously, is, that the prices of new capital goods must be equal to the value of old capital goods plus depreciation for the appropriate number of years. I shall not stop to labour the point that this statement, too, is not precise because, as we saw earlier, methods of depreciation are quite arbitrary. It is obvious that such equality could be true of all capital goods only in a stationary economy, but not in a dynamic one because – as has already been stressed – there always will be some capital goods which no longer earn their depreciation. Consequently their value is less than their original cost minus depreciation. In short, Walras' analysis is faulty because he applies the static approach to a dynamic economy. He justified this procedure by the statement that "although the economy is becoming *progressive*, it remains *static* because of the fact that the new capital goods play no part in the economy until later in a period subsequent to the one under consideration".[7] As can be seen from the preceding arguments, this claim cannot be maintained.

The question arises whether Walras would not have done better to develop his theory for the stationary state. He assumed a progressive economy because he wanted to find a market on which capital is traded; such a market, he thought, could be found only in a progressive economy. This caused Wicksell to argue at first that Walras' theory explained the rate of interest at most for a progressive, but not for a stationary econo-

[7] Walras, *Elements*, p. 283.

my[8]; however, he withdrew this criticism later in a review of Cassel's book.[9]

One could in fact assume that the supply curve for loanable funds contains not only savings as a function of the interest rate but also the depreciation quotas, and that the demand for funds stems not only from the demand for additional capital goods but also for capital goods which serve to replace old ones. If these two curves intersect at a point at which only the depreciation quotas are being invested, the result will be a stationary economy and the interest rate determined by this point of intersection will be the interest rate of a stationary state. It goes without saying that all the rest of Walras' equations must also be satisfied. In this way it would be possible to avoid the objections which we had to raise earlier against Walras' argument. But even then a fundamental difficulty remains which we have encountered several times already: one of the data in the Walrasian system consists of the existing capital goods or, rather, of the supply curve for the services yielded by these. But if the equilibrium is characterized by the condition that there be equality between the prices of new capital goods and the prices of old capital goods plus depreciation for an appropriate number of years, then it must evidently be assumed that the stock of existing capital goods has from the beginning that very composition which would make this result possible. Just as Böhm-Bawerk and his successors had to assume that the time structure of the existing subsistence fund is exactly such as is necessitated by the equilibrium to be determined, so Walras has to assume the composition of the stock of durable capital goods to be exactly that which equilibrium requires. If Walras had really started, as undoubtedly he intended to do, with a completely "random" composition of capital goods – so and so many units of the capital goods K', K'', etc. – as he did and could do in the case of land and labour, then it would be most unlikely that all capital goods could and would in fact be replaced at his (temporary) equilibrium set of prices. This set of prices consists, of course, of prices for the services of individual capital goods which would result from the wants and technical coefficients assumed to be given in the unit period under investigation.

[8] Wicksell, *Value, Capital and Rent*, pp. 167–68.

[9] Wicksell, *Lectures on Political Economy*, Vol. 1, p. 226, footnote.

CHAPTER 7

IRVING FISHER

Irving Fisher himself pointed out the similarities and differences between his interest theory and that of Walras.[1] The similarities consist not only in his use of mathematics in the exposition and in his agreement with Walras on certain points of theory, but also and above all in the fact that Fisher, too, assumes a changing economy in which saving and investment are taking place.

I. Exposition

Irving Fisher's theory of interest is built upon two fundamental concepts, those of "time preference" and "investment opportunity". For the former concept Fisher occasionally substitutes the term "impatience", but as this word carries the implication that present goods are valued more highly than future goods – which is indeed usually true, although it need not necessarily be so – he prefers "time preference" as the more neutral expression.

Fisher first expounds his theory verbally, then with the aid of diagrams, and finally in algebraic form. In each of these expositions he develops the theory in three stages. In a "first approximation" he assumes that the income flowing to an individual from his labour or his property in land and capital goods is given and can be modified only by borrowing or lending. At a second stage Fisher assumes that the income stream can be altered also by investing. In the "third approximation", finally, he investigates how uncertainty affects the results previously obtained on the assumption of perfect foresight. His method of exposition involves much repetition, some of which we may avoid by combining his first and second approach.

[1] Irving Fisher, *The Theory of Interest* (New York, 1930), pp. 518–519.

We begin with the assumption that each individual has a time horizon of only one year. We can then represent his time preference by means of indifference curves, as in Figure 7. Following Fisher, we shall measure this year's income along the x-axis and next year's expected income along the y-axis. It should be imagined that the annual income is obtained at a *single point* in time, so that the interval between "this year's" and "next year's" income is exactly one year. Any point in the quadrant represents a given combination of this year's and next year's income. The I-curve is the locus of a series of such points which have the common property that the individual is indifferent between any of the combinations of this and next year's income which they represent. The slope of the I-curve at any point is a measure of the marginal time preference of the individual at the corresponding combination of present and future incomes. For instance, the slope at point K, namely OL/OT, indicates how much future income the individual is at this point willing to forego in order to secure a small increase in present income. Thus if $OL = 105$ and $OT = 100$, the individual would be ready at the point K to exchange 105 units of next year's income for 100 units of this year's, or vice versa, his time preference thus being 5%.[2] The time preference is, of course, different at different points on the same curve.

A *higher* indifference curve reflects a better income situation of the

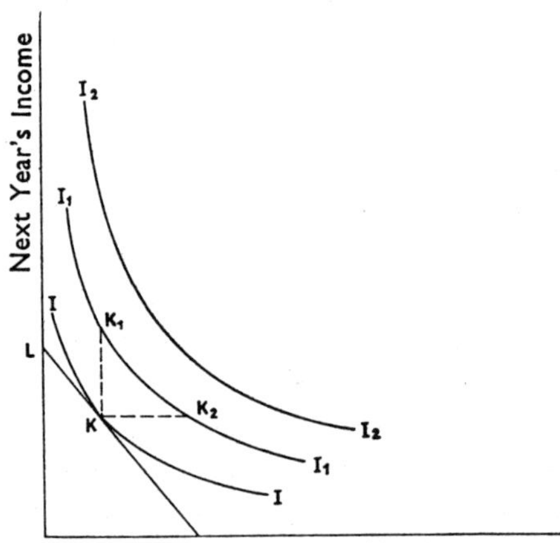

Fig. 7.

[2] The slope of the tangent is $1 + r$, where r represents the time preference (5%).

individual. Any given present income is combined with a higher future income on the I_1-curve than on the I-curve (compare, e.g., point K_1 with point K), and any given future income is combined with a higher present income on I_1 than on I (compare K_2 with K). If we go from K to K_2, we will find the higher curve at K_2 less steep than the lower curve at K, because at K_2, where the present income is larger than and the future income the same as at K, the individual will for that reason be willing to surrender 100 units of present income for fewer units of future income than at K. For analogous reasons the higher curve must be steeper at K_1 than the lower one at K. It follows that the "family" of indifference curves must have the form of that drawn in Figure 7.

Let us now assume that the individual expects to receive an income this year and next year as indicated by the coordinates of K in Figure 8. We shall now introduce the possibility of borrowing and lending. The market rate of interest is given for the individual and can be represented by the straight line MM. The slope of this line is $1+i$, where i is the rate of interest.

We might cover the diagram with an unlimited number of parallel straight lines with slopes expressing the interest factor $1+i$. Only one is drawn here, MM, which passes through the point K. By lending out the

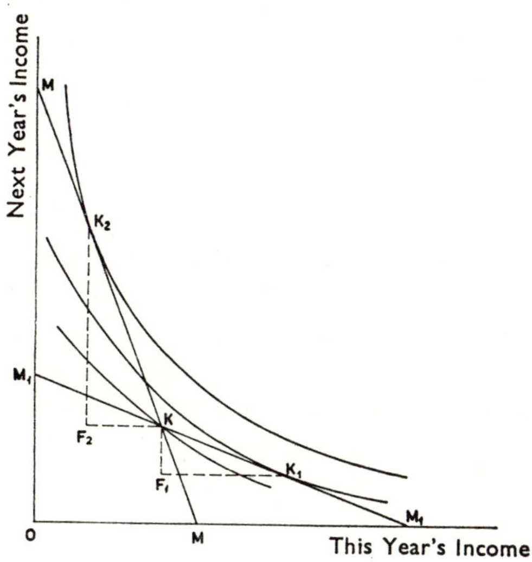

Fig. 8.

quantity F_2K the individual can improve his position, which means that he can reach a higher indifference curve. He prefers the new point K_2, which promises him a much larger income next year in return for accepting a smaller one this year, to his old position K. If, however, the rate of interest should appreciably fall – for instance, to a level which is expressed by the slope of the interest line M_1M_1[3] – he will not be a lender, but instead will borrow the amount F_1K_1 since this will lift him onto a higher indifference curve. In this way we can determine how much the individual will lend or borrow at a given rate of interest and a given time preference. The amount borrowed or lent is always determined by the rule that the marginal time preference must be equal to the given rate of interest or, expressing this geometrically, that the slope of the indifference curve at the chosen point must equal the slope of the interest line. In this manner the supply of or demand for funds in the capital market can be derived for each individual as a function of the rate of interest; the rate of interest would then be determined by the intersection of aggregate demand and supply curves obtained by addition of the individual demand and supply curves. At the market equilibrium the marginal time preference of each individual must be equal to the interest rate.

Up to this point we have not taken account of investment opportunities. How the productivity of capital affects the interest rate can be shown by a simple example. Investment means sacrificing present income in favour of future income. The greater the amount of present income sacrificed, the greater will be next year's income, or, as we shall say from here onwards, next year's product. After a certain point, however, the increase in product will slow down. How far will investment be carried? Fisher answers that it will be carried to the point at which the "marginal rate of return over cost" becomes equal to the rate of interest. In the example below the sacrifice of the first 100 units of present income brings a product (income) of 106 in the next year, the marginal rate of return over cost being 6%. For the next 100 units it is 8%, and so on. If the market rate of interest is 5%, then in our numerical example 400 units of money will be invested, the last 100 of these just earning the interest. A further 100 would earn less than the interest and therefore will not be invested.

[3] As drawn here for the sake of graphical clarity the line M_1M_1 implies a negative rate of interest.

Successively sacrificed this year:	Successively bringing in next year:
100	106
100	108
100	107
100	105
100	104

The matter can also be expressed in a different way: he who makes an investment compares different income streams and chooses the one with the greatest present value. The income stream which he sacrifices represents his investment costs which in our case amount to 400 money units. The present value of the income of 426 units obtainable in the second year, which has to be compared with these costs, is 406 units at a 5% rate of interest. If we denote the investment cost (the amount of present year's income sacrificed) by C, and the present value of next year's income obtained in exchange by V, then Fisher's approach can be described as the maximization of the difference $V - C$. This result is obtained if the investment is continued up to the point at which the marginal rate of return over cost becomes equal to the interest rate.

It must be emphasized that Fisher does not, like Böhm-Bawerk, maximize the internal *average* rate of return (Böhm-Bawerk's *ursprünglicher Zins*). In our example the latter would have to be calculated for an investment of 200 money units from the equation $214/(1+i) = 200$, for an investment of 300 units from the equation $321/(1+i) = 300$, and so on. The maximum for this internal average rate of return would be obtained not with an investment of 400, but with one of 300 money units; at this volume of investment the average rate would amount to 7%, at 400 to 6.5%, and at 500 only to 6.2%.

In Figure 9, the amount of money invested is measured along the x-axis, and the rate of return over cost as well as the market rate of interest, i, along the y-axis. The g-curve represents the marginal rate of return and the d-curve the average rate of return. According to Fisher, investment will proceed up to the point K at which the rate of interest equals the marginal rate of return. If the average rate of return were to be maximized, the investment would be only OK'. In that case the volume of investment would be entirely independent of the market rate of interest.

If the entrepreneur has enough income to save the sum OK for investment, he obviously will not have to obtain his capital in the capital market. Nevertheless, we can say that he "borrows" the capital from himself. If he saves more, he will lend the excess on the market; if he saves less, he must borrow the required amount. The statement that the entrepreneur will carry his investment to the point at which the marginal rate of return becomes equal to the rate of interest holds good, of course, only on the assumption that he has free access to the capital market and is able to lend or borrow any amount at the given market rate.

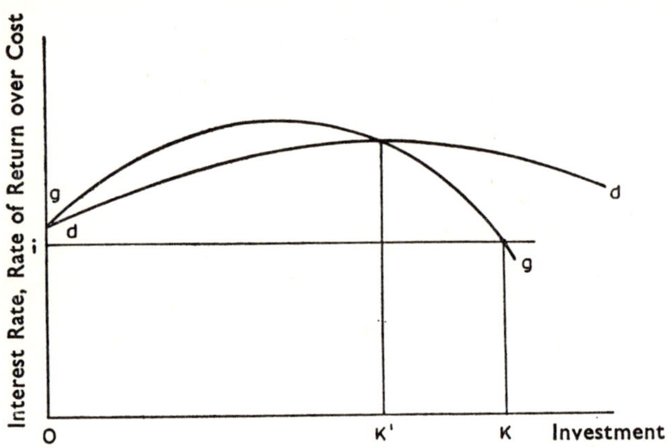

Fig. 9.

Fisher himself presents the matter in a somewhat different fashion. He measures this year's income on the x-axis and next year's income on the y-axis, as in Figure 10, and draws within this system of coordinates an optimum investment opportunity line JI.[4]

Let us, for simplicity's sake, assume that the "entrepreneur" expects an income this year equal to OI and no income at all next year. We may imagine, for instance, that his machines last one year and then "die". Then OI would correspond to the gross return from these machines, or

[4] The curve as we have drawn it here is somewhat different from Fisher's version in two respects: (1) To the left of point I on the x-axis it initially rises at an increasing rate, which Fisher's curve does not do; this means that we assume initially increasing marginal returns on investments. (2) It is carried beyond the y-axis.

to their net product plus depreciation. In accordance with Fisher's definition, the depreciation must be considered income as long as it is not reinvested.[5] Part of this income – which we will assume to be available in its entirety at the very beginning of the first year – may now be reinvested by the entrepreneur in the form of repairs, which would make it possible for the machines to yield an income again at the beginning of the next year. This income will be the greater, the more is spent on the repairs. In making such investments, the entrepreneur moves from *I* to the left along the curve *JI*. We might picture this as a continuous movement, from a few through ever more effective repairs to the full replacement of the machines and, beyond that, to better or more machines. The curve *JI* in itself says nothing about the method of financing of these investments; it simply represents the optimum investment opportunities. As we move back from *I* towards the origin through successive investments of 100 money units at a time, the corresponding points on the *JI*-line will indicate the product obtainable next year as the result of these investments. Thus, if *FI* represents 100 units of money invested, then *FL* is the product obtainable next year from this investment and the ratio $(FL - FI)/FI = (FL/FI) - 1$ is the rate of return on this investment.

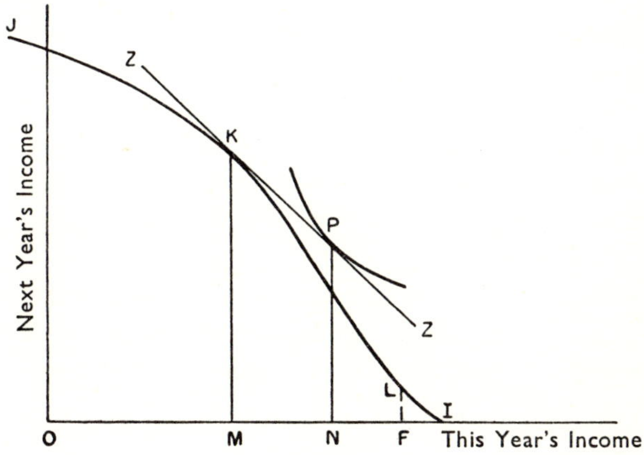

Fig. 10.

[5] It is not necessary to presuppose such a shape of the "income stream". We could start from any point on the curve. Fisher himself starts out from a point on the *JI*-curve which does not lie on the *x*-axis.

If we assume the additional investments to be made in very small doses, $(FL/FI)-1$ represents the marginal rate of return on investment, r, at L. The slope of the JI-line is $1+r$. If we now let the given market rate of interest, i, be represented by a system of parallel straight lines ZZ with the slope $(1+i)$, then one of these will be tangent to the JI-line at a point K. Here market rate of interest and marginal rate of return are equal; the total investment will be MI.[6] The funds required for the investment MI need not be taken from this year's income; the entrepreneur may choose to obtain them on the capital market. How much he will borrow depends on his time preference. Like every other individual he will try to move to the highest curve of indifference between this year's and next year's income. The highest point attainable is in our example represented by P; hence the entrepreneur will invest out of this year's income the quantity IN and borrow for investment purposes the amount MN.[7] It is, of course, also possible that the interest line is tangent to the JI-curve at a point to the left of the y-axis. In that case the entrepreneur would not be able to finance the investment himself. But how much he would borrow and how much he would take out of his income will be determined in exactly the same way as in the case discussed here.

It has thus been shown that with the aid of (1) the indifference curves for this year's and next year's income which reflect the individual's time preference, and (2) the investment opportunity lines which express the productivity of investment, it is possible to determine the demand for and the supply of funds on the part of each individual for any given rate of interest. The equilibrium between supply and demand on the capital market establishes a rate of interest which must be equal to the marginal rate of return on investment and the marginal time preference of each individual.

A detailed analysis of the determination of the interest rate in the more complicated case where several periods are considered must be deferred to the mathematical appendix.[8] Here it must suffice to point to the main

[6] In this diagram the average internal rate of return would be measured by the slope of the line joining I to K. To maximize *this* rate, we would have to join I to a point on the curve so chosen as to make this slope a maximum.

[7] Fisher chooses a situation in which the entrepreneur not only invests nothing himself, but even arranges for a consumer's loan. That is, of course, possible, but can scarcely be regarded as the rule. We have therefore altered the presentation.

[8] See Mathematical Appendix, Section 5.

consequence of such an extension of the analysis. First of all, in a progressive economy the rate of interest must be assumed to change from period to period. The investments made this year will influence the income next year, and since the time preference is a function of, among other things, the size of the income, this preference will change; furthermore, the increase in the capital stock will change the marginal rate of return on additional investments.

The fact that the interest rates will change in future periods was entirely neglected by Walras, even though he, too, had a changing economy in mind. Fisher was the first to take account of it, but he dealt with the problem only in the mathematical formulation of his theory. In the non-mathematical part he merely mentioned it. The verbal exposition of his theory is based on the assumption of a one-period horizon and therefore of a single rate of interest.

As soon as Fisher considers several periods in which the interest rate changes, he comes up against the problem of the structure of interest rates. While there are no quotations of interest rates ruling in future periods, there are quotations of interest rates on loans of different maturities, e.g., rates on one-year loans, on two-year loans, etc. which imply interest rates for future periods. If we assume perfect foresight and disregard the fact that loans give rise to costs (both in terms of effort and of money for the fees of intermediaries), we can regard the rate of interest on a long-term loan as an average of successive short-term rates over the same time span. For instance, one money unit might be lent out three times in succession at the short-term interest rates i_1, i_2, and i_3. At the end of the three unit periods the money unit will have grown to $(1+i_1)(1+i_2)(1+i_3)$. Alternatively, the money unit might be lent out with a term to maturity of three unit periods at the interest rate, J_3, per unit period; under our assumptions the market will see to it that the amount lent out in this fashion will grow to the same sum as that lent out for a short term three times in succession. Thus we obtain the equation:

$$(1 + J_3)^3 = (1 + i_1)(1 + i_2)(1 + i_3)$$

or:

$$J_3 = \sqrt[3]{(1 + i_1)(1 + i_2)(1 + i_3)} - 1 \qquad (1)$$

We assume here that the interest will not be paid until the end of the entire time span.[9] It follows that, if interest rates for future short periods were known, it would be possible to calculate the long-term rates quoted today. Thus the determination of short-term rates for the future in effect simultaneously determines the *structure* of interest rates prevailing in the present unit period.

Let us furthermore consider what effect an extension of the time horizon of the individuals over several periods has on their borrowing and lending. If we consider only one period, the individual will borrow or lend, as we know, up to the point where his marginal time preference for present income over income in the next period equals the interest rate. If an individual has definite (single-valued) expectations with respect to his income stream over *m* years, his time preference for this year's over next year's income depends not only on the incomes of these two years but also on all those expected in the more distant future. Yet it remains true, according to Fisher, that the individual will maximize the utility of his entire income stream if he lends or borrows in such fashion that in each year his marginal time preference with respect to the income of the current and the following year is equal to the interest rate prevailing in the current year. This should not, however, be taken to mean that the individual saves in each year the same amount as he would have saved if he had had only a one-year horizon.[10]

The investment opportunities, too, give rise to new problems when several periods are assumed. Fisher lays down the rule that here again the marginal rate of return on investments for each future year must be equal to the rate of interest prevailing in that year. This will appear quite evident if we imagine that all investments mature in one year, as was the case in the foregoing exposition where only one period was taken into account. The marginal rate of return on investments planned, for instance, for the beginning of the second year must then be equal to the rate of interest prevailing in the second year. According to Fisher this rule also holds for investments maturing after several periods; thus for investments which mature in two years (a tree which is cut after two years), the

[9] For the case of periodical payments the formula becomes more complicated; see F. A. Lutz, 'The Structure of Interest Rates', *Quarterly Journal of Economics*, **55** (1940–41) 36–63; reprinted in *Readings in the Theory of Income Distribution* (Philadelphia-Toronto, 1946), pp. 499–529.
[10] See the example on p. 259.

marginal rate of return in the first and in the second year must equal the interest rates prevailing in these years, and the marginal rate of return *per annum* over the two years must be related to the interest rates of the two years according to the equation

$$R = \sqrt{(1 + i_1)(1 + i_2)} - 1$$

where R represents the marginal rate of return *per annum* on the two-year investment. We shall return to this point later in our critique.

Fisher fully realized that once the assumption of perfect foresight is abandoned the rate of interest will be influenced by new factors, especially by risk and by the closely related factor, liquidity of investments. "Salability is a safeguard against contingencies which may make quick selling advisable. In other words, in a world of chance and sudden changes, quick salability, or liquidity, is a great advantage. For this reason, the rate of interest on individual mortgages will be higher than the rate of interest on more marketable securities... The most salable of all properties is, of course, money; and as Karl Menger pointed out, it is precisely this salability which makes it money. The *convenience* of surely being able, without any previous preparation, to dispose of it for any exchange, in other words, its *liquidity*, is itself a sufficient return upon the capital which a man seems to keep idle in money form. This liquidity of our cash balance takes the place of any rate of interest in the ordinary sense of the word."[11]

II. Critique

It was remarked at the beginning of this chapter that Fisher developed his theory for a changing economy. His mathematical treatment makes it particularly clear that he divides the whole time span under consideration into a series of unit periods ("years") for which he determines beforehand the rate of interest on contracts of one year's duration. And the result he obtains that the rate of interest does not remain constant from year to year, is in itself proof that Fisher assumed a changing economy. This is not to say that Fisher's theory would not be applicable to a stationary economy; but he did not set up his premises beforehand in such a manner that a stationary economy must of necessity follow – something the first

[11] Fisher, *Theory of Interest*, pp. 215–216.

group of theorists did with their assumption of a given subsistence fund. A stationary equilibrium could arise in Fisher's theory if marginal time preference and marginal rate of return happened to be exactly such that only replacement investments would prove profitable. But Fisher was not concerned with this case.

It is possible to cite evidence to the contrary – namely, that Fisher did after all have in mind a stationary economy. His "market principles" contain a statement that one of the equilibrium conditions for the capital market is that the present value of the sums of money lent out by individuals over the entire period under consideration (of n years) has to be equal to the present value of the sums (including interest) received by them in repayment, and correspondingly for the amounts borrowed. This condition implies that at the end of the period all credits have been repaid and the state of things at the beginning of the first period has been restored. This assumption might be cited as evidence that Fisher was concerned with a stationary economy. Nevertheless it remains true that Fisher analyses the movement of the interest rate over time in an economy that changes from year to year.

Let us now turn to the theory itself. Fisher assumes that this year's income, and also, of course, the income in future years, can be sacrificed in favour of still later years; and he makes the further assumption – at least in his mathematical treatment of the problem – that the investments all mature *at a definite date* (the beginning of the second, third, etc. year). The optimum investment opportunity line reproduced above also rests on this assumption. Thus Fisher bases his theory on the "point output" case. He does, indeed, also consider – by way of illustration – the case of durable goods, but this case is not taken into account in the formulation of his equilibrium conditions.

Fisher's solution for the "point output" case is that the marginal rate of return in each year must be equal to the interest rate in that year. To test this result, let us investigate the case of an investment for two years. The method which here immediately suggests itself is to calculate the rate of return over *two* years, which Fisher does not mention, and to compare it with the rate of interest on two-year loan contracts. For an investment of a money units we have

$$\frac{P}{(1+R)^2} = a$$

where P is the end-product and R the *per annum* rate of return on the two-year investment. The investment will be continued until the rate of return calculated from this formula equals the rate of interest J on two-year loan contracts. We do not take as our starting point the rates of return for each year separately, but the two-year rate. Now J, the interest rate for a two-year contract, is related to the interest rates for the first and second year by the formula $(1+J)^2=(1+i_1)(1+i_2)$, so that at the margin of the investment the relation obtains:

$$\frac{P}{(1+R)^2}=\frac{P}{(1+J)^2}=\frac{P}{(1+i_1)(1+i_2)}=a$$

At the end of the first period the value of the product obtainable from the "last" investment of amount a will be $P/(1+i_2)$. Thus it can be said that the marginal rate of return in the first year was equal to the rate of interest in the first year, and that the marginal rate of return in the second year was equal to the interest rate in the second year. To put it differently, we first assume that in the second year the investment earns i_2; then we calculate the value $P/(1+i_2)$ and consider this the "final product" of the first year; the marginal rate of return for the first year is then calculated from the formula $a=[P/(1+i_2)]/(1+r_1)$, where r_1 is the marginal rate of return for the first year. The investment will be continued until this rate of return in the first year equals the interest rate in that year. It is no wonder that the marginal rate of return in the *second* year is then also equal to the interest rate in the second year, for this was implicitly assumed beforehand in the calculation.[12]

The difference between the two procedures – one involving a two-year rate, the other two one-year rates – can be shown graphically. Let us take the case of a tree whose length of life, it is assumed, cannot be extended beyond two years for technical reasons (Figure 11). The lifetime is Ot_2. In the first approach the costs Oa are joined with the final value $P_{t_2}t_2$ by a curve whose slope in each year reflects the two-year rate of return calculated as a *per annum* rate. This line is aP_{t_2}; since we have adopted a logarithmic scale for the ordinate, it appears as a straight line. At the margin of the investment in trees this rate has to be equal to the two-year

[12] As already noted, Hayek's approach is identical with Fisher's (cf. *supra*, p. 64).

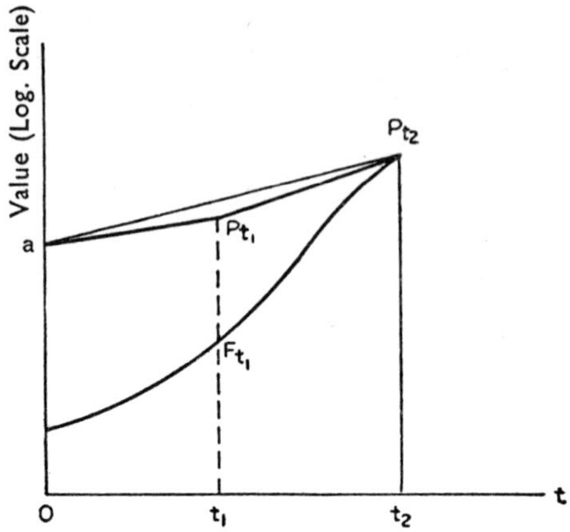

Fig. 11.

interest rate J. The second approach consists in discounting the value $P_{t_2}\, t_2$ with the market rate of interest for the second year, so as to obtain the value $P_{t_1}\, t_1$, and then connecting P_{t_1} with a. The slope of the line between a and P_{t_1} reflects the rate of return for the first year, and investment will be continued until this rate equals the interest rate for the first year. The two methods yield the same result. It is also clear that in the second case the marginal rate of return for the second year equals the interest rate in that year only for the reason that this assumption was made from the start. The original growth curve of the tree, however, does not at all show the value of the investment at the end of the first year to be $P_{t_1}t_1$. If the tree were to be cut down at the time t_1, the owner would not receive the value $P_{t_1}t_1$, but the value $F_{t_1}t_1$. If the tree were to be sold standing, on the other hand, the seller would in fact obtain $P_{t_1}t_1$. One could then regard $P_{t_1}t_1$ as this year's "income" which is reinvested in favour of next year's, so that the marginal rate of return is, indeed, in both years equal to the interest rates prevailing in those years. Yet, it seems a rather artificial approach to pretend that the value of the investment at the margin grows each year by the amount of interest of that year. It seems to us that the rate of return for the first year would have to be calculated from the formula $a = (F_{t_1}t_1)/(1 + r_1)$, where the numerator on the right-hand side of the equation represents the value of the investment at the end of the year on the assumption that the investment will really be terminated at this point (by cutting down the tree). This rate of return is, even at the margin, *not* equal to the interest rate in the first year. The natural approach, however, would surely be to take the two-year marginal rate of return as the point of departure and to compare this to the rate of interest on a two-year contract.

Let us now turn to the case of durable goods and assume that their length of life is technologically fixed. The case of durable goods is not really covered by Fisher's theory – whether we assume their lifetime to be technologically fixed or whether, as in Åkerman's theory, their life represents a variable to be determined. Durable goods "ripen out" over the entire time span of the good's "life". This proposition has the following consequences:

(1) It is not possible to undertake an investment which would bring a return in, say, the third year only. Whoever invests in durable goods having a "life" of three years will not produce an income in the third year without also having produced incomes in the first and second years.

(2) It is not known what proportion of the original expenditure on the durable good matures in each year. Therefore it is not possible to calculate the rate of return for individual years. If the good yields a quasi-rent at the beginning of the second year and another at the beginning of the third, it is not possible to determine the one-year or the two-year rate of return as we do not know the cost of this quasi-rent.

Nevertheless, up to a certain point this case can be treated analogously to that of an investment which matures at a particular date. We can set up the following equation:

$$C = Q_1 + \frac{Q_2}{1+r} + \frac{Q_3}{(1+r)^2}$$

where C stands for the cost of the durable good, r for the rate of return which we can calculate from the equation and the Q's for the quasi-rents obtainable from the durable good.

Provided that the one-year rates of interest remain the same through both years, so that the *currently* quoted one-year rate equals the currently quoted two-year rate, we can compare this rate of return r with the interest rate and conclude that the investment in the durable good will continue up to the point at which r equals the rate of interest.

The assumption of unchanged interest rates is essential. If the interest rate does not remain the same, we cannot use this procedure. We can, however, adopt a method analogous to the second approach in the tree case. We calculate the value at the beginning of the second year of the last quasi-rent Q_3 from the formula $Q_3/(1+i_2)$, where i_2 represents the interest rate of the second year. The resulting value V_2 we equate with the costs C through the formula $C = [V_2/(1+r_1)]$, where r_1 represents the rate of return of the first year. This rate we compare with the interest rate of the first year, and the investment will be continued until this rate of return equals the interest rate of the first year. In this calculation it is tacitly assumed that the quasi-rent available at the beginning of the second year can be lent out at the rate of interest of the second year. It is one of the short-comings of Fisher's theory that he did not incorporate this important case of durable goods into the body of his theory of interest even though he made use of it in occasional illustrative passages.

A further deficiency in Fisher's theory is that he confines himself entirely to the analysis of the capital market and works with the assumption that the *prices of goods and services are already determined.* His theory is thus a partial equilibrium theory. It is generally acknowledged that such partial equilibrium theories are acceptable as long as the market we are considering constitutes only a small part of the economy, so that repercussions on the rest of the economy stemming from the developments in the market under investigation can be safely disregarded. The price of tea, for instance, can be determined with supply and demand curves which are functions of the price of tea only. But this approach is not admissible if the market is of such importance that adjustments taking place in it necessarily have repercussions throughout the economy. The capital market is certainly in that class. All of the authors treated earlier have dealt with the interest problem in the framework of general equilibrium analysis. Fisher, in attempting only a partial equilibrium analysis, had an easier task than his predecessors: he could ignore many problems such as, for instance, that posed by pre-existing old capital goods, and he could work in terms of the investment of sums of money which would not have been possible if the prices of the factors of production had to be determined at the same time. This also explains why in Fisher's theory we do not find conclusions such as that the wage rate has to be equal to the discounted marginal product of labour or the rent on land to the discounted marginal product of land.

III. Addendum

Fisher's economic world is somewhat peculiar in so far as he assumes that at the end of the whole period under investigation all loans have been repaid and no claims are outstanding. "For any given persons the additions, through loans, in some time intervals must be equivalent, in present value, to the subtractions in others", as Fisher puts it in his *Summary*.[13] This is the second of his two "market principles" which he calls the "principle of repayment".

Hayek, on the other hand, assumes in his indifference-curve presentation of the saving process that the amounts saved remain invested forever, thus yielding a perpetual increment to the income stream. We shall here give an account of Hayek's exposition, concentrating on the essentials.

Hayek develops his theory for an economy ruled by a dictator. This dictator has a certain time preference with respect to goods; and, in planning production, certain investment opportunities yielding a return are available for his consideration. Under these conditions Hayek has to find some way of harmonizing the dictator's time preference with the rates of return obtainable from investments. He need not concern himself with the market interest rate which is, in an exchange economy, in some sense "interposed" between the saver and the investor. The market rate of interest is interposed inasmuch as the individual saver brings his time preference at the margin into harmony with the market rate of interest and the entrepreneur continues his investment up to the point at which that rate is equal to the marginal rate of return. Hayek further assumes that all investments mature in one year. He thus neglects both the question of the optimum investment period of inputs and the problem of durable goods.

In Figure 12, present income is measured along the y-axis and future income along the x-axis. Future income here refers to the income which can be obtained *permanently* from the next year onward. Along the line OW, present and future incomes are equal.

We start from point P. Hayek makes the assumption that at this point only current inputs are available, and if no investments are undertaken

[13] Fisher, *Theory of Interest*, Table following p. 226.

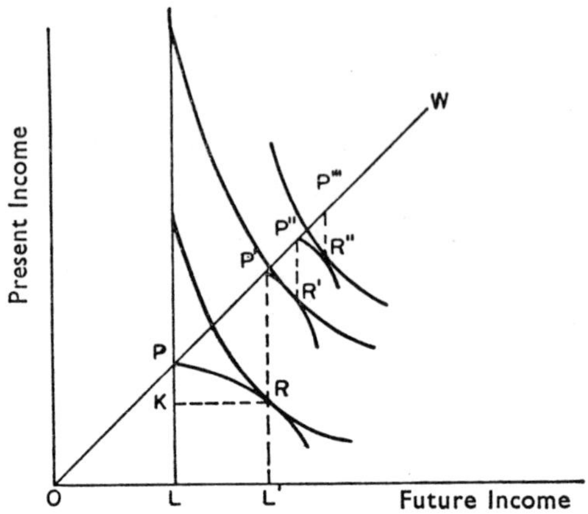

Fig. 12.

these would produce the same income – here OL – every year. On this assumption it is not possible to raise the present income at the expense of future income, and Hayek therefore disregards that part of the quadrant which lies to the left of the line PL. The indifference curves in the diagram reflect the attitude of the dictator with respect to the sacrifice of present income in favour of a permanent increase in future income. Hayek draws these curves in such a manner that at first all of them run along the vertical line LP. Evidently his idea is that a sacrifice of future income is, as was pointed out above, not possible. But indifference curves have nothing to do with the technical possibilities; the merging of the different indifference curves into a single line seems to me inadmissible as this would signify the equivalence of combinations of higher or lower present incomes with the same future income. For the purposes of our present analysis, however, this objection has no relevance. The curves PR, $P'R'$, etc., represent the investment opportunities; they show on what conditions present income can be transformed into future income. The sacrifice of the amount PK of present income for investment purposes will forever raise future income by LL', so that from the next year on the income will permanently be OL'. The transformation curves are concave to the origin[14], since increasing investments are associated with di-

[14] The individual transformation curves are not independent of one another. Since the return from an additional investment depends on the already existing total capital

minishing returns. The dictator will move from point P towards point R, a point which is characterized by equality of his marginal time preference with the marginal rate of return on investments. Once R is reached, income from the next year on will again be the same for all future years, but at a higher level than at the point P (provided, of course, that the one-year investment is replaced each year). The new income situation is reflected by point P'. This point, however, will be abandoned again in favour of R', and so on. It is evident that ultimately a point will be reached at which saving and new investment cease altogether, so that a stationary state is attained.

Thus Hayek's exposition differs from Fisher's in that saving (and investment) are looked upon as permanent. But apart from these differences Hayek arrives at the same conclusion as Fisher, namely that the marginal internal rate of return must equal the marginal time preference (with the qualification that, for reasons already stated, the market rate of interest plays no part in Hayek's solution). Hayek's solution of the interest problem in a dynamic economy also resembles Fisher's in being one of partial equilibrium. Furthermore, in this solution the investment period of inputs is assumed to be given and equal to one unit period, so that all the very difficult investment problems, which Hayek himself had earlier investigated in such detail, are in this particular context pushed aside.

---

stock, the higher transformation curves must have the same slope as the lower curves at points which reflect the *same* pre-existing capital stock. Thus at R the transformation curve PR has the same slope as the higher curve $P'R'$ at point P'.

CHAPTER 8

FRANK H. KNIGHT

It is not easy to give an exposition of Knight's theory of capital and interest.[1] Over a number of years Knight devoted many papers to the subject; and, as anyone who ever attempted to work his way through Knight's theory knows, these writings have passages which are very difficult to understand and also, either apparently or really, contradictory. I can claim no more than an earnest effort to understand his theory, but I cannot guarantee that Knight himself would accept my exposition as a correct presentation of his thought on all points. The possibility of disavowal is a risk which everyone must run who undertakes this task.[2]

[1] Knight has dealt with the problem of capital and interest in the following publications, which in this chapter are cited by the name and year of the periodicals containing them: 'Neglected Factors in the Problem of Normal Interest', *Quarterly Journal of Economics*, **30** (1915–1916) 279–310. 'Professor Fisher's Interest Theory: A Case in Point', *Journal of Political Economy*, **39** (1931) 176–212. 'Interest', *Encyclopaedia of the Social Sciences*, Vol. VIII. 'Capitalistic Production, Time and the Rate of Return', in *Economic Essays in Honour of Gustav Cassel* (London, 1933), pp. 327–342. 'Capital, Time and the Interest Rate', *Economica*, New Series, **1** (1934) 257–286. 'Professor Hayek and the Theory of Investment', *Economic Journal*, **45** (1935) 77–94. 'The Ricardian Theory of Production and Distribution', *Canadian Journal of Economics and Political Science*, **1** (1935) 3–25 and 171–196. 'The Theory of Investment Once More: Mr. Boulding and the Austrians', *Quarterly Journal of Economics*, **50** (1935–1936) 36–67. 'Comment' [on Machlup's article], *Journal of Political Economy*, **43** (1935) 625–627. 'The Period of Production: A Final Word', *Journal of Political Economy*, **43** (1935) 808. 'The Quantity of Capital and the Rate of Interest', *Journal of Political Economy*, **44** (1936) 433–463 and 612–642. 'Note on Dr. Lange's Interest Theory', *Review of Economic Studies*, **4** (1936–1937) 223–230. 'On the Theory of Capital: In Reply to Mr. Kaldor', *Econometrica*, **6** (1938) 63–82. 'The Business Cycle, Interest and Money: A Methodological Approach', *Review of Economic Statistics*, **23** (1941) 53–67. 'Professor Mises and the Theory of Capital', *Economica*, New Series, **8** (1941) 409–427. 'Diminishing Returns from Investment', *Journal of Political Economy*, **52** (1944) 26–47. 'Capital and Interest', *Encyclopaedia Britannica*, Vol. IV, 1946, pp. 779–801; reprinted in *Readings in the Theory of Income Distribution* (Philadelphia-Toronto, 1946), pp. 384–417.

[2] N. Kaldor, who quite early presented a critical appraisal of Knight's theory, begins

In order to make Knight's theory understood it will be necessary to go a little further afield and to begin with his views on the production process.

I. Knight's Concept of Production

If we want to understand the economic nature of the process of production we must abandon the old-fashioned idea that what is being produced is "wealth", that is, *goods*, and that these goods are being produced by two or three productive factors – labour and land, or land, labour, and capital. Production consists in the rendering of a flow of consumable *services*. Since, however, it serves no purpose to draw a distinction between the flow of services yielded by a good with a short length of life (e.g., food) and the good itself, we can, says Knight, regard food stuffs and similar goods as "products", so that the stream of these "products" takes the place of the stream of their services.[3] The source of this stream of perishable goods (or their services) is, then, the stock of the more durable productive capital goods which in cooperation with other productive services produce these consumer goods. This flow of services is the only kind of production going on in a stationary economy. What is *exchanged* on the market is, essentially, a variety of claims to flows of services over certain periods of time. The value of such claims is found by capitalizing the flows.[4]

Services are necessarily consumed at the moment at which they are rendered. What is more, they are also being produced as they are rendered. Thus production and consumption are simultaneous processes[5] or, to put it another way, the production period is nil. This follows immediately from the definition of production, since the delivery of "consumable services" is possible only as a current act. It is true, of course, that in each period

with the disclaimer that "this reconstruction of Knight's views ... is not necessarily a 'correct' version of his views; it should be considered as an interpretation rather than a summary; and it is possible that it will be repudiated by the author himself". (N. Kaldor, 'Annual Survey of Economic Theory: The Recent Controversy on the Theory of Capital', *Econometrica*, **5** (1937) 203). Kaldor criticizes Knight's views from the standpoint of "Austrian" capital theory.

[3] *Canadian Journal of Economics and Political Science*, **1** (1935) 13.

[4] In the case of short-lived goods the value of the services they supply is identical with the value of the goods themselves. It is for exactly this reason that we may identify such goods with the services they yield.

[5] *Economica*, **1** (1934) 276.

productive services are applied to the maintenance or replacement of capital goods. But this is merely a necessary part of the current production of consumable services. Knight remarks in support of this statement that if the capital goods were not perpetually replaced the community would be living at the expense of stored-up wealth, in which case, he says, the flow of services would no longer be produced during the current period. It is obvious that a quite different concept of production is implied by this statement since here the "rendering of services" is no longer *per se* identified with production. However that may be, according to Knight we would then be dealing with a case of consumption of "supply on hand"[6], and he concludes from this that if the services are to be currently produced as they are being consumed, then the replacement of capital goods must form a necessary component of this "current" production.

In this context Knight emphasizes that no logical difference exists between the maintenance of capital goods (by repairs) and their replacement, the latter being just a particular form of capital maintenance. From the point of view of the capital stock of the entire community, a stock which must be considered an integrated organic whole, a machine is simply a component part which needs to be replaced – just as at times parts of individual machines need to be replaced. In the first case we speak of replacement, in the second of repair, but the difference is purely terminological, not substantive.

If we now take the case of a growing economy, characterized by an expansion of real capital, we have to modify the above statements somewhat. The process of expansion of real capital, i.e., the creation of objects of "wealth" (instead of a flow of consumable services) must also be regarded as *production*. The capital so created is equal to the amount of income sacrificed for it (plus the interest accrued during the period of construction) and it must be accounted for *during* the construction period as income flowing to the productive factors which are creating it. Once it exists and has become an integral part of the community's capital endowment, it contributes to the production of consumable current services, which must then (in part) be imputed to the new capital rather than to the productive services which created the capital goods. The capital goods

[6] *Canadian Journal of Economics and Political Science,* **1** (1935) 10.

themselves are imputed to these services. The creation of new capital is the only case where objects of wealth rather than services are being "produced".

The capital endowment of the community is in practice never "liquidated". An individual often liquidates his capital by selling the capital goods and consuming the proceeds or by consuming the amortization quotas. If the community as a whole should try to liquidate its capital, it could do so only within narrow limits without bringing on a collapse of the entire production process. At any rate, as the economy which we know is not regressive but progressive, we need not consider this case any further.

If we look at the capitalistic process of production "historically", we must conclude that the productive services which create new capital never ripen into consumption goods since the capital is never liquidated. The period of production in this sense is infinite. The production period, accordingly, is zero when we are thinking of the production of current services which proceeds with the aid of the existing capital; but it is infinity when we are thinking of the investment period of productive services which create new capital. To make this conception intelligible we must add that it is, according to Knight, quite unimportant that individual capital goods wear out, as they are always replaced so that the capital as such never ripens into consumption goods. Capital is thus, as with J. B. Clark, a permanent fund of value, the size of which is found by capitalizing the income stream which it yields.

An expansion of the capital endowment of society presupposes "abstinence", not "waiting". Since the new capital will last forever, it will not in fact be used up later as the expression "waiting" would imply. Even if we look at the process of capital formation from the standpoint of the individual, it is as a rule true that he invests without any intention of later disinvesting. Individuals, who are weighing the question whether they should save, compare "large, short segments of income-flow with thinner streams reaching out to the indefinite future".[7] This approach to the saving process is the natural counterpart to the notion that capital, once created, lasts forever.

"Production" is the result of the cooperation of the productive services

[7] *Economica,* **1** (1934) 278.

rendered by all kinds of productive factors. We can, if we wish, divide these productive factors into two groups: on the one hand those factors which can be owned – real capital – and on the other hand the factors which cannot be anyone's property – labour. From the economic standpoint there is no sharp line separating these two groups. The notion that capital goods, in contrast to people, are produced for economic reasons cannot provide such a dividing line – not only because considerations other than economic ones often do play a part in the creation of real capital goods, but also because economic considerations are not entirely absent in the "production" of people, above all in their occupational training. Moreover, people have to be maintained just as capital goods do. Despite these similarities, it is convenient to distinguish between labour and capital goods, if for no other reason than that capital accounts are not kept for free persons as these cannot be bought and sold. Knight in fact treats the creation of capital goods but not the creation of men as an economic problem. In his later publications the similarity between labour and capital is stressed more strongly than in his earlier writings.

Although labourers should not be counted as part of real capital, it would nevertheless be wrong to maintain that real capital is created by labour and land and to juxtapose these to real capital as the "original" factors of production. Consumable "produced" services as well as newly produced additional capital goods are the result of the co-operation of all productive services of which none can be claimed to be "primary" in any sense. However far back we go into history in analysing the production of the existing real capital, we shall never reach a point at which only the services of labour and land were used.

It is within this general framework that Knight's theory of capital and interest has now to be considered.

II. First Version of the Theory of Interest

Following Knight's procedure, we may begin by writing down a few equations for simple cases of investment.[8] Let us assume that an investor, for the purpose of creating real capital, sacrifices one dollar of his income

[8] *Economica*, **1** (1934) 265f.

per year for t years. The last dollar is invested at the beginning of year t. Then the total costs of the investment up to the beginning of year t are

$$1 + (1 + i) + (1 + i)^2 + \cdots + (1 + i)^{t-1}$$

forming a geometric series of which the sum is

$$\frac{1 - (1 + i)^t}{1 - (1 + i)}, \quad \text{or} \quad \frac{(1 + i)^t - 1}{i}$$

If S dollars are invested each year, the expression becomes:

$$\frac{S[(1 + i)^t - 1]}{i}$$

Let us now assume that the investment, once completed, yields a uniform return (after deduction of repair costs, but not of depreciation) for n years of R per year. The present value of these incomes at the beginning of the income stream is[9]:

$$\frac{R[(1 + i)^n - 1]}{i(1 + i)^n}$$

To obtain the rate of interest, we equate the costs of the capital good to the present value of the returns:

$$\frac{S[(1 + i)^t - 1]}{i} = \frac{R[(1 + i)^n - 1]}{i(1 + i)^n}$$

or

$$S[(1 + i)^t - 1] = \frac{R[(1 + i)^n - 1]}{(1 + i)^n} \tag{1}$$

From this equation the rate of interest can be calculated. The rate in question is obviously the internal rate of return. It is assumed in the equation that the interest rate charged during the construction period of the capital good is equal to that earned by the capital good.

[9] The value of an income stream of R per annum over n years (obtainable at the beginning of each year) is $R\,[(1 + i)^n - 1]/i$ at the beginning of the n-th year. On discounting this sum back to the beginning of the income stream we obtain, according to Knight, the expression reproduced in the text. Actually the expression should be $R\,[(1 + i)^n - 1]/[i\,(1 + i)^{n-1}]$.

In equation (1) the capital good is treated as having a limited length of life; it is assumed that it will wear out. We know, however, that according to Knight it is necessary to regard an investment as permanent, i.e., to assume that it will yield a "perpetual" flow of income. This is achieved by reinvesting the amortization quotas. The "perpetuity" of an investment can be expressed by means of an equation which takes proper account of this reinvestment.

As before, the cost of the investment is $S[(1+i)^t-1]/i$. Let us now assume that a constant amount x is written off each year in such a way as to make the total, to which these amortization quotas will have grown by the end of the life of the capital good, equal to the costs of that good. We must accordingly write off each year an amount equal to[10]:

$$x = \frac{S[(1+i)^t - 1]}{(1+i)^n - 1}$$

It is assumed that the amortization quotas can be reinvested at the same rate of interest as that yielded by the capital good. Then the absolute value E of the annual net return is given by

$$E = R - S\frac{(1+i)^t - 1}{(1+i)^n - 1}$$

The net return expressed as a percentage of the cost of the capital good equals the rate of interest:

$$i = \frac{R - S\dfrac{(1+i)^t - 1}{(1+i)^n - 1}}{S\dfrac{(1+i)^t - 1}{i}} \tag{2}$$

This expression, which can be reduced to equation (1), can be solved for i.

[10] Let us denote by x the amount to be written off annually and to be reinvested. These amounts x, which are annually put aside and reinvested until the n-th year, must grow to a sum equal to the cost of the capital good. Hence

$$\frac{x[(1+i)^n - 1]}{\mathrm{i}} = \frac{S[(1+i)^t - 1]}{\mathrm{i}}.$$

By solving this equation for x we obtain the expression for x found in the text.

If we make less simplifying assumptions with regard to the rate at which income is sacrificed during each unit period, or as to the time structure of the income stream obtainable from the investment, the equations become more complicated. But nothing essential will be changed thereby.

The equations clearly show that the interest problem is in reality a problem of capital valuation and not at all a problem of distribution. Each capital good earns a return which we call its rent. In order to determine this rent we have first to solve a problem of imputation. The solution to this problem answers the question, which part of the product produced with the aid of the capital good is to be imputed to the latter? In other words, the problem of distribution must already have been solved before we can undertake to write equations of the type presented above and to use them for determining the rate of interest.

A practically unlimited number of investment opportunities are open to the individual investor. For each of these opportunities he can equate the cost of the investment and the present value of the future returns. These equations show him which of the investment opportunities yields the highest interest rate (internal rate of return), and thus which of them is the most profitable. The rate of return obtainable from the best investment expresses the marginal productivity of capital, provided that this investment does not involve a significant addition to the capital existing in the system as a whole so that this "marginal investment" cannot notably affect the rate of interest. In a competitive economy the rate of return achieved at this "margin of growth" will be the rate prevailing in the system as a whole. "The rate of return on 'capital' is the maximum perpetual income obtainable under the given conditions, through the creation of a new source of income, or the maintenance of old sources, measured as a rate per unit of time, divided by the aggregate present consumption sacrificed in making any such investment. An 'investment' is, of course, to be understood as an increment of investment, made or maintained at the margin for the total productive plant of an economy."[11]

In this solution of the interest problem we think of the economy as a growing one and analyse it at a single point in time (or in a short unit

[11] *Economica*, **8** (1941) 421.

period). Knight assumes, moreover, perfect foresight and a constant purchasing power of money.

Knight puts the emphasis on the productivity of capital. As regards saving, he basically confines himself to the statement that "all that any individual or any society can do is to save and invest, or disinvest, as the case may be, up to that point at which his preference of present over future goods, at the margin, is measured by the rate of return".[12]

When the capital endowment of society increases, the interest rate will fall as a consequence of diminishing returns on capital investments. The growth of capital will not take place through additions of more capital goods of the same kind as those already available; types other than the existing ones will be added, and all worn-out capital goods will be replaced by different types. Therefore we cannot ascribe the diminishing returns on capital to those changes in the relative proportions of the various means of production which the law of diminishing returns assumes. "There is no measurable change in the physical proportions of anything to anything else."[13]

As a consequence, Knight is forced to look for some other reason for the diminishing returns on capital investments. He finds it in the diminishing marginal utility of income to the individual, a consequence of the growth of incomes. "Even if increased production took the form of increasing the output of the same identical goods and services, without change in proportions, and if these were produced by use of the same productive agencies in the same proportions, all agencies being freely augmentable, investment would still be subject to diminishing returns, because of the diminishing utility of total economic income to the individual."[14]

Knight seems to have abandoned this position later, however, for in another place we find him remarking that "if all productive agents can be freely augmented by the use of all those which already exist, there will not be diminishing returns, for, if the growth of investment leads to progressive satiation of wants, it will affect in the same way the cost and the yield and consequently will not affect the rate".[15]

[12] *Economica*, **8** (1941) 415.
[13] *Econometrica*, **6** (1938) 80.
[14] *Econometrica*, **6** (1938) 80.
[15] *Journal of Political Economy*, **52** (1944) 36.

III. Second Version of the Theory of Interest

The statement that the rate of interest is determined at the "margin of growth" by equality between the costs of the optimum investment and the present value of the future income stream does not, according to Knight, suffice for a theory of interest: "Equality does not prove causality, still less show the direction of causality. To deal with this problem, it is necessary to consider the rate of return, or the valuation of income sources, in the usual terms of value or price theory, in the terms of demand and supply."[16]

There are two ways of approaching the analysis in terms of supply and demand. Either we regard the rate of interest – that is, a perpetual income expressed as a certain percentage rate on the capital – as the price of the capital, or we regard the capital as the price of the perpetual income. As it is the income stream which is really desired, it would be natural to look at the matter from the second point of view. Knight develops his theory under both aspects. We shall first present his exposition of the usual view, according to which interest is the price of capital.

We may regard the supply of capital at any given point in time as consisting of the whole stock of capital, assuming that we have some way of measuring this stock. In Figure 13 the quantity of capital is measured along the x-axis and the rate of interest along the y-axis.[17] The supply is

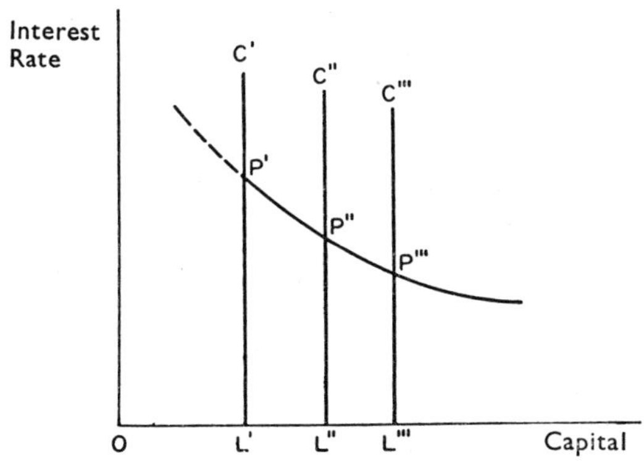

Fig. 13.

[16] *Economica*, **8** (1941) 421.
[17] *Journal of Political Economy*, **44** (1936) 619ff.

then represented by a vertical line which cuts the x-axis at a certain distance from the origin. We assume that at a given point in time the system is in equilibrium, and that $P'L'$ represents the interest rate prevailing in that equilibrium. We then proceed to draw a demand curve for capital which begins at point P'. This will be sloping downwards to the right as additional investments bring diminishing returns. Since demand curves have to be drawn on the assumption of *ceteris paribus*, it would be meaningless, according to Knight, to extend the curve to the left of the point P' (this would imply disinvestment), and equally meaningless to carry it very far to the right because the other conditions cannot be assumed to remain constant if investment takes place on a large scale. As the capital stock grows, the vertical line shifts to the right and, taken in conjunction with the demand curve, indicates the successive interest rates which result from this accumulation of capital.

According to Knight, there is no point at which saving and, consequently, capital accumulation will cease. Saving is a function of income; income grows with the accumulation of capital; the growth in income causes further capital accumulation which once again increases income, and so on. There is, therefore, no tendency towards a stationary state in a capitalistic economy. Such an economy is of necessity characterized by growth.

In the alternative approach, it is the future income obtainable through investment which is regarded as the "commodity" in demand[18]; the price of this commodity is then the present value of such future income, or the market value of the sources yielding it. The supply is regulated by the cost of producing this perpetual income, i.e., by the cost of producing capital goods which are the sources of such income. The demand is represented by the volume of saving which becomes available in the time period under consideration. As the volume of saving can change only with the lapse of some time, it may be thought of as constant in a short period and can then be represented by a vertical line. The supply curve is exceedingly elastic. If the sources of future income can be produced at constant cost, the supply curve appears as a horizontal line; if they are produced at slowly decreasing cost, as Knight seems to suppose[19], the curve slopes slightly downward. As saving increases, we shift the vertical

[18] *Journal of Political Economy*, **44** (1936) 642.
[19] *Journal of Political Economy*, **44** (1936) 642.

line towards the right so that it intersects the supply curve at ever lower points.

One more of Knight's theses remains to be mentioned. He maintains that the rate of interest could fall to zero only if all capital goods were to become free goods. His proof for this statement will be given in the following section.

IV. Critique

We shall not attempt a detailed critique of Knight's views on the nature of the production process in a capitalistic economy. For our purpose, it will suffice to bring out those points which are significant for his interest theory.

It follows from the definition of production as the "rendering of consumable services", that the production period is zero. If this definition is accepted, it will appear natural to regard capital as a perpetual fund yielding such consumable services. It will then seem unnecessary, and indeed meaningless, to speak of investment periods of productive inputs; and, if we construct a theory of interest with the help of these concepts time no longer seems a necessary element in the explanation of the interest rate. To be sure, Knight agrees that in the case of an individual capital good we can determine both the time at which the inputs used in the construction of the capital good are applied and the time at which the services of the capital good are rendered.[20] If we wish, we can construct an investment period for these inputs. But on the whole he treats this possibility as unimportant and prefers to look upon capital as a permanent fund yielding a perpetual income. "Wherever resources, i.e. any useful things whatever, are actually produced, or maintained, any resource or bit of capital which we choose to consider as a unit, viewed as the marginal increment of productive capacity in an economy, is actually self-perpetuating, hence essentially perpetual, regardless of the durability of the concrete agent or agents of which it is composed."[21]

Despite such pronouncements, Knight's analysis proceeds quite differently. The construction period of capital goods and the time of waiting for their services form an essential part of his analysis. His own equations,

[20] E.g., in *Economica,* **1** (1934) 274f.
[21] *Economica,* **8** (1941) 418.

which must be solved for the interest rate, are based on the assumption that both the time at which the inputs are applied and the time at which the returns become available is known. This applies also to equation (2) which is intended to express the fact that capital is a permanent fund. Here we may cite Knight himself as the chief witness: "But each increment of investment must yield its return at the same rate (in the sense of 'ratio'), either in consumed service or as an addition to the investment, and *for as long as it remains invested...* Because the process of investment must be spread over time and because, in general, there is more or less disinvestment in connection with the direct yield of any particular capital good, it is necessary to recognize the separate period of investment, from zero to infinity, of each infinitesimal increment of capital invested in any source or capital good. Only in this way can different investments be made at the same rate and the maximum yield obtained on the whole capital, which is possible under the given economic conditions."[22] Thus in his theory Knight cannot dispense with dating the productive expenditures on individual capital goods or with dating the yields. Since this is so, only confusion can arise by a terminology according to which the production period is zero and capital is a permanent fund.

The latter concept also obscures another important fact: namely, that the replacement of the machines ought to be treated in exactly the same way as the acquisition of additional machines. Either action involves abstinence, and there can be no question of the replacement of machines being "automatic". Here again Knight's actual analysis, at least in his later writings, conflicts with his terminology. In one of his earlier publications he had characterized it as absurd to say "that the *re*production of instruments of any kind can be considered as economic production".[23] Later, however, he tried to ward off the criticism raised against him for asserting that replacement of capital goods takes place automatically by saying that "all that is necessary is that the individual owner of any income-yielding capital good or quantity of capital shall distinguish between consuming its yield and consuming the capital itself".[24] But this can mean nothing other than that the individual has to choose between consumption and replacement, which is the same sort of choice as con-

[22] *Journal of Political Economy,* **44** (1936) 447.
[23] *Economica,* **1** (1934) 280.
[24] *Journal of Political Economy,* **44** (1936) 457.

fronts him in the case of new capital formation. This Knight implicitly admits in another passage where he argues that in a stationary state abstinence must be interpreted as a sacrifice "continuously incurred" by the owner of capital goods who abstains from consuming the amortization quotas.[25]

Thus Knight's treatment of the time element in production contradicts his definition of the production period, which is supposed to be zero, as well as his definition of capital as a permanent fund. The latter definition also conflicts with his treatment of the replacement problem.

Let us now turn to Knight's interest theory itself. His most important statements, at least according to the first version, can be summarized as follows: The rate of interest prevailing in the system as a whole is determined by the highest internal rate of return which can be obtained from investments made at "the margin of growth" of the system. As the capital endowment increases, the interest rate falls. The interest rate can, however, never fall to zero; it could attain that level only if all goods became free goods.

We shall consider the three parts of this summary separately: (1) The rate of return at the "margin of growth" can be calculated only if we know the value of the inputs used in the construction of the capital good in question as well as the value of its yield. The substantive content of Knight's solution, whose correctness is of course indisputable, is thus rather thin. Only a general equilibrium analysis which determines these values together with the other unknowns of the system can be regarded as a satisfactory solution of the interest problem. We must maintain, therefore, that the first version of Knight's theory gives us no clear answer to the question: which factors in particular determine the level of the interest rate at the "margin of growth"? All we learn on this question is that the rate depends in some way on the amount of existing real capital, and that it falls when the latter rises.

(2) The interest rate falls with the expansion of the capital stock. Knight, believing that this fact cannot be explained by the law of diminishing returns, had to account for it in some other way. He himself abandoned his first explanation, according to which the drop in the rate of interest was connected with the diminishing marginal utility of income

[25] *Journal of Political Economy,* **44** (1936) 632.

as the latter increases as a result of capital accumulation. But he did not replace this explanation by another one that could be called satisfactory. It is undoubtedly correct that if all means of production – capital, land and labour – were increased proportionally there would be no diminishing returns on additional investments. If decreasing yields on a productive resource are to be the result of the law of diminishing returns, the resource in question must increase relative to the others used in production. Knight saw that, in the case of an expansion of capital, such a change of proportions requires a special explanation, since, given the amount of land and labour, new investment does not as a rule increase the stock of machines by adding machines of the same type as those already in use but rather by adding new types. Knight ultimately concludes: "The successively smaller increments of income must result from successive equal increments of investments as measured by cost in sacrificed income from productive agents (or some form of capacity) other than those (or that) in which the new investment is embodied. Investment which takes the same form (in the aggregate for 'society') as the source of the income sacrificed in making it cannot be subject to diminishing returns."[26] The last sentence in this quotation is evidently nothing but a different way of stating that no diminishing returns would occur if all means of production ("productive agents", which include capital goods) could be increased proportionally. The first part of the quotation, however, does not make it clear what are the proportions that would be altered by new investment. Probably the simplest solution would be to point out that in consequence of the accumulation of capital the ratio of workers employed in the capital goods industry to those employed in the consumer goods industry increases, from which it follows that the value of future consumer goods which will be produced with the aid of these capital goods must fall relative to the value of present consumer goods. This implies a lower rate of interest.

(3) Finally, we have to examine Knight's conclusion that the interest rate could be zero only if all goods were free goods. His argument is as follows: "No agent would be maintained at a cost, in the absence of some incentive, which is a return on the cost. The 'gross' yield (the imputed service value or rental) of any agent which is not naturally immortal,

[26] *Journal of Political Economy*, **52** (1944) 37.

must be greater than its 'net' yield, the difference being the cost of provision for maintenance. Hence if the service has any value (marginal utility) at all, the gross yield must be preferable to the net yield, since the difference will have some value for consumption. In other words, 'resources' of limited life will be maintained, in the absence of a return on investment, only if their services are free goods, which means that the resources themselves are not resources in the economic sense."[27]

The fact that there would be a zero interest rate if all goods were free goods is indisputable. But is the obverse of this also true, namely, that the interest rate can be zero only if all goods are free goods?

Knight's argument, if we understand it correctly, runs along these lines: someone who owns a capital good which yields no interest can consume the gross return from the good without suffering any harm, since thereby he increases his present consumption without diminishing his future consumption to which the capital good, if maintained, does not contribute anything. If the interest rate were zero, capital goods would be consumed, which would have the consequence that a positive rate of interest would eventually re-emerge. The interest rate could be zero only if the capital goods were free goods, since only then would the consumption of capital goods not force a reappearance of the rate of interest.

There will, however, always be individuals who would not consume their capital goods even if they brought no return – for instance, individuals who are expecting a diminishing income stream which they want to replenish at a later date by postponing the consumption of their capital goods until then. There will even be people who will create capital goods even though these bring no return because they find themselves in a period of increasing income and expect diminishing incomes later. By this means they even out their income stream. Thus it is quite possible that even with a zero rate of interest the existing capital will not be used up or, indeed, that new capital may be formed – i.e., that the formation of new capital will exceed the consumption of capital – even if capital goods are not free goods. One may object that it is quite possible to even out the income stream by first hoarding money and then liquidating these hoards rather than by first accumulating and then consuming capital goods. However, the assumption that under stationary conditions and

[27] *Economica*, **8** (1941) 415.

with a zero interest rate individuals would hoard rather than reinvest the depreciation quotas does not appear to us a sensible assumption. The real capital goods engaged in the production process create, jointly with labour – that of the manager-owner included – a flow of goods from which the owner-manager may derive, if not an income from interest, at least an income from work. And it is reasonable to assume that this income from work would become smaller if the owner were to consume his real capital.

Let us now turn to Knight's second version of his theory of interest.

In Figure 13 the supply of capital is regarded as consisting of the entire real capital. The supply curve therefore is a vertical line. The demand curve begins at point P', which lies on this supply line. The distance of P' from the x-axis measures the rate of interest corresponding to this capital stock. This interest rate is *not* found as the intersection of the demand curve with the supply curve, but rather is determined at the "margin of growth" and simply serves as the starting point for the demand curve.

I can see no justification for the supply curve of capital in Knight's presentation. As he himself has repeatedly stressed, the value of capital can be found only by capitalizing the returns, and this would require knowing the rate of interest. A higher interest rate would imply a smaller, and a lower interest rate a larger, supply of capital, even if the quantity and composition of real capital goods remained the same. The construction of this supply curve presupposes that we already know the interest rate which, in the further course of Knight's presentation, is to be determined by the intersection of the supply and demand curves.

Furthermore, it is not permitted to draw an aggregate demand curve for capital: as Knight himself emphasizes, demand curves must be drawn subject to the assumption of *ceteris paribus* – an assumption which cannot be made in the case of a demand curve for an aggregate like total capital. If aggregate capital increases, there will be changes in wages, in commodity prices and in income distribution – all factors which influence the demand for capital. Knight's remedy – not to extend the demand curve to the left and to draw it only "a short distance" to the right from the point P' – is a dubious expedient which does not satisfy the reader.

Knight's second method of using supply-and-demand analysis is still more puzzling. It is based on the notion that the future income itself is the good demanded and supplied, the price of which is the price of the source yielding that income. The demand is here represented by new saving, and since in any small unit period the quantity of saving is practically constant it can be regarded as given (independent of the interest rate). The supply is a function of the cost of this "source" and is accordingly represented by a horizontal straight line if costs are constant, by a falling

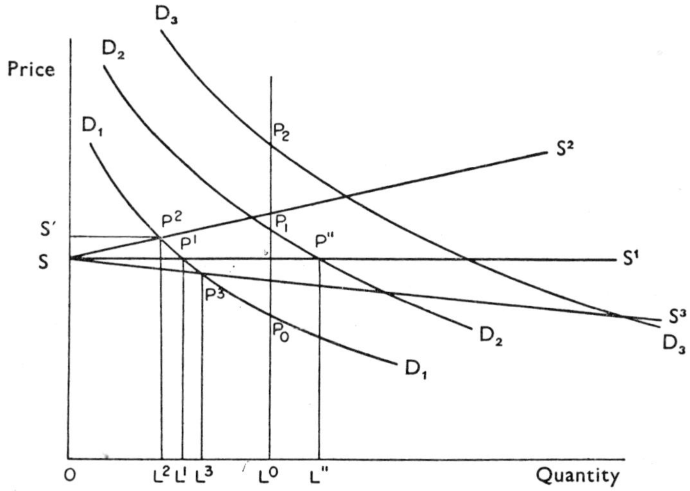

Fig. 14.

line if they are decreasing, and by an upwards sloping line if they are increasing. This construction is open to three objections:

1. In the first place, it is not at all clear why it should be possible to expand the production of capital goods at will during a unit period which is too short to permit an expansion of saving. An expansion of the production of capital goods, too, cannot occur without the passage of a certain time; hence during a very short period the supply of capital goods must also be inelastic.

2. What are the units of measurement on the x-axis? We are obviously dealing with physical units. Then the given amount of savings must be expressed as so and so many physical units of capital goods which can be bought with the amount saved, and this quantity depends, of course, on

the price of the goods. The supply must also be expressed in units of capital goods. But what kind of units can we use here, considering the fact that the stock of real capital goods consists of many different types?

3. The entire approach rests on the notion that real capital goods produce an income stream of a certain definite magnitude. Under this assumption constant costs would imply constant marginal efficiency of capital, decreasing costs would imply increasing marginal efficiency and increasing costs diminishing marginal efficiency of capital. But, as already stressed, it is not acceptable to lump the costs of real capital goods of all kinds into a single variable, such as could be plotted in a diagram, unless the problem of finding a single physical denominator for all real capital goods could be solved.

The relationship between the costs of a capital good and the interest rate can be shown diagrammatically for *one particular type* of capital good in the following manner: on the x-axis of Figure 14 we measure the supply in units of the real capital good and on the y-axis the supply price. We obtain a horizontal straight line in the case of constant costs, a rising curve in the case of increasing costs and a falling curve in the case of decreasing costs (SS^1, SS^2, SS^3). To these curves let us now juxtapose a family of demand curves (D_1D_1, D_2D_2, D_3D_3) which reflect the capitalized stream of quasi-rents obtainable from the capital good, each curve being based on a different interest rate. The farther a curve lies to the right, the lower is the rate of interest on which the curve is based. For a given quantity of the capital good, say OL^0, the demand price will be the higher, the lower the rate of interest – compare P_2, P_1, and P_0.

We can now reconstruct from this diagram the customary presentation of the demand for capital as a function of the interest rate. The total sum required for the purchase of the capital good at the interest rate reflected in the demand curve D_1D_1, assuming constant costs, will be $OSP'L'$; at the interest rate reflected in D_2D_2 it will be $OSP''L''$, and so on. If we plot the values so obtained in a new diagram which measures total values on the x-axis and the interest rate on the y-axis, we obtain a demand curve for loan-capital for the purchase of this particular capital good, the demand being expressed as a function of the interest rate. It is immediately obvious that we can make no general statement about the effect of increasing or decreasing costs of the capital good: this effect evidently depends on the elasticity of both the SS- and the DD-curves. For instance, at the interest rate reflected in D_1D_1, the rectangle OL^2P^2S' relevant in the increasing cost case could be either larger or smaller than the rectangle $OL'P'S$ which represents the sum required in the constant cost case at the same interest rate.[28]

[28] This derivation of the demand curve for capital, which was contained already in the first edition of this book, is now also to be found in an article by J. G. Witte. He concludes from it that the macroeconomic investment function or the marginal efficiency of capital curve for society as a whole is not a demand curve in the usual sense at all. It connects points of total capital outlay that arise at different interest rates under the assumption that the supply of and demand for capital goods is in equilibrium at these different rates. The macroeconomic marginal efficiency curve is a curve connecting equilibrium points in the market for capital goods. See J. G. Witte, 'The Microfoundations of the Social Investment Function', *Journal of Political Economy*, **71** (1963) 447.

CHAPTER 9

CONCLUSIONS

The analysis of the interest theories put forth by the first group of authors – those who had tried to explain the interest rate for a stationary economy – showed that their explanation was not completely satisfactory. We were forced to the conclusion that a different approach would have to be found, i.e., we concluded that the starting point should be a unit period in the "life" of a progressive economy. The economy enters the period with an arbitrary structure of real capital goods which must be considered one of the data. Starting from such data, the theorist has first to analyse the investment plans of the entrepreneurs and the saving plans of the savers and then to determine, with the help of this analysis, the interest rate in the period by way of general equilibrium analysis.

The authors whose works have been analysed in this second part of our investigation in fact take such a unit period as their point of departure. This approach is most clearly seen in Irving Fisher's work; but it is also used by Walras and, even though less clearly, by Knight. Basing the theory of the first group on the assumption of a growing rather than a stationary economy would help to bridge the gap between their analysis and that of the second group.

The treatment of the interest problem by our second group of writers contains another basic contribution which should be included in all theories of interest. Once we assume a changing economy, we are led automatically, as was Irving Fisher, to the problem of the term structure of interest rates – a problem which the first group did not even touch. They could not, in fact, consider the problem, since in a stationary economy only *one* rate of interest can exist. But once the theory of the first group is developed along the lines suggested in Chapter 5 it necessarily runs into the problem of the structure of interest rates, as was apparent already in Hayek's work; this seems to indicate that the two groups of theories could be fused into *one* theory.

An essential condition for making this synthesis, however, is that the interest problem be dealt with in terms of general equilibrium analysis, as the first group attempted to do and as Walras did. As soon as one attempts such an analysis, it is no longer possible to work simply with the investment of sums of money, as Fisher did; it then becomes necessary to explore the investment periods of the individual productive inputs, in so far as these can be determined. For example, it is possible to explain the price of a productive input and to conclude that the price must be equal to the discounted marginal product of the input only if the investment period of the productive inputs is known. In brief, a general equilibrium analysis requires that the core of the explanation attempted by the first group – namely, the time structure of production – should be incorporated into the theory of interest.

PART THREE

MONEY AND INTEREST

CHAPTER 10

OLDER THEORIES

So far we have had no opportunity to consider the influence of money on the interest rate. Not all of the authors which we have considered up to now expressed their views on this problem, but those who did were far from denying the existence of such an influence. The reason they did not introduce the monetary factor into their own theories of interest was their conviction that the influence of money on the interest rate is only of a temporary character, a view which can be traced back to the English classical economists. Böhm-Bawerk expressed this as follows: "The level of the interest rate prevailing in a country does not in the long run depend on whether that country has a large volume of coins or other types of money, but on whether it is rich in real capital, in stored-up products available for productive investment or for lending. Nevertheless, the stock of money, taking this term quite literally, does exert a certain influence on the movements of the interest rate – an influence which, although not profound, is very conspicuous and therefore often overestimated, especially by the layman."[1] Böhm-Bawerk goes on to explain the connexion between money and the interest rate by pointing out that, as a rule, the additional money flows initially into the banks, causing a reduction of the interest rate on bank credit. However, this effect will not be a lasting one, for "then the excess quantity of money, to the extent that it pours into the channels of the commodity markets, will in a well-known fashion reduce the purchasing power of money. Money prices of all commodities – and, thus, prices of real capital goods – will rise; and ultimately more units of money than previously will be required to transfer the same amount of real capital goods. Once matters have come to this point, the increased supply of money which initially pressed on the market as excess supply will be completely absorbed by the demand for

[1] Böhm-Bawerk, art. 'Zins' in *Handwörterbuch der Staatswissenschaften* (3rd ed., Jena, 1911).

money capital which rises for the above reason. Eventually the disturbed equilibrium between supply and demand will be restored, and the normal interest rate corresponding to the actual supply of real capital (*der reellen Kapitalfülle entsprechend*) will also be re-established."[2]

Wicksell develops a similar line of thought in much more detail in his book *Interest and Prices.*[3] After explaining how the "natural" rate of interest is, as we have already seen, determined by the subsistence fund, by the supply of productive factors and the function which relates the volume of output produced by a labourer to the period of production, he introduces money as a means of payment. He shows how the banking system can keep the interest rate on bank credit – i.e., the money rate of interest – below the natural rate of interest. This condition leads to a general rise in prices which can be brought to a standstill only when the money rate of interest is raised to the level of the natural rate. Conversely, when the money rate is above the level of the natural rate, deflation will set in and will continue until this discrepancy between the two rates of interest is again removed. On Wicksell's assumptions, nothing changes in the economy but the price level. His distinction between the natural and the money rate of interest provoked an extensive discussion which turned mainly on the question whether equality between the two rates of interest in a progressive economy would guarantee stability of the price level, and whether it would be identical with the ex ante equality between saving and investment. This discussion, in turn, led to the question, what kind of interest policy a central bank ought to pursue.[4] However, we shall not follow this line of thought any further.

Alfred Marshall was also, in principle, a proponent of the point of view presented by the authors just mentioned. "The supply of gold exercises no permanent influence over the rate of discount. The average rate of discount permanently is determined by the profitableness of business. All that the influx of gold does is to make a sort of ripple on the surface of the water. The average rate of discount is determined by the average level of interest in my opinion, and that is determined exclusively by the profit-

[2] Böhm-Bawerk, art. 'Zins' in *Handwörterbuch der Staatswissenschaften.*

[3] Knut Wicksell, *Interest and Prices*, trans. R. F. Kahn (London, 1936).

[4] On this problem see especially: G. Myrdal, 'Der Gleichgewichtsbegriff als Instrument der geldtheoretischen Analyse', in F. A. Hayek (ed.), *Beiträge zur Geldtheorie* (Vienna, 1933).

ableness of business, gold and silver merely acting as counters with regard to it."[5] And his later description of this "ripple on the surface"[6] shows that his theory is not very different from that of Böhm-Bawerk.[7]

For the sake of our later discussion it should be added that, consciously or unconsciously, these authors also assumed competition in the labour market and, thus, perfectly flexible money wages. They did not examine the question whether, and to what extent, their results might be affected if money wages were to be regarded as fixed.

The theories of these authors about the influence of money on the interest rate can, no doubt, be taken as typical of the views prevailing in their days; nevertheless, different ideas on the subject of money and interest began to make their appearance in that period.

First of all, we find the admission that the influence of money on the interest rate is, or at least can be, more than temporary. Wicksell himself recognized this possibility which had been stressed, among others, by Cassel. "There is no doubt that when a sudden violent rise in prices has set in, people with fixed incomes or with incomes which have not increased sufficiently are compelled to curtail consumption. This process is equivalent to a real accumulation of capital, and to that extent should lower the real rate. In normal conditions, however, such a reaction should only be of secondary importance."[8]

This statement reflects a well-known line of thought which can be expressed as follows: if during a general rise in prices certain incomes are left behind, the income distribution in the economy is altered: if those individuals who experience a more than proportional rise in their incomes

[5] Alfred Marshall, *Official Papers* (London, 1926), p. 41.

[6] Marshall, *Official Papers*, p. 52.

[7] A *Dogmengeschichte* of theories on the influence of money on the interest rate before Keynes would probably show as its main result that in the mercantilist period the interest rate was thought of as being determined by the quantity of money; that the classical economists in their desire to remove the "money veil" regarded the interest rate as primarily determined in the "real" sector of the economy, although there were exceptions, especially among authors dealing with problems of money and banking; and that the modern theorists before Keynes indeed granted money an influence, but only a temporary one.

[8] Wicksell, 'Professor Cassel's System of Economics', reprinted in *Lectures on Political Economy* (London, 1934), Vol. 1, p. 251. A detailed analysis of the Wicksellian cumulative process under various assumptions is to be found in J. Niehans, 'Interest Rates, Forced Saving, and Prices in the Long Run', *Review of Economic Studies*, **32** (1965) 327–338.

proceed to save the additional income entirely or in part; and if with no rise in prices the group whose income is lagging behind would have saved less, then real capital will grow more and the natural rate of interest will fall further than would have been the case without inflation. This influence of money on the natural rate of interest must, accordingly, be ascribed to two factors:

1. to the existence of time lags in the adjustment of certain incomes to the price level; and

2. to the assumption that the income recipients who are favoured will save more than the recipients of incomes now lagging behind would have saved if the price rise had not in fact taken place.

It is necessary to emphasize this second assumption in order to bring out that there is nothing automatic about the process whereby real capital is increased as the result of inflation. Besides, the acknowledgement of such a potential influence of money on the natural or equilibrium rate of interest does not make the theory a monetary theory of interest. To call it a monetary theory of interest simply because money's influence is recognized would have as much justification as designating an interest theory as a "population theory of interest" because one recognizes that an increase in population might lower wages and increase the return on capital.

Antedating Keynes but still in recent times, we find theories of interest which allot money a really essential role. Here Schumpeter is the first who should be mentioned. His famous thesis that in a stationary economy there would be no interest need not detain us long. This claim rests on a double assumption: first, that the individuals in a stationary economy, because they expect an unchanging income, will not value present goods higher than future goods, so that their time preference will be zero; second, that there will be no investment opportunities other than those already realised. On these assumptions Schumpeter's result is correct.[9] Whether one accepts it depends, therefore, on whether one finds the assumptions to be acceptable. Schumpeter, indeed, was of the opinion that the first point does not constitute an assumption but, rather, that it follows from the postulate of rational behaviour. He considers it a corollary of this postulate because anyone who valued present goods more highly than future goods and who acted on this basis would, under these

[9] On this point, see G. Haberler, 'Schumpeter's Theory of Interest', *Review of Economics and Statistics*, **33** (1951) 122–128.

circumstances, find "that he had obtained a smaller total satisfaction than he might have done".[10] But this conclusion is valid only if it is assumed *a priori* that the individual does not value present goods more highly than future goods. Thus we are indeed dealing with an assumption which may, but need not, be correct. The second hypothesis, namely, that no investment opportunities exist, is possibly connected with Schumpeter's concept of the "static manager" (*statischer Wirt*) who simply does not think of trying out new methods of production. "Given the necessary quantities of labour and natural agents, production by this method (i.e., by the method already in use) will be repeated indefinitely without any exercise of choice..."[11] But once a "rational" type of entrepreneur is assumed, as is usually the case in economic theory, the approach of Böhm-Bawerk, Fisher, Knight, Cassel and others seems to us better justified: namely, that even in the absence of technical progress practically unlimited investment opportunities exist, the adoption of which is solely a question of the level of the interest rate. If the rate of interest were zero, advantage would be taken of these opportunities, and the resulting increase in the demand for capital would push the interest ratc above zero again.

In Schumpeter's positive theory the interest rate is a result of the dynamic development caused by the entrepreneurs' attempts to exploit innovations. These undertakings create "surplus value", since the value of the products produced by the innovating firms will be above their costs of production – even if only temporarily for the individual firm. Entrepreneurial profits arise which are always liable to be swept away by competition; but which, so long as the dynamic development lasts, do not disappear in the economy as a whole since profits will keep reappearing in ever different sectors. In order to put the innovations into effect, the entrepreneurs need purchasing power because they are not in possession of the necessary means of production. Initially they obtain this purchasing power from the credit-creating banks. Later in the development process the purchasing power supplied by the banks will be augmented to a considerable extent by funds stemming from new saving – which occurs in the wake of development – and from working capital temporarily lying idle. The profits the entrepreneurs earn enable them to

[10] Schumpeter, *The Theory of Economic Development*, trans. Redvers Opie (Cambridge, 1951), p. 35.
[11] Schumpeter, *The Theory of Economic Development*, p. 36.

pay interest on the purchasing power borrowed from the banks. Schumpeter describes the demand and supply relations in this market, constructing the demand curve for capital on the basis of the entrepreneurs' expected rates of return and juxtaposing it to the limited supply. So far as credit creation by banks is concerned, the supply is limited by the need of banks to stay liquid, and in so far as savings are offered on the market, by the insistence on the part of savers to be compensated for the "disturbance" of their consumption plans.

Obviously, Schumpeter here develops what would nowadays be called a "loanable funds" theory, that is to say, a theory which explains the interest rate on the basis of supply and demand for credit in the capital market. We shall return later in more detail to this subtype of the so-called monetary theories of interest. Undoubtedly it explains quite correctly the surface phenomena observable in the capital market. In fact, it would seem to us that no theorist could have an objection to it. By itself, however, it does not carry us very far. Interest theories may be distinguished by the extent to which they advance the analysis of the supply and the demand for capital. In this respect Schumpeter differs considerably from his predecessors in that he derives the demand for credit from the need for capital occasioned by the introduction of innovations and refuses to admit that even in the absence of such innovations an unlimited need for capital would exist. The supply, on the other hand, he basically derives from credit creation – thus emphasizing the monetary factor alone, although he does not deny the existence of a supply of saved funds, provided the economic development is in full swing. His predecessors, by contrast, either disregarded the monetary factor altogether or held it to be of importance only in the short run.[12]

Very similar to Schumpeter's theory of interest was that of Albert Hahn, particularly in the first edition of his *Volkswirtschaftliche Theorie des Bankkredits.* Hahn formulated the core of his interest theory in the Keynesian sentence that "the interest, i.e. the price to be paid for credit, must be regarded as the compensati on for the loss of liquidity occasioned

[12] I shall not here enter upon a detailed critique of Schumpeter's theory, but I do not wish to conceal my opinion that in the controversy between Schumpeter and Böhm-Bawerk the latter had the best of the argument in all essential points. (See Böhm-Bawerk, 'Eine dynamische Theorie des Kapitalzinses', in *Kleinere Abhandlungen über Kapital und Zins*, edited by Franz X. Weiss (Wien-Leipzig, 1926), pp. 520–585.)

by the granting of the credit".[13] In his later writings, however, Hahn considerably modified his views, so that a detailed appraisal of his theory can be dispensed with here.

The discussion about the relation between money and the interest rate received a new impulse from Keynes' *General Theory of Employment, Interest and Money*, and in the next few chapters we shall concentrate entirely on the "Keynesian" literature. In these chapters it will be necessary to abandon the approach we have hitherto followed. The Keynesian literature consists largely of articles in periodicals, and, apart from a few exceptions, it contains no original contribution to the theory of interest which would have to be discussed as such. Hence we can no longer expound and analyse the theories of each author separately. Instead we shall, after the presentation of Keynes' theory, take up particular problems and deal with the views of the principal authors who took part in the discussion under the various problem headings.

[13] Albert Hahn, *Volkswirtschaftliche Theorie des Bankkredits* (2nd unchanged ed., Tübingen, 1924), p. 102.

CHAPTER 11

JOHN MAYNARD KEYNES

Let us prepare the ground for a detailed discussion of Keynes' theory of interest by presenting first his main theses in broad outline.

The ultimate independent variables of the Keynesian system are, in Keynes' own words, the following: "1. the three fundamental psychological factors, namely, the psychological propensity to consume, the psychological attitude to liquidity and the psychological expectation of future yield from capital assets; 2. the wage-unit as determined by the bargains reached between employers and employed; and 3. the quantity of money as determined by the action of the central bank..."[1] These variables determine national income and employment roughly in the following way:

If we initially assume national income to be given, the level of the interest rate will be determined by the curve reflecting the demand for cash at different rates of interest (the liquidity preference schedule) and by the given money supply. The interest rate, together with the marginal efficiency of investment[2], determines the volume of investment. The volume of investment together with the consumption function (on which the multiplier depends) determines national income (and employment). If this national income is the same as that which we initially assumed as given, the system is in equilibrium and the interest rate is the equilibrium rate of interest. If, however, the resulting national income is larger or smaller than that with which we started, the liquidity curve will shift, and consequently the interest rate and the volume of investment will change, until the system reaches an equilibrium position.

For what might be called didactic reasons we started out by assuming

[1] J. M. Keynes, *General Theory of Employment, Interest and Money* (London, 1936), pp. 246–247.

[2] We are using this expression rather than Keynes' "marginal efficiency of capital", because we want to reserve the latter term for the marginal product of the existing capital stock.

a given level of national income and then described the process of reaching equilibrium as it would occur through time. Keynes, however, views all these changes as taking place at once, so that the equilibrium levels of national income, of the rate of interest and of investment and consumption are all determined simultaneously.

Keynes assumes that the technical apparatus of production and the quantity of the factors of production are given and that the money wage rate is determined "from the outside", i.e., by negotiation between workers and employers, so that it can be regarded as a datum. The economy in this model is not a stationary, but a progressive one in which investment and saving occur. Thus the analysis refers to a unit period (or strictly speaking to one moment of time) in the development of a progressive economy, as did the analyses of Walras, Fisher, and Knight; and the equilibrium which Keynes has in mind is the (temporary) equilibrium in this unit period (or at a single point of time). The method applied in his analysis might be called static, in so far as time-lags are ignored and all adjustments to changing data occur immediately and simultaneously. The economy under investigation, however, is not stationary.

Let us now concentrate on those factors which, within this general framework, determine the level of the interest rate; and let us assume with Keynes that there is only one rate of interest.

According to Keynes, interest is the price paid for the willingness to part with cash. "It is the price which equilibrates the desire to hold wealth in the form of cash with the available quantity of cash."[3] The desire to hold cash can be expressed in the form of a demand curve for cash, a curve which reflects the liquidity preference at different hypothetical rates of interest. For two reasons this curve slopes downwards to the right:

1. Because more money will be required for transaction purposes when the rate of interest is low: "...for if the fall in the rate of interest increases the national income, the amount of money which it is convenient to keep for transactions will be increased more or less proportionately to the increase in income."[4]

2. Because a reduction in the rate of interest tends to increase the amount of cash "which certain individuals will wish to hold because their

[3] Keynes, *General Theory*, p. 167.
[4] Keynes, *General Theory*, pp. 172–173.

views as to the future of the rate of interest differ from the market views."[5]

These two reasons for the downward slope of the liquidity preference curve call for a critical appraisal.

1. Let us first consider the demand for money for transaction purposes. If we have in mind a very short period of time, for which we regard national income as given, and if we draw the liquidity preference curve for that period, it is obviously not permitted to explain the downward slope of the curve by saying that lower interest rates promote a larger national income in *later* periods so that in these *later* periods more cash is necessary to cope with the increased volume of transactions. Robertson put the same thought as follows: "This is, to my mind, to confuse the amount of money which people will wish to hold in the face of a given rate of interest now existing with the amount of money which they will wish to hold as an indirect consequence of a given rate of interest prevailing at some previous time..."[6]

In answer to this objection Keynes could claim that he does not regard national income as a datum, but rather as a variable which is determined at once and simultaneously with all other variables. The amount of money necessary for transaction purposes will be larger or smaller, depending upon the level of income which results for the period under investigation. Since the interest rate does influence national income, as explained above, it seems indeed permitted to associate a falling interest rate with a growing demand for transaction money and vice versa. Nevertheless, it is not correct to combine in a *single* curve the demand for transaction money and the demand for money required for speculative purposes since one cannot represent three variables (money, interest rate, and income) in a two-dimensional diagram. We should have to use a three-dimensional diagram; but as such diagrams are awkward we may make do with two dimensions by drawing a separate demand curve for money for each level of income, as in Figure 15. Here the distances OO', OO'', etc., represent the demand for transaction cash at different income levels; OO' for the relatively low income Y', OO'' for the higher income Y'', and so on. The downward sloping curves which "lean" against each of the vertical lines

[5] Keynes, *General Theory*, p. 172.

[6] D. H. Robertson, 'Mr. Keynes and the Rate of Interest', in D. H. Robertson, *Essays in Monetary Theory* (London, 1940), p. 8; reprinted in *Readings in the Theory of Income Distribution* (Philadelphia-Toronto, 1946), p. 432.

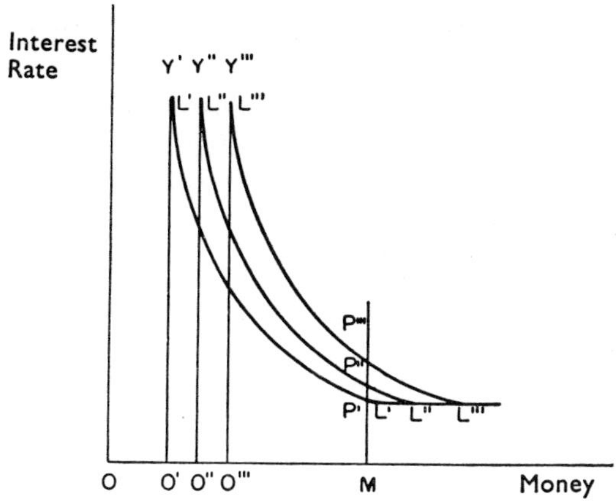

Fig. 15.

erected over O', O'', O''', etc., represent the demand curves for money held for speculative purposes.

2. Let us now turn to the speculative demand for money, that is, to an analysis of the curves $L'L'$, $L''L''$, etc., in Figure 15. Keynes explains the downward slope of these curves by the expectations about the future of the interest rate. An exceptionally high rate of interest will be connected, as a rule, with the expectation that it will fall in the future, i.e., that the prices of securities will be higher in the future than at present. The owners of wealth will thus prefer securities to cash. Accordingly, a high rate of interest will be connected with a small demand for cash. For the contrary reason an exceptionally low rate of interest will be associated with a large demand for cash. With a rate between the extremes, expectations will be divided: some of the owners of wealth will expect a rise in the rate and will therefore want to hold cash, whereas others, expecting a fall, will prefer securities; hence the demand for cash must be somewhere between the low demand associated with a high interest rate and the high demand associated with a low interest rate. This is Keynes' explanation of the downward slope of the LL-curves. Sooner or later, however, a point will be reached after which these curves will no longer fall, but will run parallel to the x-axis. For at a very low rate of interest owners of wealth will prefer to hold cash rather than to invest because the interest rate, once it has reached this level, cannot be expected to fall any further. It can only rise.

The quantity of money OM, together with the demand curve for speculative cash, determines the rate of interest for any given level of income; for instance, the interest rate MP' for income level Y', MP'' for income level Y'', and so forth. Superficially, therefore, the interest rate appears to be a purely monetary phenomenon determined by the demand for and supply of money.

To derive this downward slope of the LL-curve from the expectations as to the future of the interest rate and then to determine the rate of interest with the aid of this curve runs up against an objection which Robertson expressed as follows: "Thus the rate of interest is what it is because it is expected to become other than it is; if it is not expected to become other than it is, there is nothing left to tell us why it is what it is. The organ which secretes it has been amputated, and yet it somehow still exists – a grin without a cat."[7] Or, as Hicks put it: "... to say that the rate of interest on perfectly safe securities is determined by nothing else but uncertainty of future interest rates seems to leave interest hanging by its own boot-straps; one feels an obstinate conviction that there must be more in it than that."[8]

This objection would be valid if, in Keynes' system, the rate of interest were in fact determined simply and solely by this curve and the quantity of money, so that if nobody expected the interest rate to change, there would be nothing to explain this rate. But this is not so, as we shall see. Keynes' theory is in fact not a purely monetary theory. As soon, however, as other factors are brought in to help determine the rate of interest, there can be no objection to introducing into the theory as an additional factor expectations as to the future of the interest rate – just as there could be no objection to a price theory which takes account, among other things, of the influence exerted by expected future prices on present prices. If the interest is not expected to change, the other factors still remain to determine it.

What are these other factors in Keynes' theory of interest? The answer is actually implied in what has already been said. Figure 15 shows that the level of income has an influence on the interest rate. In Keynes' system this level of income is determined with the help of the marginal efficiency of investment and the propensity to save, which determines the multiplier.

[7] D. H. Robertson, *Essays*, p. 25; *Readings in the Theory of Income Distribution*, p. 448.
[8] J. R. Hicks, *Value and Capital* (2nd ed., Oxford, 1946), p. 164.

The equilibrium rate of interest is thus governed not only by the demand for money, but also by saving and by the marginal efficiency of investment. Hence, Keynes' theory is *not* a purely monetary theory. Designating it as purely monetary might be justified in one case only: if the interest rate has fallen to its minimum so that we are moving along the horizontal portion of the *LL*-curve, for then an expansion of income – such as might be caused by a rise in the marginal efficiency of investment – evidently cannot influence the rate of interest. In this extreme case the interest rate is indeed determined solely by the quantity of money and the demand for money. These relationships were clearly brought out in the discussion after Keynes; and the following chapters, in which the post-Keynesians are treated, will throw further light on them.

What has been said so far can best be summarized by presenting Lange's exposition of Keynes' theory.[9] Lange deviates from Keynes only in so far as he assumes consumption to be dependent not only on income but also on the interest rate, and investment to be dependent not only on the interest rate but also on consumption.

Lange uses the set of three diagrams here reproduced in the three panels of Figure 16. The first shows the demand for money as a function of the interest rate. Since the amount of transaction money required is different at various income levels (Y_0, Y_1, etc.), a separate curve is drawn for each level of income, the higher ones denoting higher incomes. The second

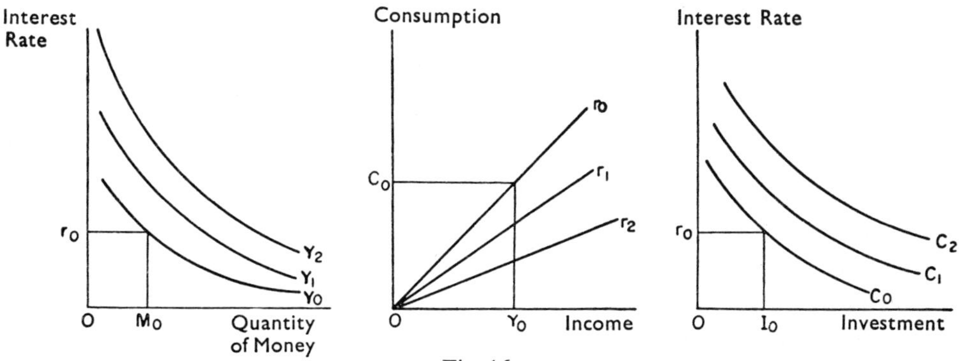

Fig. 16.

[9] Oscar Lange, 'The Rate of Interest and the Optimum Propensity to Consume', *Economica*, New Series, **5** (1938) 12–32; reprinted in *Readings in Business Cycle Theory* (Philadelphia-Toronto, 1944), pp. 169–192.

diagram represents the consumption function – that is to say, it shows how consumption rises with income. As in Lange's model consumption depends not only on income but also on the interest rate, a separate consumption function is drawn for each rate of interest r_0, r_1, etc. ($r_0 < r_1 < r_2$). The third diagram shows investment as a function of the rate of interest. Since, however, investment depends not only on the interest rate but also on the level of consumption, a separate marginal efficiency of investment curve is drawn for each level C_0, C_1, etc., of consumption ($C_0 < C_1 < C_2$).

If we now take income to be given at Y_0, and likewise the supply of money at OM_0, the rate of interest, determined solely by the liquidity preference and the quantity of money, will be r_0 (panel 1 in Figure 16); this rate of interest then determines the consumption function which we must use in the second panel, where we obtain for the given income Y_0 the level of consumption OC_0. Once we know this, we also know the marginal efficiency curve to be used in panel 3 which, in conjunction with the rate of interest r_0, gives us the investment OI_0. Consumption plus investment constitute aggregate income. We now return to panel 1 and take from there the liquidity curve corresponding to this new income (unless, of course, this is identical with the initial income – in which case we have immediately reached the equilibrium position). We continue in this manner until the income has become the equilibrium income. In each short unit period for which we consider income to be given, the interest rate seems, according to panel 1, to be determined solely by the liquidity preference and the quantity of money; but at the same time it is evident that the marginal efficiency of investment curve and the propensity to consume (or to save) play their role in the course of the adjustment process and help to determine the final equilibrium rate of interest.

What remains to be done at this point is to discuss in somewhat more detail the concept of marginal efficiency of investment and the part played by saving in the Keynesian system.

The marginal efficiency of investment is obtained from an equation already known to us.[10] The equation relates the expected returns from the "last" capital good acquired, discounted at the internal rate of return which is to be calculated from the equation itself, with the purchase price of the capital good. Let us imagine a machine which lasts three years and

[10] See the chapter on Irving Fisher.

which yields the quasi-rents Q_1 in the first, Q_2 in the second and Q_3 in the third year (always at the end of the year). Then, as we already know, the internal rate of return on the investment in the machine can be obtained from the equation:

$$C = \frac{Q_1}{(1+r)} + \frac{Q_2}{(1+r)^2} + \frac{Q_3}{(1+r)^3}$$

where C represents the original cost of the machine and r the internal rate of return. These quasi-rents are equal to gross revenue less current expenditures (variable costs). As more machines are installed, the purchase price will rise and the expected quasi-rents will fall. The acquisition of machines will continue until the internal rate of return on the last machine equals the given rate of interest. We can thus let the internal rate of return on additional investments be represented by a falling curve in a system of coordinates in which the marginal internal rate of return is measured along the vertical axis and the volume of investment in machines along the horizontal axis. The problem of how much an entrepreneur should invest reduces to a comparison of the marginal efficiency with the given rate of interest.

This solution of the volume-of-investment problem is obviously inadequate. The most important "sins of omission" involved are the following:

1. It is assumed that capital goods have a certain definite length of life. The problem, how durable a capital good ought to be made, is either disregarded or is presumed to have already been solved.

2. Circulating capital is disregarded. In calculating the quasi-rents it is assumed that the production process in which durable goods are used does not require any circulating capital – i.e., that no time elapses between the input of labour and raw materials and the emergence of the finished product. The introduction into the model of circulating capital would make the marginal efficiency of investment dependent on the interest rate, because the interest on circulating capital would have to be deducted from gross revenue along with the expenditures on labour and materials *before* the quasi-rents attributable to the capital good could be calculated. This, however, means nothing other than that the curve of the marginal efficiency of investment changes with the interest rate: if the interest rate increases, the quasi-rents will be smaller and the marginal efficiency of investment will be reduced.

3. Durable capital goods have different lengths of life even if these are considered technically fixed. If all capital goods, regardless of their various lengths of life, are incorporated in a single marginal efficiency curve, a new problem will arise if the rate of interest changes in the course of time.[11] A single marginal efficiency curve for *all* capital goods can, however, be constructed with the method already outlined in the chapter on Fisher. If we take a capital good which has a life of three years and assume three successive (expected) one-year rates of interest i_1, i_2, and i_3, we can calculate the value V_2 of the capital good at the end of the first year from the equation

$$V_2 = \frac{Q_2}{(1 + i_2)} + \frac{Q_3}{(1 + i_2)(1 + i_3)}$$

With the aid of the value V_2 we can then calculate an internal rate of return r for the first year from the equation $C = [V_2/(1 + r)]$ and compare this rate with the rate of interest for the first year. This procedure can be used for all capital goods regardless of their respective lengths of life, and we can say that the investment in capital goods will be continued until the internal rate of return for the first year equals the interest rate of the first year. This approach does not, of course, overcome the difficulty referred to in paragraph (2) above. Moreover, this result is dependent on what rates of interest are expected in the future and hence cannot be obtained unless these interest rates are known.

4. Keynes constructed the marginal efficiency of investment curve for the economy as a whole, not for a single industry. This, too, is open to question. Keynes himself attacked the notion of a demand curve for *labour* for the system as a whole with the following remarks: "For the demand schedules for particular industries can only be constructed on some fixed assumption as to the nature of the demand and supply schedules of other industries and as to the amount of the aggregate effective demand. It is invalid, therefore, to transfer the argument to industry as a whole unless we also transfer our assumption that the aggregate effective demand is fixed. Yet this assumption reduces the argument to an *ignoratio elenchi*. For, whilst no one would wish to deny the proposition that a reduction in money-wages *accompanied by the same aggregate effective de-*

[11] Keynes recognized this problem but did not deal with it; see *General Theory*, p. 137, note 1.

mand as before will be associated with an increase in employment, the precise question at issue is whether the reduction in money-wages will or will not be accompanied by the same aggregate effective demand as before measured in money."[12]

The same argument applies to the schedule of the marginal efficiency of investment, which represents the demand curve for investment funds. The point at issue is one with which we had to deal earlier – namely, the inadmissibility of using the tools of partial equilibrium analysis for the purposes of general equilibrium analysis. It has become customary to circumvent this difficulty by drawing a separate marginal efficiency curve for each level of income, and thus for each aggregate effective demand. This procedure will be used here also, but it should be stressed that basically there is no justification for assuming that the aggregate demand for goods or the national income should remain the same regardless of how far we move along on such a marginal efficiency curve, since different volumes of investment imply different levels of income.

5. The connection between the demand for investment funds and the market for capital goods is not made clear. We have touched on this point in our criticism of F. H. Knight's theory and shall return to it again in the fifth part of this book.

Since the entire Keynesian literature makes use of the marginal efficiency of investment curve, we too shall have to use it in our account of that literature.

We now turn to the role of saving in the Keynesian theory. The multiplier is the reciprocal of the marginal propensity to save. Thus, if this propensity is one-third the multiplier is three, and an additional investment of 100 money units will raise national income by 300 units. Keynes assumed that the multiplier takes effect *immediately*, so that the additional income arises simultaneously with the investment. Under some conditions this assumption may lead to absurd results, as, for instance, in the case of a marginal propensity to save which is zero: a small investment would then not only bring about the absorption of all unemployment, but lead to an infinite inflation.

It has become customary to show the effect of the multiplier (and therefore of saving) on national income by making use of a diagram of the

[12] Keynes, *General Theory*, p. 259.

type represented by Figure 17.[13] Income, Y, is measured along the x-axis, consumption, C, plus investment, I, and saving, S, along the y-axis. It has here been assumed that individuals save one-third of their income in excess of 40 billion, so that the consumption function is

$$C = 40 + 2/3\,(Y - 40).$$

This function is represented by the line $C(Y)$. It has further been assumed that the volume of investment is 10 billion; if we add this to the consumption function, we obtain the curve $I + C(Y)$.

Now, income is by definition equal to consumption plus investment. This is the case along the 45 degree line. The income actually realised must lie on this line; it is given by the intersection of this line with the $I + C(Y)$-line. National income will here amount to 70 billion. Thus, owing to the effect of the multiplier, the investment of 10 billion has raised income by 30 billion as compared with a state in which nothing was invested and income was equal to consumption (40 billion). The $S(Y)$-curve shows saving as a function of income. With an investment of 10 billion saving

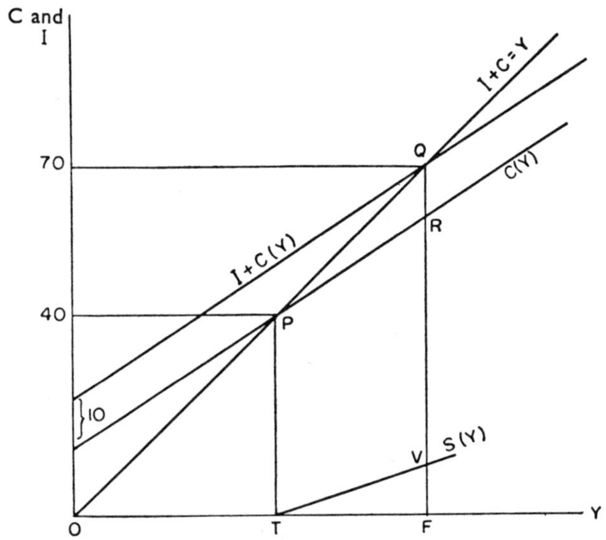

Fig. 17.

[13] I am using here the graphical presentation found in Abba P. Lerner, *Economics of Employment* (New York, 1951), p. 82.

likewise amounts to 10 billion. The saving curve is obtained as the vertical difference between the $I+C=Y$-curve and the $C(Y)$-curve. This diagram is based on the assumption that the marginal propensity to save is constant. It is measured by the slope of the curve $S(Y)$, and the multiplier by its reciprocal, FT/FV.

The determination of national income in this diagram rests on the equations $I=\bar{I}$ (constant), $C=C(Y)$, and $I+C=Y$. The interest rate does not enter into the picture at all, and for this reason the diagram cannot be said to give an adequate account of the Keynesian income determination. It either presupposes that investment is not a function of the rate of interest or that the level of national income, and with it the demand for transaction cash, does not affect the interest rate. In Keynes' theory this could be so only if national income were so low that the demand for money remained within that range where the interest rate stays at its minimum level. Otherwise the increase in the demand for transaction cash caused by the increase in national income will raise the interest rate. The smaller the marginal propensity to save, the greater is the multiplier and the higher is the rate of interest, and vice versa.

We shall later frequently make use of the saving function in the expanded form $S=S(Y, r)$, instead of $S=S(Y)$, and also of the equality between saving and investment in the form of an equation $I(Y, r)= S(Y, r)$, where r is the rate of interest. It is important to realise exactly what these functions and equations are intended to express. First of all, it should not be thought that saving, expressed here as a function of income and of the interest rate, represents the supply of saved funds on the capital market. This function tells us nothing as to whether the amounts saved will be offered for investment or whether, to use the old terminology, they will be hoarded. The consequences are, of course, quite different according to which of these alternatives occurs. In the Keynesian system hoarding finds its expression in the demand curve for cash. Whereas, in the method of presentation that was customary before Keynes, hoarding would have been expressed by shifting the *supply* curve for funds on the capital market towards the left, in Keynes' presentation the demand curve for money is moved to the right. The result is a higher interest rate, less investment, a smaller national income, and less saving as the latter is a function of national income. All these adjustments must be thought of as taking place simultaneously. Thus, hoarding does not influence the saving function through its effect on national income; but hoarding does affect the absolute volume of saving. To put it in a different way, the larger the share of hoarding in aggregate saving, the smaller will the latter be.

In Keynes' system equality between saving and investment does not have the meaning which it had in classical theory where, on the assumption that all savings were offered on the capital market, equality was brought about by the rate of interest. For Keynes it is an *ex post* equality; hence we are dealing here with an *identity* of saving and investment. But when, in the literature after Keynes, equality between saving and investment appears as a *condition* for equilibrium, this equality must evidently express something more than a mere identity which would be valid regardless of whether the system were in equilibrium or not.

The matter may be clarified by a graphical presentation devised by Modigliani.[14] The panel in the centre of Figure 18 shows saving S (on the vertical axis) as a function of income Y.[15] With an income of Y_2 saving will be F_2Y_2. In the left panel investment I (measured along the vertical axis) is shown as a function of the interest rate r (along the horizontal axis) for different levels of income. If a line is now drawn from F_2 in the middle panel horizontally across to the left panel, this line will cut

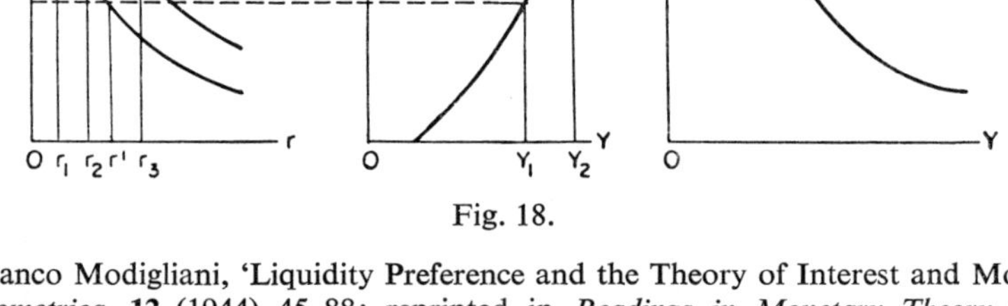

Fig. 18.

[14] Franco Modigliani, 'Liquidity Preference and the Theory of Interest and Money', *Econometrica*, **12** (1944) 45–88; reprinted in *Readings in Monetary Theory* (New York-Philadelphia-Toronto, 1951), pp. 186–239.

[15] In this treatment the fact that saving is also a function of the interest rate is disregarded. It could be expressed by drawing a separate saving curve for each rate of interest.

the investment curves for different levels of income at the points A_3, A_2, and A_1. At each of these points saving is equal to investment, but only one of them is an equilibrium point, namely A_2, as it is only there that the income Y_2 is the same as the income which corresponds to a level of saving Y_2F_2. Therefore only r_2 is an equilibrium interest rate. To every rate of interest there corresponds such a state of equilibrium; for instance, at the interest rate r' the volume of investment and saving is $r'B$ and the income is Y_1. When we now say that in equilibrium saving must equal investment, we mean equality at an income level at which no further adjustments are required; and this statement is identical with the other one that in equilibrium *ex ante* saving and investment must be equal. Clearly, there are a large number of income levels at which *ex ante* saving and investment can be equal – viz., one for each interest rate. In the right-hand panel of Figure 18 a curve *IS* has been drawn which connects all the equilibrium points so defined and shows the equilibrium income as a function of the interest rate.[16]

With these remarks we have already gone beyond Keynes, as we have been describing tools of analysis which were not developed until after Keynes. We shall now turn to the literature which followed the publication of his work.

[16] This curve was first used by J. R. Hicks in his paper 'Mr. Keynes and the Classics; A Suggested Interpretation', *Econometrica*, **5** (1937) 153; reprinted in *Readings in the Theory of Income Distribution* (Philadelphia-Toronto, 1946), p. 469.

CHAPTER 12

THE DISCUSSION AFTER KEYNES

In presenting the discussion which followed the publication of Keynes' work, we shall not proceed in chronological order. Instead, we shall analyse the consequences of three different assumptions, taking account, in so doing, of the contributions of the most important authors. The three different assumptions are:

1. the money wage rate is given,
2. the money wage rate is flexible, hence competition exists in the market for labour,
3. the real wage rate is given.

Under all three assumptions we shall make use of a system of equations which, in one form or another, has been used by various authors participating in the discussion. The system chosen here is that of Modigliani.[1]

I. The Assumption of Given Money Wage Rates

We shall now turn to the analysis of the determinants of the rate of interest on the assumption of a given money wage rate. The symbols in the system

[1] Franco Modigliani, 'Liquidity Preference and the Theory of Interest and Money', *Econometrica*, **12** (1944) 45–88; reprinted in *Readings in Monetary Theory* (New York-Philadelphia-Toronto, 1951), pp. 186–239. A somewhat different system of equations was used by J. R. Hicks in 'Mr. Keynes and the "Classics"; A Suggested Interpretation', *Econometrica*, **5** (1937) 147–159; reprinted in *Readings in the Theory of Income Distribution* (Philadelphia-Toronto, 1946), pp. 461–476. See also the system of equations in Oscar Lange, 'The Rate of Interest and the Optimum Propensity to Consume', *Economica*, New Series, **5** (1938) 12–32; reprinted in *Readings in Business Cycle Theory* (Philadelphia-Toronto, 1944), pp. 169–192. As can be seen from our discussion of Lange's presentation of the Keynesian theory (pp. 141–142), Lange uses only four equations which broadly correspond to the first four equations of the system used in the text. A. C. Pigou, in his *Employment and Equilibrium* (2nd ed., London, 1949), also makes do with four equations.

of equations below have the following meanings:

$\bar{M}$ = quantity of money (given)
r = rate of interest
Y = national income
X = production of consumer goods and of new capital goods
N = number of employed
I = investment
S = saving
C = consumption
P = price level
$\bar{W}$ = money wage rate (given)

The unknowns are r, Y, I, S, C, N, X, P.

The system of equations is as follows:

$$\bar{M} = L(r, Y) \quad (1) \qquad S = Y - C \quad (5)$$
$$I = I(r, Y) \quad (2) \qquad Y = PX \quad (6)$$
$$S = S(r, Y) \quad (3) \qquad X = f(N) \quad (7)$$
$$S = I \quad (4) \qquad W = f'(N)P \quad (8)$$

Some explanatory remarks on these equations may be added:

ad (1): The demand for money (right-hand side of the equation) is a function of the interest rate and of national income and must be equal to the given quantity of money $\bar{M}$. The demand for money includes both the demand for speculative and that for transaction purposes. If we so wish, we can split up equation (1) into three equations:

$$M_1 = L(r) \qquad (1a)$$
$$M_2 = kY \qquad (1b)$$
$$M = M_1 + M_2 \qquad (1c)$$

where M_1 and M_2 denote the quantity of money demanded for speculative and for transaction purposes respectively, the latter expressed as a percentage k of national income Y. Thus we have two additional unknowns, namely M_1 and M_2, and two additional equations.

ad (2): The volume of investment depends not only on the interest rate, but also on national income, as it is the latter which determines the demand for the products produced with the help of the investment goods. Some authors – Oscar Lange, for instance – substitute consumption for national income, but as this is itself a function of national income we have used the latter in the equation. Investment is a decreasing function of the rate of interest and an increasing function of national income.

ad (3): Saving is an increasing function of the rate of interest and of national income.

ad (4): In a state of equilibrium, saving is equal to investment. The meaning of this equation has already been explained. We made it clear that the equation expresses the *ex ante* equality of saving and investment. It would be possible for the saving and investment functions to have a shape such that they could be equal to one another only at a rate of interest lower than the minimum below which the rate cannot fall, but for the present we shall disregard this possibility.

ad (6): National income is equal to the value of the final goods produced – i.e., consumer goods and newly created capital goods that are added during the period to the existing capital stock.

ad (7): Production is an increasing function of employment.

ad (8): The money wage rate must be equal to the marginal product of labour times the value of this marginal product. The marginal product is a decreasing function of employment. We postulate competition in the market for products.

The first four equations by themselves constitute a self-contained system, sufficient to determine the four unknowns: interest rate, investment, saving and income. The remaining equations then permit the determination of the other unknowns, especially price level and employment. All of the first four equations are necessary to determine the rate of interest; this means that the interest rate is affected by saving and investment as well as by the quantity of money and the liquidity preference, which again proves that the interest rate is not determined by the quantity of money and the liquidity preference alone.

Hicks has developed a graphical method which helps to throw further light on these relationships.[2] The *IS*-curve in Figure 19 is already familiar to us. It shows the income at which saving and investment are in equilibrium as a function of the interest rate. The lower the rate of interest, the higher is the income level at which this equality between saving and investment occurs. The *MM*-curve shows the levels of income and the interest rates at which the demand for money equals its supply (equation

[2] Hicks, *Econometrica*, **5** (1937) 153; *Readings in the Theory of Income Distribution*, p. 469.

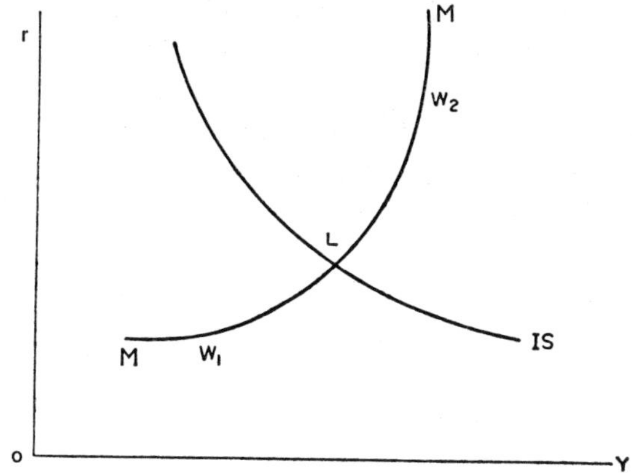

Fig. 19.

(1)). When income rises, more money will be required for transaction purposes and less is left for speculative purposes. Accordingly, the rate of interest must rise as income increases if the money market is to stay in equilibrium. The equilibrium interest rate and the equilibrium income are then determined by the intersection of these two curves.

The *MM*-curve can be divided into three sections. Starting from the left, the first runs as far as point W_1, thus covering the horizontal part of the curve. The second reaches from W_1 to W_2, covering the section of the *MM*-curve which is rising to the right. The third begins at W_2 and covers the vertical section of the curve. Let us first consider the middle section: here a rise (fall) of the marginal efficiency of investment or a fall (rise) in the propensity to save – which move the *IS*-curve towards the right (left) – raise (lower) income as well as the interest rate. In the case of a rise in the marginal efficiency of investment the adjustment process should be pictured as follows: the increase in the marginal efficiency leads to more investment which will be financed with money previously held for speculative purposes. The additional investment brings about a higher level of employment and thus also a larger income. The interest rate will rise. The new equilibrium will be reached when, out of the increased income, an amount is saved which is equal to the investment.

Let us now assume that the *IS*-curve cuts the *MM*-curve in its initial horizontal segment. In that case a shift of the *IS*-curve will obviously not affect the interest rate, provided that the point of intersection with the *MM*-curve remains on the horizontal segment of this latter curve. In this situation the interest rate is at its minimum level. If the *IS*-curve were to shift to the left, the only result would be a reduction in income. In this extreme case it can thus be said that saving and investment have no influence on the interest rate but affect only income. If, for instance, the marginal efficiency of investment curve falls and investment is reduced, the transaction money freed will simply be added to the money held for speculative purposes as the demand for the latter is here infinitely elastic. Income will then fall until saving has dropped to the level of investment. The necessary adjustment takes place only through income, not through a fall in the interest rate.

As regards the third or vertical segment of the *MM*-curve, the reverse is true. Here all the money is being used for transaction purposes and the income cannot rise above the level already reached. Saving and investment alone determine the rate of interest; we are back in the "classical" world.

The *MM*-curve itself would shift to the left if the liquidity preference increased or the money supply were reduced. The interest rate would then rise and income would fall. The opposite result would emerge if the liquidity preference fell or the money supply increased.

II. The Assumption of Flexible Money Wage Rates

If we assume free competition in the labour market, we have to postulate either that the workers offer the same amount of services no matter what the wage rate is, or that the supply of labour services is a function of the real wage rate. We shall adopt the first assumption, which is the simpler one. Hence, instead of taking the wage rate as a datum as we have hitherto done, we shall now assume that the number of workers N is given.

Furthermore, we shall express the relevant variables in the system of equations in real terms, adopting the wage unit for this purpose as the unit of measurement, as did Keynes. Since wages are assumed to be flexible, we must proceed in this fashion if we want to give expression to the assumption that individuals are not subject to money illusion in Modigliani's sense, i.e., that real saving and real investment are functions of real and not of money income. We then obtain the following system of equations, where W represents the money wage rate[3]:

$$M = L(r, Y) \qquad (1)$$

$$\frac{I}{W} = I\left(r, \frac{Y}{W}\right) \qquad (2)$$

$$\frac{S}{W} = S\left(r, \frac{Y}{W}\right) \qquad (3)$$

$$\frac{S}{W} = \frac{I}{W} \qquad (4)$$

$$\frac{S}{W} = \frac{Y}{W} - \frac{C}{W} \qquad (5)$$

$$\frac{Y}{W} = \frac{PX}{W} \qquad (6)$$

$$X = f(N) \qquad (7)$$

$$\frac{W}{P} = f'(N) \qquad (8)$$

We are now no longer able to consider the first four equations a determinate system as they contain five unknowns – namely, r, Y, S, I, and W. Equations (2)–(8), however, do form a self-contained system sufficient to determine the seven unknowns:

$\frac{S}{W}$ = real saving

$\frac{I}{W}$ = real investment

$\frac{Y}{W}$ = real income

$\frac{C}{W}$ = real consumption

X = output

$\frac{W}{P}$ = real wage rate

r = rate of interest

Thus the interest rate is determined by all these equations reflecting the "real" sector taken together, and neither liquidity preference nor the quantity of money has any influence on it. If the interest rate, determined in the real part of the system, is inserted into equation (1) – which can also be written

$$M = L\left(r, \frac{Y}{W} W\right)$$

[3] Modigliani, *Econometrica*, **12** (1944) 67–68; *Readings in Monetary Theory*, pp. 213–214.

where Y/W has already been determined – we obtain the money wage rate. With the money wage rate the price level is also determined via equation (8). Thus, the money equation (1) determines the money wage rate or the price level but has no influence on the interest rate. If, for instance, the liquidity preference were to increase, the money wage rate and the price level would fall; but the interest rate, determined solely by the "real" equations, would not be affected.

Hicks has applied his diagrammatical apparatus, which we presented above, also to the case where prices and wages are perfectly flexible, so that real income – identical with the full-employment income – remains constant.[4] Here the *IS*-curve familiar to us from Figures 18 and 19 (the combinations of interest rates and money incomes at which saving equals investment) runs horizontally at the level of the interest rate which is determined exclusively by productivity and thrift (Figure 20). The *MM*-curve shows, as in Figure 19, the combinations of interest rates and incomes at which the demand for money equals the supply. Let us disregard for the moment the horizontal section of that curve at the level of the minimum interest rate. If we shift the *MM*-curve to the right or to the left, the interest rate does not change; only the money income (together with the price level and the wage rate) rises or falls. All this is only an-

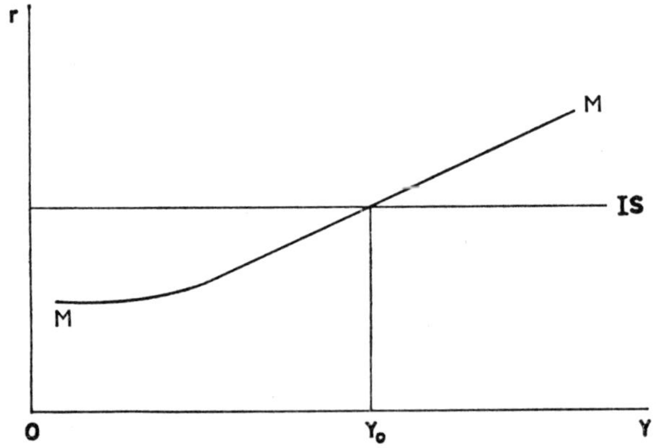

Fig. 20.

[4] J. R. Hicks, 'A Rehabilitation of "Classical" Economics?', *Economic Journal*, **67** (1957) 278–289.

other way of showing that the interest rate is determined solely by the real factors.[5]

This conclusion which Modigliani has drawn from his system of equations is, of course, an old one. Before Keynes it was always supposed that two economies in which only the quantity of money and/or the liquidity preference were different, while all the real factors were the same, would also have the same rate of interest. The foregoing considerations seem to strengthen this conclusion.[6] It depends, however, on the assumption that saving is a function of real income only, and not also of real wealth. As soon as a dependence of saving on real wealth is admitted, the rate of interest will, in the case of flexible wages, also be influenced by the monetary factor, because a drop in the price level will affect the real value of cash balances and hence the rate of saving.

We have not yet reached the end of our exposition. It might happen that the interest rate reaches the minimum level without full employment having been attained. Under these circumstances, a further reduction of the wage rate would not lead to full employment, because the money no longer needed for transaction purposes would simply be hoarded and therefore would not stimulate effective demand. Pigou has shown, however, that with flexible wages this danger does not exist. In the following section we shall examine the Pigou effect in somewhat greater detail.

III. The Pigou Effect[7]

Assuming flexible wages and disregarding the Pigou effect, we obtained the result that the interest rate is determined by the real factors of the system and that full employment will be maintained as long as the equilibrium interest rate is above its minimum level.

[5] If the monetary factor thus determines only the monetary but not the real variables, it does not follow that a change in the latter has no effect on the former. This would be the case only if the *MM*-curve were a vertical line. If, however, it rises to the right, a rise of the *IS*-curve resulting, say, from a rise in the marginal efficiency of investment causes an increase in money income.

[6] Pigou's system of four equations also yields this result. Cf. A. C. Pigou, *Employment and Equilibrium* (2nd ed., London, 1949), p. 66ff., and especially p. 71.

[7] The Pigou effect is discussed in the following works: A. C. Pigou, 'The Classical Stationary State', *Economic Journal,* **53** (1943) 343–351. Pigou, 'Economic Progress in a Stable Environment', *Economica,* New Series, **14** (1947) 180–188; reprinted in

Let us now take the case in which saving and investment could only be in equilibrium at full employment if the interest rate stood below its minimum. This is the case of the so-called secular stagnation. The system would have no tendency towards a full-employment equilibrium unless it could be shown that some mechanism is at work which pushes the equilibrium rate of interest above the minimum level.

This situation is represented in Figure 21. The *EE*-curve reflects the marginal efficiency of investment in real terms on the assumption that the income for which the curve is drawn is the full-employment income. The curve shows the planned real investment at different rates of interest. The *SS*-curve, on the other hand, shows planned real saving as a function of the interest rate for the same income. The height *OZ* of the horizontal line indicates the minimum level of the interest rate which is supposed to prevail in the economy. The level of wages and prices is assumed to be given.

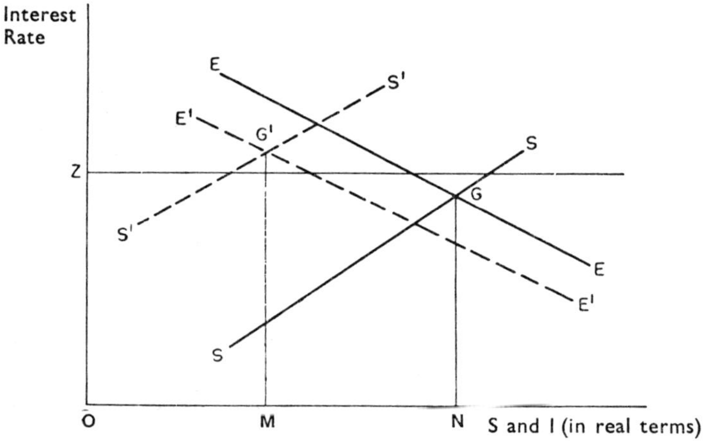

Fig. 21.

Readings in Monetary Theory (New York-Philadelphia-Toronto, 1951), pp. 241–251. Pigou, *Employment and Equilibrium* (2nd ed., London, 1949), in particular Chapter 9. Don Patinkin, 'Price Flexibility and Full Employment', *American Economic Review*, **38** (1948) 543–564; reprinted in *Readings in Monetary Theory*, pp. 252–283. L. A. Metzler, 'Wealth, Saving, and the Rate of Interest', *Journal of Political Economy*, **59** (1951) 93–116. V. C. Lutz, 'Real and Monetary Factors in the Determination of Employment Levels', *Quarterly Journal of Economics*, **66** (1952) 251–272. G. Haberler, 'The Pigou-Effect Once More', *Journal of Political Economy*, **60** (1952) 240–246. G. Ackley, 'The Wealth-Saving Relationship', *Journal of Political Economy*, **59** (1951) 154–161.

It is evident that in this situation planned saving at the given rate of interest will be greater than planned investment. They are equal to one another at a rate of interest *GN* which is lower than the minimum rate. The full-employment income cannot be realised. If we continue to take the money wage rates as given, income will fall and the saving curve will consequently shift to the left. If the position of the marginal efficiency curve is also considered to be dependent on income, this curve, too, will shift to the left, and a stable equilibrium will be reached (at an interest rate *G′M*) which is characterized by underemployment. However, if money wage rates are not given, these and the price level will fall. An equilibrium would not be attained unless it could be shown that in this case, too, the saving curve would shift to the left.

Figure 20 can also be used to throw light on the problem. If the *MM*-curve at its left end has a horizontal segment at the level of the minimum rate of interest, and if the *IS*-curve falls below this level, a reduction in money wages cannot stop the deflationary process and restore equilibrium – unless the deflationary process itself releases tendencies which will raise the *IS*-curve above the horizontal stretch of the *MM*-curve so that the latter is cut in its rising section. Pigou and Haberler have shown how this result comes about.

The prerequisite for this result is that saving is not, as was assumed so far, a function only of real income and the interest rate, but also a function of wealth, i.e., of the real value of the assets in the possession of people. If the real value of these assets rises, less will be saved and more will be consumed. A drop in the price level causes a rise in the real value of money balances and of fixed-interest securities, and with this rise the real saving curve will shift to the left; so that finally a rate of interest higher than the minimum level will materialize, at which rate planned saving and planned investment are in equilibrium. The fall in prices and wages will come to a stop, and full employment equilibrium will be attained. This is Pigou's conclusion. It calls for a more detailed examination.

The first objection that comes to mind arises from the fact that to each creditor there corresponds a debtor. Let us consider first the case of fixed-interest securities. If the rise in the real value of these has a stimulating effect on the expenditures of their owners, it must also be supposed that a depressing effect is exerted on the debtor, so that, on balance, there is no stimulus. If a positive effect on spending is to be obtained, one must suppose that there are debtors who do not react "negatively". The government is such a debtor; hence we must confine ourselves to fixed-interest securities issued by the government.[8]

Much the same thing applies to cash balances. To the extent that these consist of bank deposits which are matched by credits to entrepreneurs, there exist debtors whose reactions to a fall in the price level cancel those of the creditors. Only a rise in the real value of notes and coins in circulation and of bank deposits, the counterpart of which are government bonds held by the banks or reserves held with the central bank, can have a stimulating effect on expenditures in the economy as a whole. We must, however, also take into consideration the increased burden of real interest charges on the national debt caused by a rise in the value of money. This implies a change in the income distribution in favour of creditors of the government; and, if these have a smaller propensity to consume than the individuals whose incomes are reduced by the increased tax load, the Pigou effect will be weakened.

It must also be remembered that private debtors may be bankrupted by the fall in the price level. It might at first sight be inferred from this that the demand for investment funds would also be changed, so that (in Figure 21) a leftward shift of the marginal efficiency curve accompanies the leftward shift of the real saving curve. This will indeed occur temporarily, since the bankruptcies will cause a loss of confidence and expectations will become more pessimistic. For the long-run analysis, however, which alone concerns us here (comparative statics), we need not take this factor into account. Since a general fall in prices affects the prices of the firms' inputs as well as those of the goods which they produce, the "real" marginal efficiency of investment will not change, and once the transition period is over the demand for investment funds in real terms will be the same as before. The fall in prices will, however, change the proportion between debts and equity of the firms. Credits to entrepreneurs are now riskier than before, and at each interest rate the supply of funds offered to them will be smaller than before. The supply of funds curve will shift to the left and for this reason the Pigou effect will be intensified.[9]

[8] See also footnote 4 on p. 194.

[9] See V. C. Lutz, *Quarterly Journal of Economics*, **66** (1952) 266.

Metzler has attempted to prove, with the aid of the Pigou effect, that open-market purchases by the central bank can *permanently* lower the interest rate.[10] His argument runs as follows:

If saving depends not only on the interest rate but also on the real wealth owned by individuals, there will evidently be more than one rate of interest at which saving can be equal to investment in a state of full employment. A high real value of the assets held by individuals is, according to Pigou, associated with less saving – at a given income level – than a lower real value. In the first case the interest rate is higher and investment (equal to saving) is lower than in the second case. In both cases, however, the market for goods and services may be in equilibrium in the sense that full employment exists at a stable price level. This enables us to construct a curve, Metzler's "wealth-requirements schedule", which shows how large the real value of the assets, consisting of bonds provided with a purchasing power clause[11] and money, must be at different interest rates in order that saving and investment may be equal and full employment equilibrium may prevail. This curve, which rises with a rising interest rate, thus indicates the real value of the *total assets* required. It is represented by the *WW*-curve in Figure 22. We can subdivide it into a curve for securities and one for money. If we assume the quantity of securities to be given, the real value of these securities will fall as the interest rate rises (see curve *AA* in Figure 22). In order for the total value of assets (securities *plus* money) to be maintained at the level indicated by the "wealth-requirements schedule", the volume of money must increase as the interest rate rises. The required money supply is measured by the horizontal distance between the schedule of the total real value of securities at different rates of interest and the "wealth-requirements schedule" at the same interest rates. In this manner we can construct a "money-requirements schedule" which shows how much money must be held at each rate of interest in order to bring the real value of wealth (total assets) up to the amount indicated by the "wealth-requirements schedule". This schedule is entered in the right-hand diagram of Figure 22 as the *MM*-curve. The *LL*-curve in the same diagram represents the liquidity preference (the demand for money) at different rates of interest. The interest

[10] L.A. Metzler, *Journal of Political Economy*, **59** (1951) 93–116.

[11] Metzler calls the securities he has in mind "common stock". In fact he is dealing with fixed-interest securities provided with some type of purchasing power clause.

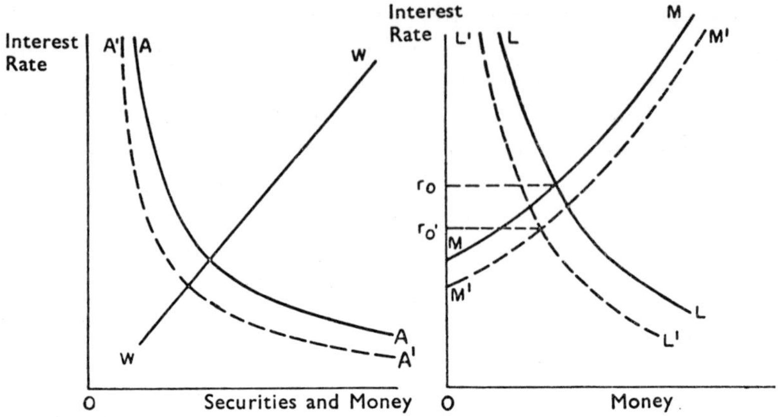

Fig. 22.

rate r_0 is the rate which, under the assumed conditions, makes saving equal to investment at full employment.

If the central bank now bought, say, one third of the securities held by the public, the *AA*-curve would shift a corresponding distance (one-third) to the left and become the *A'A'*-curve. The distance between the *A'A'*-curve and the *WW*-curve will be larger and accordingly the *MM*-curve in the right-hand diagram will be shifted to the right to the position of the *M'M'*-curve. At the same time the *LL*-curve shifts one-third to the left, because, under Metzler's assumption, people will wish to maintain the ratio of security holdings to money holdings unchanged. Under these new conditions the rate of interest necessary to achieve equilibrium between saving and investment will be r_0', which is lower than the old rate r_0. Only at this rate will the market for securities as well as the market for goods and services be in equilibrium.

Metzler sees the process by which this result is obtained roughly as follows. When the central bank buys securities, the interest rate will fall and the prices of securities will rise. The sellers of securities exchange these for cash. The increase in the prices of securities gives rise to capital gains and inflates the total value of privately held assets. The immediate result, owing to the Pigou effect, is a reduction of saving. At the same time, the temporarily lower rate of interest leads to increased investment. An expansion will set in, the price level will rise and the real value of the supply of money will be correspondingly reduced. "The rise in the prices and the reduction in the real value of private money holdings must continue until the real value of security-and-cash holdings combined is low enough to encourage a sufficient amount of saving to make full-employment saving once more equal to full-employment investment."[12] As can be seen from the diagram, the new equilibrium will be reached at a lower rate of interest.

We do not wish to evaluate here the practical significance of Metzler's theory. On the theoretical side, however, there seems to be a gap in his reasoning which requires comment. In the transition period, once the interest rate has fallen in consequence of the purchase of securities by the central bank, investment will increase, as Metzler himself admits. In order to finance this investment the entrepreneurs issue new securities which will be taken up by those individuals who, having sold securities to the central bank, are now in possession of large money balances. This, of course, presupposes that the interest rate will rise again, since we cannot assume that these individuals will buy the new securities at the price at which they have just sold their old ones. The price level will then rise, since the money now enters the transaction sphere. Prior to this rise in prices the real value of financial assets held in the economy will evidently have increased by the issue of new securities. And Metzler would have to prove that the rise in prices will be so large that, in the final outcome, the real value of the total financial assets, including the new securities, will have fallen *below* the level at which it stood prior to the purchase of securities by the central bank. Only under these circumstances does increased saving occur in his model. This proof has not been supplied unless one is willing to disregard the creation of *new* financial assets (securities) which is connected with the expansion of investment.

IV. The Assumption of Given Real Wage Rates

The argument can be briefly stated. If the real wage rate is fixed, entrepreneurs will employ workers up to the point where the real marginal product of labour becomes equal to the given real wage rate (assuming free competition). In principle, employment cannot be influenced by

[12] Metzler, *Journal of Political Economy,* **59** (1951)110.

changes in the quantity of money and in the liquidity preference. Employment being determined in this way, real income is also determined, and with it real saving which is a function of real income. The marginal efficiency of investment, measured in real terms, is also independent of changes in the monetary factors. Hence the rate of interest is determined by the "real" factors, just as in the case of flexible money wage rates. The Pigou effect may also become operative if changes in the money supply or the liquidity preference lead to changes in the price level and in the money wage rates.

CHAPTER 13

LIQUIDITY PREFERENCE THEORY *VS.* THEORY OF LOANABLE FUNDS

Soon after the appearance of Keynes' *General Theory*, an article was published by Bertil Ohlin contrasting Keynes' liquidity preference theory with the Swedish theory of loanable funds, according to which the interest rate is determined by supply and demand in the market for credit. Ohlin's paper initiated a debate on the relative merits of the two theories, and on the question whether both theories might, in fact, be saying the same thing.[1] After a first flare-up of the discussion in 1937, the year Ohlin's paper was published, contributions have continued to appear, though at a somewhat slower rate, up to the present day. Although more than a quarter of a century has passed since the question as to the equivalence of the two theories was first raised, no answer has as yet found general acceptance. One of the reasons is that the controversy broadened into a discussion about the much more fundamental problem whether theorizing in terms of "stocks" would lead to the same results as theorizing in terms of "flows". As a rule the liquidity preference theory has been classified as a "stock" theory and the loanable funds theory as a "flow" theory.

Before turning to the controversy about the two interest theories, let us have a look at this more general problem.

I. Stock and Flow Magnitudes

In order to examine this problem, we shall take as our starting point a single market: the market for perpetual bonds – consols –, each unit of which carries a yield of one dollar per unit of time. The price of one such

[1] B. Ohlin, 'Some Notes on the Stockholm Theory of Savings and Investment', *Economic Journal*, **47** (1937) 53–69 and 221–240; reprinted in *Readings in Business Cycle Theory* (Philadelphia-Toronto, 1944), pp. 87–130. J. M. Keynes, 'Alternative Theories of the Rate of Interest', *Economic Journal*, **47** (1937) 241–252. B. Ohlin, D. H. Robertson, R. G. Hawtrey, 'Alternative Theories of the Rate of Interest, Three Rejoinders', *Economic Journal*, **47** (1937) 423–443. J. M. Keynes, 'The "Ex-Ante" Theory of the Rate of Interest', *Economic Journal*, **47** (1937) 663–669.

security will be $1/r$ if r is the rate of interest per unit of time. Let the period we are considering start at the moment t-1 (the end point of the preceding period) and end at the moment t. Following L. R. Klein's way of posing the question[2], our problem is then this: does the interest rate change during this period because, at the rate of interest of the preceding period, the *stock* of bonds at t is larger or smaller than the demand for this stock; or does it change because, at this interest rate, the *addition* to the bonds outstanding at t-1 (i.e., the new issues *during the period*) is larger or smaller than the demand for this addition? Expressing this in symbols, the question is whether we should base our theory on equation (1), the equation for stocks, or on equation (2), that for flows?

$$r_t - r_{t-1} = G(B_t^S - B_t^D) \qquad 0 = G(0) \qquad (1)$$

$$r_t - r_{t-1} = G^*[(B_t^S - B_{t-1}^S) - (B_t^D - B_{t-1}^D)] \quad 0 = G^*(0) \qquad (2)$$

Here the letter r is used to designate the rate of interest, G and G^* denote the respective functions, B^S is the supply of bonds (considered as a stock) and B^D the demand for the same, and the subscripts t and t-1 designate the points in time at which the various magnitudes are measured.

Fellner and Somers answered this question as follows: if at the end of each short period, and thus also at moment t-1, equilibrium is reached so that $B_{t-1}^S = B_{t-1}^D$, equations (1) and (2) will be identical.[3] However, Klein[4] and also Brunner[5], who entered the debate, were not willing to leave matters there. If one were to assume that at moment t-1 no equilibrium existed, and thus $B_{t-1}^S \neq B_{t-1}^D$, a stock theory would give a result different from that of a flow theory. According to Brunner we have to hold that in a market in which the stock of the commodity is large and the increment is relatively small – as is true for the securities market – the price is determined in the short run by the stock magnitudes and not by the flow magnitudes. "In general, a flow equilibrium price will still be accompanied by a stock disequilibrium, which will force a change in price till short-run stock equilibrium has been achieved. This situation will then be accom-

[2] L. R. Klein, 'Stock and Flow Analysis in Economics', *Econometrica*, **18** (1950) 240.
[3] W. Fellner and H. M. Somers, 'Stock and Flow Analysis: Comment', *Econometrica*, **18** (1950) 243.
[4] L. R. Klein, 'Stock and Flow Analysis: Further Comment', *Econometrica*, **18** (1950) 246.
[5] K. Brunner, 'Stock and Flow Analysis: Discussion', *Econometrica*, **18** (1950) 247 ff.

panied by a flow disequilibrium which will change the underlying stock relationship. So a new stock equilibrium will be formed, with a new price and a new flow disequilibrium, and so on until the whole short-run system has eventually been adjusted."[6]

In order to evaluate this thesis of a potential discrepancy between the results of the two approaches we shall take, first, a situation in which both approaches, as all participants in the discussion would certainly agree, yield the same result. In the left graph of Figure 23 the price of a bond, (1/r), is shown on the y-axis and the number of bonds on the x-axis. The bonds outstanding at moment t-1 are given by $S_a(=OM)$, while the S_n-line shows the bonds newly issued during the period from t-1 to t as a function of the interest rate. Correspondingly, the D_a-line shows the bonds which bondholders would wish to hold at moment t-1 at various interest rates (reservation demand), and the D_n-line reflects the new demand during our period as a function of the interest rate. In the situation depicted by this half of Figure 23, the stock OM at the moment t-1 is at the interest rate r equal to the reservation demand of bondholders (D_a). At moment t, at the same interest rate, the supply or stock of bonds $S'_a(=ON)$ is equal to the aggregate demand D_a+D_n (which we have to consider as reservation demand once all transactions of the period have been concluded). Thus, at the end of our period the stock S'_a is equal to

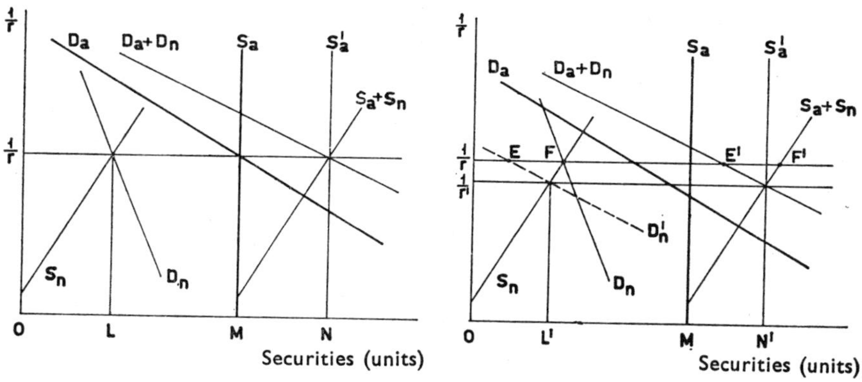

Fig. 23.

[6] K. Brunner, 'Stock and Flow Analysis: Discussion', *Econometrica*, **18** (1950) 247–248.

the demand for this stock $D_a + D_n$ at the interest rate of the preceding period; and at the same time the increment OL during our period (t-1 to t) is equal to the demand for this increment at this same interest rate. Both stock analysis and flow analysis yield the result that the rate of interest does not change.

Let us now drop the assumption that a stock equilibrium prevailed at moment t-1. The current period thus begins under circumstances in which not all bondholders are willing to hold on to their securities at the still prevailing interest rate r of the preceding period. This situation is depicted in the right-hand graph of Figure 23, in which S_a and D_a do not intersect at the interest rate r. We leave the supply curve for new bonds S_n and the corresponding demand curve D_n unchanged. The new interest rate r' is obtained at the intersection of the aggregate demand curve $D_a + D_n$ and the supply curve $S_a + S_n$. At the end of our period, at the moment t, the aggregate supply of bonds considered as a stock, S_a', is ON'. This stock together with the aggregate demand for it, $D_a + D_n$ (which we view as the new reservation demand at t) obviously give us the same interest rate r', which is higher than r. The change in the interest rate was caused by the fact that at the old interest rate r a positive discrepancy developed between the stock and the demand for it.[7]

Let us now look at the flows. Both the supply curve for newly issued bonds and the new demand for them are represented in the right-hand graph of Figure 23 as they are in the left-hand part of the graph. By themselves, they would re-establish the old interest rate r. However, the decline in the reservation demand of bondholders also has an effect on the "current" supply or the "current" demand, i.e., on the flow magnitudes. We can take account of this effect by subtracting from the new demand any negative difference between the reservation demand and the stock of bonds at the moment t-1 (and by adding a positive difference). In this way we obtain a net demand for new issues which is different from the gross

[7] If one determines the interest rate in a stock analysis at time t with the help, on the one hand, of the stock expressed by the perpendicular erected over N' and, on the other hand, with the help of the curve $D_a + D_n$ which represents the reservation demand at time t, one has introduced the new issue of bonds into the analysis "not as something separate which influences matters *qua* 'flow', but simply as what brings about a change in stocks and requires additional willing bond-holders to be found". (G. L. S. Shackle, 'Recent Theories Concerning the Nature and Role of Interest', *Economic Journal*, **71** (1961) 226.)

new demand, since part of the latter merely serves to fill the gap caused by the shrinkage in the reservation demand of old bondholders. The intersection of this net new demand curve D_n' with the S_n-curve also yields the new interest rate r'. In this flow analysis the change in the interest rate was caused by the fact that at the old rate of interest r the increment of bonds would have been larger – by the amount EF – than the net demand for this increment. Thus here, too, stock analysis and flow analysis lead to the same result – in our case, an increase in the interest rate.[8] However, in the period following the one ending at t, if the supply and demand curves for new issues were to shape up in the same way as in the preceding period, a lower interest rate than r' would result in that period, so that old securities would be offered in the market. The situation depicted in the left-hand part of Figure 23 would develop only over a stretch of many periods. But to characterize this process as a divergency, maintained over many periods, between the flow equilibrium and the stock equilibrium would be admissible only if by flow equilibrium we meant equilibrium between the supply of new securities and the new demand rather than the net new demand.

Don Patinkin set forth the proof that theorizing with stocks leads to the same result as theorizing with flows in a much simpler fashion. The demand for bonds at time t, C^D, is equal to the stock of bonds at the beginning of the period, C_0, plus the credit granted through the purchase of new bonds during the period, L. Thus:

$$C^D = C_0 + L \tag{3}$$

The supply is

$$C^S = C_0 + B \tag{4}$$

where B stands for the credit obtained during the period through the sale of new securities. It follows that

$$C^D - C^S = L - B \tag{5}$$

"Thus the excess demand in the bond market considered from the view-

[8] R. W. Clower, 'Productivity, Thrift and the Rate of Interest', *Economic Journal*, **64** (1954) 107 ff., is also concerned with the problem of stock and flow equilibria on the bond market. Clower comes to the – to us incomprehensible – conclusion that "... the current rate of interest is determined independently of the net supply of new issues..." (p. 110).

point of stocks must necessarily equal the excess demand considered from the viewpoint of flows."[9]

At the interest rate r in the right-hand graph of Figure 23, $C^D - C^S = E'F'$ and $L - B = EF$; the two distances $E'F'$ and EF are equal. One could, of course, be of the opinion that the magnitude C^S (the $S_a + S_n$-curve in Figure 23) is not really a stock magnitude since it has been obtained by adding a flow magnitude – namely, the supply curve for new securities S_n – to C_0, the stock of securities existing at the beginning of the period ($= OM$). We consider it more appropriate to view the stock of securities as a given magnitude which is independent of the interest rate. The quantity of securities ON' is a stock magnitude, but not the supply of securities as a function of the interest rate (the curve $S_a + S_n$). As already stressed, we then have to view the demand $D_a + D_n$ as a "reservation demand" – an approach which is quite acceptable once all transactions of the period are over. There does not seem to be full agreement on what should be considered a stock and what a flow.

II. The Equivalence of the Two Theories under Static Conditions

In the literature, a number of attempts have been made to prove the equivalence of the theory of loanable funds and the liquidity preference theory. These proofs have been given for static conditions, if we interpret the term "static" to refer to situations of temporary short-run equilibria.

We shall first deal with an unsuccessful attempt by A. P. Lerner.[10] Lerner combined his proof of the equivalence of the two theories with a proof of his thesis that saving and investment do not affect the interest rate – a statement which directly contradicts the conclusion to which we were led by our analysis of the Keynesian theory. In our presentation of Lerner's equivalence-proof, we shall also discuss his claim that the interest rate is a purely monetary phenomenon.

[9] Don Patinkin, 'Liquidity Preference and Loanable Funds: Stock and Flow Analysis', *Economica*, New Series, **25** (1958) 305.

[10] See A. P. Lerner, 'Alternative Formulations of the Theory of Interest', *Economic Journal*, **48** (1938) 211–230, and Lerner, 'Interest Theory – Supply and Demand for Loans or Supply and Demand for Cash', *Review of Economic Statistics*, **26** (1944) 88–91. Both papers were reprinted in S. E. Harris (ed.), *The New Economics* (New York, 1947), pp. 634–661, and in A. P. Lerner, *Essays in Economic Analysis* (London, 1953), pp. 277–304 and 318–327.

Lerner first gives a presentation of what might be called the "expanded classical" theory, according to which the interest rate is determined by the demand for and the supply of funds. The supply may derive not only from saving, but also from dishoarding and from newly created bank credit. The demand may result from the need for investment funds and for hoards. As far as hoarding and dishoarding are concerned, it is of course possible that the savers hoard and the investors dishoard. We need only consider the net result of hoarding and dishoarding. If for the economy as a whole hoarding is going on, we add this on the demand side; if the economy as a whole dishoards, we add the cash released on the supply side. On these premises the market for funds can be represented by the following diagram, used by Lerner, which is intended to express the fact that "the rate of interest is the price that equates the supply of 'credit', or saving *plus* the net increase in the amount of money in a period, to the demand for 'credit', or investment *plus* net 'hoarding' in the period."[11]

In Figure 24 the *S*-curve shows saving and the *I*-curve investment as functions of the interest rate. If there were neither hoarding nor additional bank credit, the interest rate would be P_0A. The *L*-curve shows hoarding

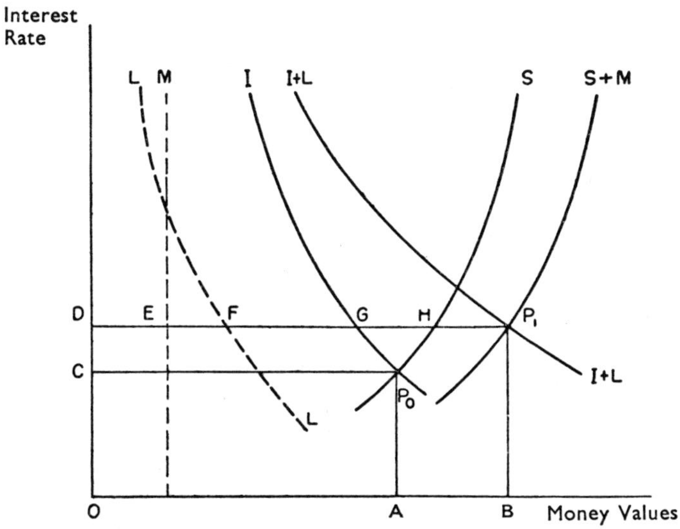

Fig. 24.

[11] A. P. Lerner, 'Alternative Formulations of the Theory of Interest', *The New Economics*, p. 637; *Essays*, p. 281.

– here assumed to be positive – as a function of the interest rate, and the M-line shows the increase in the amount of money here considered as independent of the rate of interest – an assumption made only for the sake of convenience. If the hoarding curve is added to the investment curve, we obtain the $I+L$-curve; and the addition of the newly created credit to the savings curve yields the $S+M$-curve. The interest rate will then be P_1B and will thus be different from the rate obtained if only saving and investment were taken into account.

Lerner rejects this presentation as contrary to some Keynesian definitions. In the first place, saving, at the interest rate P_1B, is not equal to investment. Instead, it is larger, as the diagram shows, whereas the two must necessarily be equal according to Keynes' definitions. Secondly, the additional quantity of money DE is not equal to the hoarding DF as ought to be the case; for, although an individual can increase his cash balance, he can do so only at the expense of someone else's cash balance if the total quantity of money remains the same. Hence, with an unchanged money supply there cannot be a net excess of hoarding. Net hoarding can take place only if new money is being created, and it must of necessity be equal to this new money.

Lerner now proceeds to give the "correct" presentation, which satisfies the basic postulate that saving must be equal to investment.

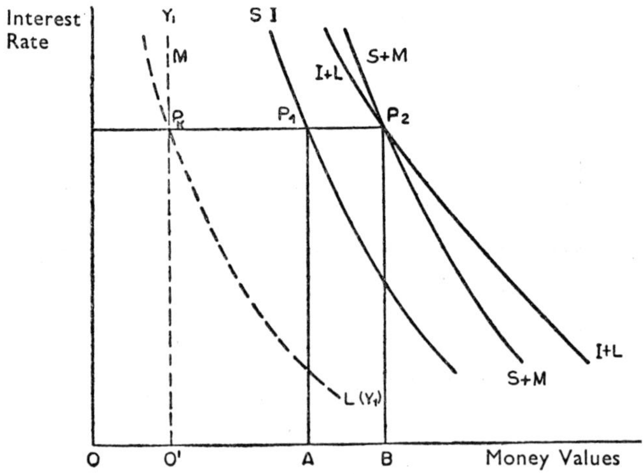

Fig. 25.

In Figure 25, all points on the *SI*-curve are equilibrium points at which saving equals investment. The idea underlying such a curve is that to any given rate of interest there corresponds a certain level of aggregate income at which the amount saved is exactly equal to the amount invested. These amounts are plotted against the corresponding rates of interest. It should be emphasized that the different points on the *SI*-curve correspond to different levels of aggregate income. The $L(Y_1)$-curve represents the hoarding of new money at the income level Y_1, and OO' shows the newly created quantity of money. The curves $S+M$ and $I+L$ are, as in Figure 24, obtained by adding the curves *SI* and *M* and *SI* and *L*, respectively. According to Lerner it is more expedient, for reasons we need not go into here, to regard the distance OO' as denoting the total quantity of money (rather than as the additional quantity only), and correspondingly to consider the *L*-curve as reflecting the schedule of the total demand for money (rather than the demand for new money). The resulting interest rate is P_2B.

It can then be clearly seen, (1) that the interest rate is determined by the liquidity preference curve and the quantity of money; (2) that the addition of saving on the "supply side", and of investment on the "demand side", does not alter the rate of interest; and, accordingly, that the loanable funds theory and the liquidity preference theory of interest both lead to the same result; and (3) that neither saving nor investment can have any influence on the interest rate, for it is evident that whatever distance we shift the *SI*-curve to the right, the interest rate will not be changed as the amounts added to the *L*-curve and to the *M*-curve are always equal.

This presentation by Lerner contains several blunders:

1. The *L*-curve is a genuine demand curve; it shows the demand for cash balances at various hypothetical rates of interest and presumes a *given* level of income. The *SI*-curve which is added on to this genuine demand curve represents a function of a different sort: it represents equilibrium points for saving and investment, each of which corresponds to a *different* level of income. It obviously makes no sense whatever to add up two such disparate things. Robertson has phrased this objection as follows: "Mr. Lerner, in a recent geometrical fantasia appears to me to have overlooked these considerations. Starting with an apparatus designed to register human choices, he proceeds to graft on to it concepts

from which choice is excluded, and expects us to share his naïve glee at the confusion which results."[12]

2. How does Lerner obtain the result that saving and investment do not influence the rate of interest, whereas in our earlier discussion we arrived at the opposite conclusion? Patently he assumed from the start that Y_1 is the equilibrium income. At the corresponding equilibrium interest rate, the supply of and the demand for money are equal and so are saving (*ex ante*) and investment (*ex ante*). Point P_1 on the *SI*-curve is thus, by assumption, the only point on this curve which is valid simultaneously with the $L(Y_1)$-curve as both S and I are equal to OA only at the equilibrium income Y_1 and the equilibrium interest rate P_1A. Because the interest rate does not change if we add S and $I(OA)$ to the respective money curves, Lerner draws the conclusion that saving and investment do not influence the interest rate. For the equilibrium income, we could equally well have drawn a saving and an investment curve (marginal efficiency of investment curve) as functions of the interest rate, which would have given us the equilibrium rate of interest. And we could have added an *LM*-curve combining all points at which the demand for and the supply of money are equal at different interest rates (and different incomes). On the *LM*-curve, only that point which corresponds to the interest rate as determined by the saving and investment curves would be valid simultaneously with the *S*- and *I*-curves. We could then have concluded that saving and investment determine the interest rate, as the rate does not change if account is taken also of the supply of and demand for money. This procedure would have as much justification as Lerner's but would be equally wrong. As soon as we cease to take the equilibrium income as initially given, we find that the money equation as well as the saving-investment equation are necessary to determine the interest rate.

In spite of the objections raised against it, Lerner held on to his theory that saving and investment do not influence the interest rate. In a later publication he again presented this view very strongly and even sharpened

[12] D. H. Robertson, 'Mr. Keynes and the Rate of Interest', in D. H. Robertson, *Essays in Monetary Theory* (London, 1940), p. 5; reprinted in *Readings in the Theory of Income Distribution* (Philadelphia-Toronto, 1946), p. 429. Others have also pointed to this fault in Lerner's argument. Cf. G. Haberler, *Prosperity and Depression* (5th ed., London, 1964), pp. 184 ff. and 200 ff.; L. R. Klein, *The Keynesian Revolution* (New York, 1949), pp. 119 ff.; S. C. Tsiang, 'Liquidity Preference and Loanable Funds Theories, Multiplier and Velocity Analyses: A Synthesis', *American Economic Review*, **46** (1956) 539 ff.

the formulation: "If we take these repercussions into account we find that it is only when borrowing is *not invested* or otherwise spent that it tends to increase the rate of interest and it is only when lending is *not out of saving* that it tends to lower the rate of interest."[13] "Thus we see that neither borrowing for investment nor lending out of saving has any net effect on the rate of interest."[14] According to Lerner, those who take the contrary view are simply neglecting the repercussions of investment or of saving. Investment raises the level of income, and from this income exactly as much will in the end be saved as the investment requires. Conversely, saving reduces the aggregate income – and correspondingly less will be invested. Hence the interest rate can only be explained by the liquidity preference and the quantity of money – indeed a "purely monetary" theory. Unfortunately, such a theory is vitiated by the fact that it completely disregards the dependence of the liquidity preference curve on income – an income which, in turn, is codetermined by the marginal efficiency of investment and the propensity to save. Because of these shortcomings of Lerner's presentation, his proof of the equivalence of the theory of loanable funds and the liquidity preference theory (illustrated in Figure 25) also must be considered a failure.

There are two ways of proving the equivalence of the two theories. The first starts from general equilibrium theory and is based on Walras' law. This proof was first given by J. R. Hicks.[15]

If we assume n goods, one of which is money, we have to determine n-1 commodity prices and the rate of interest – hence a total of n prices. For this purpose we have n-1 equations which equate supply and demand as functions of all prices on the n-1 commodity markets; we have one equation which equates supply and demand for claims in the form of, let us say, consols; and one further equation which does the same for money. We thus have $n+1$ equations. But since, as Walras has shown, one of the equations follows from the others, we have for the determination of the $n-1$ commodity prices and the interest rate only n independent equations. It does not matter which market is disregarded in counting the equations. For instance, we can leave out the market for consols. Then the interest rate will appear as determined with the aid of the money equation. But we

[13] A. P. Lerner, *Economics of Employment* (New York-Toronto-London, 1951), p. 116.
[14] A. P. Lerner, *Economics of Employment*, p. 108.
[15] J. R. Hicks, *Value and Capital* (2nd ed., Oxford, 1946), chapter 12.

can equally well, without affecting the result, leave out the money equation; the interest rate will then appear to be determined with the aid of the equation for bonds. If we now identify the procedure in which we use the money equation with the liquidity preference theory, and the other one in which we use the equation for bonds with the theory of loanable funds, it is proven that both theories lead to the same result – i.e., to the same rate of interest.

The critique of this type of proof frequently starts out from the question ascribed to A. P. Lerner: But what if instead of the money equation or the bonds equation we were to leave out the equation for peanuts?[16] This question indeed strikes at the Achilles' heel of this type of argument. In a general equilibrium analysis all independent equations are necessary for the determination of each individual price, including the interest rate; the latter is indeed determined "with the aid" of the money equation if the bonds equation were to be eliminated, but no more so than it is determined "with the aid" of the peanuts equation or any other commodity equation. The liquidity preference theory and the theory of loanable funds should have more substantive content than is found in a theory asserting that either the money equation or the bonds equation, just like any other equation, can be used or eliminated in the determination of equilibrium. One will therefore have to agree with Don Patinkin when he says that it is not advisable to identify the two theories with the use of the corresponding equation – money or bonds – in the determination of general equilibrium.[17]

More recently a very different objection has been raised against the Hicksian approach to the problem. "Unfortunately the fact that the current rate of production is equal to the current rate of consumption does not mean that the market is in equilibrium. There still exists the possibility that the current existent stock of the good is not equal to the current demand to hold the good. This being the case, price will change because total

[16] The question was attributed to Lerner by L. R. Klein (*The Keynesian Revolution* (New York, 1949), p. 118) and has ever since made the rounds through the literature. For a critique of the Hicksian theory, see in particular L. R. Klein, *The Keynesian Revolution*, and L. R. Klein, 'Stock and Flow Analysis in Economics', *Econometrica*, **18** (1950) 238; further, S. C. Tsiang, 'Liquidity Preference and Loanable Funds Theories, Multiplier and Velocity Analyses: A Synthesis', *American Economic Review*, **46** (1956) 540 ff.

[17] Don Patinkin, 'Liquidity Preference and Loanable Funds: Stock and Flow Analysis', *Economica*, New Series, **25** (1958) 301.

demand (consumption plus the demand to hold) will not be equal to total supply (production plus existent stocks). In equilibrium, not only must the rate of production equal the rate of consumption, but total supply must be equal to total demand."[18] Accordingly, such a commodity will have to be represented in the general equilibrium analysis not with *one*, but with *two* equations. The Hicksian proof based on the elimination of only *one* equation can, on this argument, be accepted only under very restrictive conditions which we do not need to specify here. Brunner, as we saw, had already asserted that a discrepancy could exist between a stock equilibrium and a flow equilibrium; but we could not accept this reasoning. In the right-hand part of Figure 23 we have equilibrium at the interest rate r' not only between the current (net) demand for new securities – the curve D_n' – and the new supply, but also between the total demand $D_a + D_n$ and the total supply.

A second proof of the equivalence of the two theories which can be found in the literature is of a macroeconomic type. Let us assume a period which is so short that the money can be used only once during the period, be it for the purchase of commodities or of securities. We could identify our short period with a "week" and assume that all transactions take place on "Monday", as Hicks did in a different context.

Households and firms enter into the current period with their assets – capital goods, securities and money balances. In order to avoid the problem of the structure of interest rates, we shall assume that only one type of security exists, a bond of the "consols" type. Let us further assume that a given amount of money is required for transaction purposes; the remaining quantity of money is then available to satisfy the speculative motive.

The demand for cash balances for speculative purposes can be divided into two parts. First, some households and firms may wish to simply hoard part of the money which is left over after they have set aside their transaction money; i.e., they will hold it through the current period. Second, others may demand additional cash balances which they obtain by selling securities. These cash balances are thus made available by the buyers of the securities. Both kinds of demand for money can be viewed as functions of the rate of interest. The demand for money (through

[18] Cliff L. Lloyd, 'The Equivalence of the Liquidity Preference and Loanable Funds Theories and the *New* Stock-Flow Analysis', *Review of Economic Studies*, **27** (1959–60) 207.

hoarding or through the sale of securities) rises when the interest rate falls. The two schedules which reflect these two types of demand for cash balances can be added to form the demand curve for speculative cash balances. This total demand for speculative cash balances together with the quantity of money available for speculative purposes determines the interest rate. In Figure 26 the *h*-curve shows the quantity of money which households and business enterprises are willing to hold through the period at different interest rates; the *n*-curve shows the new demand for money (through sales of securities), and the horizontal addition of both, the *l*-curve, represents the total speculative demand for cash balances. The latter cuts the *m*-line, which reflects the quantity of money available for speculative purposes, at *L*. The rate of interest will then be *GL*.

The demand for money arising from the sale of securities has, as its counterpart, a supply curve for money resulting from the purchase of securities. Obviously we can obtain the latter by subtracting the *h*-curve horizontally from the *m*-line. The total quantity of money available for speculation less the quantity held throughout the period is clearly identical with the quantity of money which will be offered on the market for securities. This supply schedule for money is represented by the *SS*-curve in Figure 26. It follows from the construction of the diagram that the intersection of this supply curve with the corresponding demand curve (demand for cash balances as expressed by the sale of securities) at point *P* will yield a rate of interest which is the same as that obtained at the

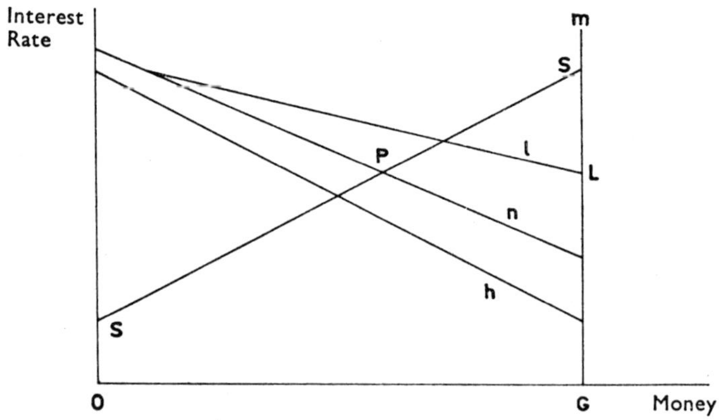

Fig. 26.

intersection of the total demand curve (the *l*-curve) with the supply of money for speculative purposes. Thus the point *L* stands at the same level as the point *P*. If we identify the demand for money through the sale of securities with the demand for loanable funds, and the supply of money through the purchase of securities with the supply of such funds, then it will be evident that the theory of loanable funds and the liquidity preference theory yield the same rate of interest.[19]

One could, of course, present the argument without such narrow assumptions. Thus, we could assume that commodity market transactions – i.e., the money receipts from the sale of commodities – are not given, but rise with a falling interest rate. We would then have to introduce an additional curve with the shape of the *h*- and *n*-curves, namely, a *c*-curve which reflects the demand for cash balances through the sale of commodities; the *l*-curve would be the addition of the three curves, $c+h+n$; and *OG* in Figure 26 would be the total money supply, not only that for speculative purposes. Further, we could assume that the quantity of money itself increased with a rising interest rate because banks are ready to sacrifice more liquidity at higher interest rates. The *m*-line in Figure 26 would then rise towards the right. The difference between the vertical line erected over *G* and this new *m*-curve would then represent the additional credit. A diagram expanded in this manner is used by S. C. Tsiang to prove the equivalence of the two interest theories.[20] The demand for money by the sellers of securities, however, is replaced by the demand for money by the sellers of investment goods which are all bought with loanable funds; his *c*-curve, accordingly, does not reflect the demand for money via the sale of all commodities, but only via the sale of consumer goods.

It should be noted that Tsiang would not accept this interpretation of his curves. He would consider it an *ex post* analysis because it regards the demand for money as resulting, *ex post*, from the sale of commodities –

[19] This proof of the equivalence of the two theories has been taken over unchanged from the first German edition of this book (*Zinstheorie*, Zürich-Tübingen, 1956); it is different only in the form of presentation, but not in its essence, from that given by Fellner and Somers (W. Fellner and H. M. Somers, 'Alternative Monetary Approaches to Interest Theory', *Review of Economic Statistics*, **23** (1941) 43–48). On this subject, see also E. Schneider, 'Zur Liquiditätstheorie des Zinses', *Weltwirtschaftliches Archiv*, **62** (1949) 123–131.

[20] S. C. Tsiang, 'Liquidity Preference and Loanable Funds Theories, Multiplier and Velocity Analyses: A Synthesis', *American Economic Review*, **46** (1956) 549.

a fact which, according to him, has no causal significance. Tsiang would rather have his curves understood as the *ex ante* demand for "finance" which is needed to effect the expenditures planned on the various markets at different interest rates. If we assume only one turnover of money during the period, these planned purchases will, in Tsiang's opinion, give us the *ex ante* demand for money to make the purchases. However, Tsiang is in error if he believes that his approach constitutes a fundamental difference between his analysis and that of his two predecessors, Fellner and Somers. If Tsiang shows the money expenditures on commodities planned for each "Monday" as a decreasing function of the interest rate, this curve can be nothing other than the locus of all points reflecting combinations of money expenditures and interest rates at which the commodity market is in equilibrium – i.e., at which the price mechanism has seen to it that supply and demand for goods are equal Unless this assumption is made, it would be necessary to have a separate expenditure curve, as a function of the interest rate, for each hypothetical level of prices – or it would be necessary to have a different expenditure curve, as a function of the price level, for each interest rate.

Figure 27 may serve to clarify the statement just made. In the left-hand graph we show on the y-axis the price level and on the x-axis the planned money expenditures on goods. The S-line represents the supply of goods in money terms on the assumption, made for simplicity's sake, that the *quantity* of goods supplied is independent of the price level. The curve D_{i_1} represents the planned expenditures on commodities at a given interest

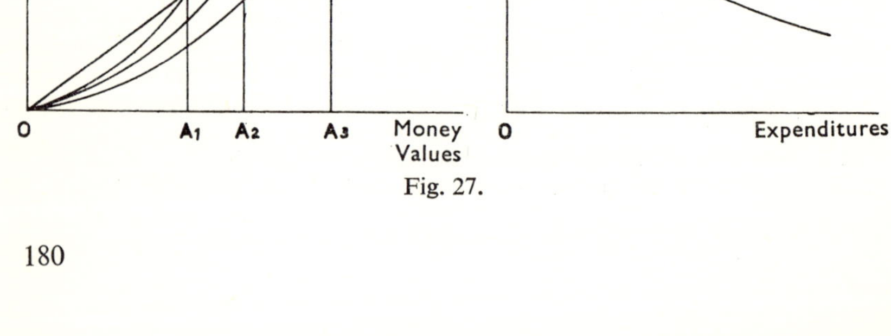

Fig. 27.

rate i_1, the curve D_{i_2} the planned expenditures at a lower interest rate i_2, and correspondingly for D_{i_3} and i_3. If we now plot the equilibrium expenditures for the various interest rates – A_1, A_2, A_3 – against those rates of interest, as in the right-hand graph of Figure 27, we will obtain Tsiang's curve of "planned" expenditures.

Thus the quantity of transaction money put aside by households and business firms is only determined on the assumption of an equilibrium situation in the commodity market. Once it is recognized that Tsiang's demand curve for "finance" has been drawn on the assumption of equilibrium in the commodity market, it follows that the quantity of money demanded by the sales of goods is merely the mirror image of Tsiang's demand for "finance" to carry out money expenditures on goods. The curves are identical, regardless of whether they are interpreted as Fellner, Somers, and we did, or interpreted in Tsiang's fashion.

Neither the macroeconomic nor the microeconomic proof of the equivalence of the two interest theories has much substantive content. The macroeconomic proof supposes that the entire economic system is divided into a very small number of markets (instead of an infinite number, as in microeconomics) which are reflected in a corresponding number of equations. If one takes three markets – the market for commodities, the market for securities, and the money market – and if one assumes, as Fellner and Somers, Tsiang (even though *malgré soi*) and the writer all do, that the commodity market is always in equilibrium, then, if the securities market is in equilibrium at a certain interest rate, it follows from Walras' law that the money market must also be in equilibrium, and vice versa. Thus the macroeconomic proof basically rests on the same principle as the microeconomic one although one cannot make it look as absurd as the latter. For there can here be no question of eliminating an equation of the type of the "peanuts equation". We are inclined to conclude that the entire discussion about the equivalence of the theory of loanable funds and the liquidity preference theory was hardly worth the bother.

III. Equivalence under Dynamic Conditions?

L. R. Klein has, with some justification, little regard for the proof of the equivalence of the two theories under static conditions. And he asserts that under dynamic conditions the theory of loanable funds and the liquidity preference theory will not yield the same result.[21]

Klein's argument, reduced to its essentials, runs as follows: According to the liquidity preference theory, the rate of interest changes if there is an excess demand for or an excess supply of money. Let us designate the quantity of money – assumed to be given – by K, the demand for money by M^D, the rate of interest by r, the end of the period under consideration by the subscript t, and correspondingly the end of the preceding period by the subscript $t-1$. According to the liquidity preference theory:

$$r_t - r_{t-1} = h_1(K_t - M_t^D) \qquad 0 = h_1(0) \tag{1}$$

r_t is greater than r_{t-1}, if M_t^D, at the interest rate r_{t-1}, is larger than K_t, and vice versa.

By contrast, according to the theory of loanable funds, the cause of a change in the rate of interest is an excess demand or an excess supply in the securities market. If we designate the demand for bonds in money terms (*not* in terms of the number of bonds) by B^D and the supply by B^S, then according to this theory:

$$r_t - r_{t-1} = h_2(B_t^D - B_t^S) \qquad 0 = h_2(0) \tag{2}$$

r_t is larger than r_{t-1} if B_t^S, at the interest rate r_{t-1}, is larger than B_t^D, and vice versa.

But an excess supply of money must be equal to the excess demand for securities plus the excess demand for goods and services (and vice versa in the case of an excess demand for money), so that

$$K_t - M_t^D = (B_t^D - B_t^S) + p_t(x_t^D - x_t^S) \tag{3}$$

where x^D represents the quantity of goods and services demanded, x^S the quantity supplied, and p their price level. Inserting (3) into (1), we obtain

$$r_t - r_{t-1} = h_1[(B_t^D - B_t^S) + p_t(x_t^D - x_t^S)] \tag{4}$$

Thus, if we start from equation (1) which states the liquidity preference theory and, in place of the excess demand for money in that equation, substitute an expression in which the excess demand for bonds appears, we

[21] L. R. Klein, 'Stock and Flow Analysis in Economics', *Econometrica*, **18** (1950) 236–241.

obtain by no means equation (2) which reflects the theory of loanable funds. We obtain a more complicated expression. Accordingly the two theories are not equivalent.

If, conversely, we begin with equation (2) and insert equation (3) in which the money market appears, we do not obtain equation (1), but rather

$$r_t - r_{t-1} = h_2\,[(K_t - M_t^D) - p_t(x_t^D - x_t^S)] \tag{5}$$

It should first be stressed that the results here differ from those reached in the static analysis because in that approach, as noted above, it is assumed that the market for commodities is always in equilibrium – i.e., that $p_t(x_t^D - x_t^S)$ always equals zero. In a dynamic analysis, if we drop this assumption, the choice between liquidity preference theory – equation (1) – and loanable funds theory – equation (2) – will undoubtedly have to be decided in favour of the theory of loanable funds. In order to show the reasons for deciding in this way, let us begin with the case of an excess supply of money. We shall initially assume that the counterpart to this excess supply consists exclusively in an excess demand for commodities. According to the liquidity preference theory (equation (1)) this would lead to a fall in the interest rate, even though by assumption no excess demand had arisen in the market for securities – i.e., $(B_t^D - B_t^S)$ in equation (4) still stood equal to zero. The interest rate would thus fall *even though* supply and demand in the market for securities were in equilibrium.[22]

The liquidity preference theory would yield an even more absurd result if we were to assume that the excess supply of money was accompanied by an excess supply of securities because people intended to finance their increased purchases of goods not only by reducing their cash balances but also by selling securities. In this case the liquidity preference theory as expressed in equation (1) would still yield a fall in the interest rate, even though the sale of securities should bring about a rise of that rate.

The theory of loanable funds, by contrast, yields reasonable results. If the effects of an excess supply of money are evident exclusively in an ex-

[22] Already Fellner and Somers have pointed to this problem (W. Fellner and H. M. Somers, 'Stock and Flow Analysis: Comment', *Econometrica*, **18** (1950) 242–245). Patinkin also decided in favour of the loanable funds theory (Don Patinkin, 'Liquidity Preference and Loanable Funds: Stock and Flow Analysis', *Economica*, New Series, **25** (1958) 310 ff.).

cess demand for goods (no changes occurring in the market for securities), the interest rate, according to this theory, will not fall. In equation (5), $(K_t - M_t^D) - p_t(x_t^D - x_t^S)$ will be equal to zero. If the excess demand for goods is larger than the excess supply of money because securities are being sold, a rise of the interest rate will result, as can be seen both from equation (2) and from equation (5).

Whatever other initial assumption one might wish to make – excess demand for money, excess supply of securities, excess demand for securities, etc. –, one will always find that the theory of loanable funds gives reasonable results, whereas the liquidity preference theory does not. This is not surprising; it merely demonstrates what should not need to be stressed, namely, that the immediate cause of a price change has to be sought in changes of supply or demand in the market of the good in question and not in other markets.

Rose has attempted to reconcile the two theories by explaining the discrepancy under dynamic conditions as due to a time lag.[23] To save ourselves the construction of a new model with new symbols, we shall expound his basic idea as well we can, retaining the present framework.

According to the liquidity preference theory, an excess supply of money will change the interest rate; and, what is the disquieting aspect of that theory, the interest rate will change even if this excess supply makes itself felt solely in an excess demand for goods, no changes taking place in the market for securities. Rose now argues that the immediate effect of such an excess demand for goods will be a decrease in inventories. Instead of holding the additional undesired cash balances, entrepreneurs will buy securities. Therefore, an excess demand will develop, although with a time-lag, in the securities market, which will cause a drop in the interest rate. The excess supply of money will turn into an excess supply of credit (excess demand for securities). Conversely, an excess demand for money will lead to an accumulation of inventories which will require financing; and, in Rose's model, it will be financed through the sale of securities. The interest rate will rise in both theories. Even under dynamic conditions it thus seems that, if we neglect the time-lag, both theories give the same result.

In answer to this proposition we can, first of all, argue that although

23 H. Rose, 'Liquidity Preference and Loanable Funds', *Review of Economic Studies*, **24** (1956–57) 111–119.

this may be the case, it does not necessarily follow. For instance, owners of inventories who accumulate cash because their inventories are decreasing can equally well use the additional money during the second stage for the purchase of a larger volume of goods to replenish their stocks rather than for the purchase of securities. Even if it could be proved (which seems to us impossible) that ultimately somewhere in the system an excess demand for securities must develop, the time-lag might be so large that a dynamic analysis could not neglect it.[24]

[24] F. H. Hahn, 'The Rate of Interest and General Equilibrium Analysis', *Economic Journal*, **65** (1955) 52–66, attributes the potential discrepancy between the results of the two theories to a difference in the periods which allegedly underly the two theories. However, we were not convinced by his argument.

CHAPTER 14

DON PATINKIN

I. Exposition

In our presentation of Patinkin's analysis[1] we shall confine ourselves to his macroeconomic theory. Patinkin expounds it in two parts. We shall concentrate principally on the first part in which he assumes full employment and takes the gross national product as a datum.

Patinkin describes the equilibrium of the system with the help of four equations which we shall reproduce below with the necessary explanations.

$$Q\left(\frac{w}{p}, K_0\right) = R\left(\frac{w}{p}\right) \qquad \text{(labour)} \qquad (1)$$

This equation reflects the market for labour. On the right-hand side the supply of labour is presented as a function of the real wage rate w/p (w=money wage, p=price level). On the left-hand side we have the demand for labour, also as a function of the real wage rate; the quantity of capital K_0 is given. Patinkin assumes that supply and demand in the labour market react so rapidly to a disturbance of equilibrium that we can consider this market as in permanent equilibrium.

$$F\left(Y_0, r, \frac{M_0}{p}\right) = Y_0 \qquad \text{(goods)} \qquad (2)$$

On the right-hand side we have the full employment supply of goods in the form of the real gross national product Y_0, which is given. The expression on the left-hand side represents the demand for goods as a function of the real gross national income, the interest rate r, and the real

[1] Don Patinkin, *Money, Interest, and Prices* (1st ed., Evanston, Ill., and White Plains, N.Y., 1956; 2nd ed., New York, 1965).

cash balances. The gross national product has not been split up here into investment and consumption goods.

$$rp \cdot H\left(Y_0, \frac{1}{r}, \frac{M_0^H}{p}\right) = rp \cdot J\left(Y_0, \frac{1}{r}, \frac{M_0^F}{p}\right) \qquad \text{(securities)} \qquad (3)$$

This equation represents the market for securities. The securities in question are consols, a unit of which carries a yield of one dollar per period; thus the price of the bond is $1/r$, and its real value $1/rp$. If we designate the supply of bonds (i.e., the number of bonds outstanding) by B^s, its real value will be B^s/rp. According to Patinkin this supply is a function of the real gross national product Y_0 (assumed to be given), the price of bonds $1/r$, and the real cash balances held by business firms, M_0^F/p; hence the supply function for bonds can be written $(B^s/rp) = J[Y_0, (1/r), (M_0^F/p)]$. If rp is brought over to the right-hand side, we have the expression for the supply of bonds (in terms of numbers) on the right-hand side of equation (3). In a similar manner we obtain the left side of equation (3), the demand for bonds, where M_0^H/p represents the real cash balances of households. The distribution of the total money supply M_0 between households and business firms is assumed to be given.

$$p \cdot L\left(Y_0, r, \frac{M_0}{p}\right) = M_0 \qquad \text{(money)} \qquad (4)$$

On the right-hand side we have the supply of money in nominal units. The demand for real money balances – $L(Y_0, r, M_0/p)$ – is a function of real income, the rate of interest, and the real cash balances M_0/p; since M_0 is given, it is the price level, p, which is the variable in this expression. If the demand for real cash balances is multiplied by the price level, as in equation (4), we obtain an expression for the demand for money M^d in terms of nominal money units which must, in equilibrium, be equal to the existing quantity of money.

At first sight it may seem surprising to find in the demand function for money the expression M_0/p. This fact requires some further explanation. If the term M_0/p were lacking, the demand for money M^d would, with a constant real income and rate of interest, vary proportionally to changes in the price level – e.g., it would double if the price level doubled.

The demand for money in nominal units as a function of the value of money would always have unit elasticity, while the demand for money in real terms, M^d/p, would be independent of the price level. For Patinkin, however, the demand for real balances is dependent also on the price level; and this implies that the demand for cash balances in nominal units cannot have unit elasticity. How does Patinkin arrive at this conclusion? Let us imagine a household confronted with a doubling of the price level. Since its real income is to remain constant, we must, in a money economy, assume that its money income doubles. If the household now continues to spend its entire income during the income period, keeping no cash balances except those stemming from current income receipts (balances which, in the course of the income period, will fall to zero), it will at any given moment be holding twice the amount of money as previously – amounts which will, of course, have the same purchasing power as did the smaller amounts at the lower price level. This would be in agreement with the classical view, according to which the demand for money in terms of nominal units always has unit elasticity. Let us now, however, make the assumption that the household holds, for the sake of liquidity, some cash which was accumulated earlier and is now carried along from period to period without serving to defray regular expenditures. The assumption that real income remains the same after the doubling of the price level does not require that *this* amount of money, too, will be doubled. Since the purchasing power of its cash balances has now declined, the household will seek to replenish its real balance, but not up to the old level. The household will go up to the point at which the utility which it derives from the liquidity of the last money unit added to its cash balance equals the utility of the consumer goods which it could have financed with this money unit. This point will be reached, with normal utility functions, before the cash balance has been built up to its original real value.[2] It seems indeed quite plausible that the household will not make up a loss in its real cash balance in full by abstaining to that extent from consumption: one would expect it to spread the sacrifice over both consumption on the one hand, and its real cash balance on the other. The demand for real

[2] This presentation does not correspond exactly to that of Patinkin, as the latter does not explicitly speak of the necessity to assume that money incomes and, with them, the quantity of money will rise if real incomes are to remain constant at a higher price level.

cash balances thus changes with the price level: it will fall if the price level rises, and vice versa. This is how the real-balance effect makes itself felt. It follows that the demand for money in nominal units as a function of the price level will not have unit elasticity.

Of Patinkin's four equations only three are independent, for – as was pointed out in the preceding chapter – if out of n markets $n-1$ are in equilibrium, then the n-th market is also in equilibrium. These three equations are sufficient to determine the three unknowns: the price level p, the rate of interest r, and the wage rate w.

From the four equations we can immediately see that the interest rate will stay unchanged and that general equilibrium will be maintained if, with a doubling of all cash balances, the price level and the money wage rate double. The number of outstanding bonds will double, and thus also their nominal aggregate value, but their real value will stay the same. Patinkin assumes either that all capital goods in the hands of firms have to be replaced during the period under consideration – so that new bonds, corresponding to the rise in the price level, will have to be issued to finance the replacement purchases –, or that the book value of the existing capital assets is written up, new bonds being issued to the extent of this increase in capital values.

During the transition period from one equilibrium situation to the other, however, the interest rate will temporarily fall, as the classics had also maintained. According to Patinkin this fall of the interest rate comes about because households, which after the increase in the quantity of money are provided with larger cash balances, will now demand not only more commodities but also more securities, while firms, which will also demand more commodities, will at the same time buy back some of their own securities. They will thus be supplying fewer bonds in the face of a larger demand. However, eventually the real-balance effect of the price increase in the commodity market will reduce the real demand of households for bonds, B^d/rp, while the real supply from firms, B^s/rp, will increase again, until an equilibrium is established at the old rate of interest. There will be twice the number of bonds which, however, will have the same real aggregate value as half their number had previously.

Patinkin stresses that these results will not be changed if we assume that the real-balance effect affects only the bond market, but not the commodity market. It can be readily seen from the four equations that the elimination of the term M_0/p in the commodity market equation (2) will not affect the conclusion that a doubling of the quantity of money will cause a doubling of the price level and leave the interest rate unchanged.

Let us now change the liquidity preference. We assume that households and firms wish to hold larger cash balances. Let this desire, in the case of households, be achieved at the expense of diminished purchases of both goods *and* securities – i.e., let the relative desirability of goods and securities remain unchanged. The larger balances are not obtained, as Keynes assumed, at the expense of the securities alone. The new equilibrium price level will have been reached when prices have fallen so far that the desire of individuals for a larger real value of their cash balances is satisfied. Households will then be buying the same commodities as before and will be holding the same real value in bonds, while firms will have the same real sales turnover and the same real value of bonds outstanding. This implies that the rate of interest will be the same as previously. The nominal value of the securities outstanding will, of course, be smaller, but at a lower price level the demand for finance will also be correspondingly smaller. During the transition period, however, the interest rate will rise temporarily, since the householders' desire for larger cash balances will at first shift the demand not only for goods but also for bonds to the left. Firms, in turn, will initially be supplying more bonds in order to increase their cash holdings. Once the fall of the price level takes hold, the real-balance effect will, according to Patinkin, cause an increase in the demand for bonds and a reduction in the supply since households and firms will now find themselves in possession of larger real balances than they wish to hold[3]; these changes in demand and supply of bonds will continue until the rate of interest has returned to the initial level.

If, however, the increase in liquidity preference affects only the bond market – as Keynes assumed – , the rate of interest in the new equilibrium situation will be higher than in the initial situation. The speculative balances will have increased at the expense of the transaction balances, and the price level will be lower than in the initial situation.

[3] If the households, for instance, add a certain sum of money to their cash balances instead of spending it in order to bring the real balances up to the desired level, and if, as a result of this abstention from spending, prices fall, the households will be holding larger real balances than they desire; their demand for goods and securities will consequently increase again.

Patinkin thus reaches the following results: 1) A change in the money supply leads in the long run to a proportional change in the price level but leaves the rate of interest unchanged. 2) A change in liquidity preference which leaves the relative desirability of goods and securities unaffected leads to a change in the price level but the rate of interest remains unchanged. 3) If a change in the liquidity preference has a primary effect only on the bond market (or only on the commodity market), the rate of interest in the new equilibrium will be different. In the transition period from one equilibrium to the other temporary changes in the rate of interest will occur also in the first two cases.

These results, however, depend on the following assumptions: 1) Prices and money wage rates are flexible. 2) Nobody is subject to money illusion; this means that the demand for commodities, bonds and real cash balances of each individual depends only on his real income, his real cash balance, the real value of his bonds, the relative prices of commodities, and the rate of interest. 3) The result of the collective behaviour of households and firms is not affected by any redistribution of incomes, bonds and cash balances – in other words, absence of net distribution effects is assumed. In particular, it is assumed that when a rise in the price level shrinks the real value of bonds held by households, and when the demand for goods decreases because households want to restore, at least in part, the real value of their security holdings, there is a corresponding increase in the demand for goods by the firms which are the debtors. This presumes that no government bonds are outstanding. 4) Interest and price expectations are held with certainty; prices and interest rate are expected to remain in the future what they are now.

Patinkin clarifies the significance of these assumptions by investigating what effect their absence would have in the case of a doubling of the quantity of money. On the first assumption – that of price and wage flexibility – we do not need to spend any time since the consequences of a lack of such flexibility have been dealt with in chapter 12.

The second assumption is the absence of money illusion. Patinkin investigates two cases: first the situation when purchasers and sellers of securities are subject to the illusion; and, second, when workers are subject to it.

In the case of money illusion among the individuals participating in the bond market, for whom speculative cash balances are the immediate alternative to holding securities, the equation of demand and supply for money must, according to Patinkin, be written as follows:

$$p \cdot L_1(Y_0) + L_2(r) = M_0$$

This equation reflects Keynes' assumption in that the first term on the left-hand side shows the real demand for transaction money as a function of income alone and the second term the demand for speculative balances as a function of the rate of interest exclusively. In the absence of money illusion, Keynes' equation would, according to Patinkin, have to be written:

$$p \cdot L_1(Y_0) + p \cdot L_2(r) = M_0$$

in which case the new equilibrium that will emerge after a doubling of the quantity of money will be characterized by double the price level and an unchanged rate of interest. This is not true for the Keynesian equation. Logically, we have two possibilities here. After the doubling of the quantity of money, either the price level rises so strongly that the entire amount of additional money will be tied up in transaction balances, while the (nominal) speculative balances and the rate of interest remain unchanged; or the interest rate falls and the demand for speculative balances increases until this increased demand for speculative balances, together with the additional demand for transaction money (due to the rising price level of commodities), completely absorbs the increased supply of money. According to Patinkin only the second of these two possibilities can materialize. This follows from the equilibrium condition in the commodity market, which in real terms is expressed by the equation $F[Y_0, r, (M_0/p)] = Y_0$. Let us assume that all the additional money finds its way into the commodity market (which means that the transaction money will more than double), and let us replace the term M_0/p in the commodity market equation by $(2M_0)/(2+x)p$, so that the real value of cash balances is now smaller than prior to the doubling of the quantity of money. Owing to the real-balance effect, the real demand for goods, at an unchanged rate of interest, will then be smaller than the real supply; a deflationary gap will arise and the price level will fall again. Some part of the increased money supply will therefore seek an outlet in the purchase of securities and the interest rate must fall. According to Patinkin the new equilibrium will be reached at a lower rate of interest and at a price level which, although it is more than twice as high than it was prior to the doubling of the quantity of money, is not high enough to absorb the entire additional amount of money in transaction balances.

In the second case of a money illusion, it is assumed that the workers are subject to this illusion in that they let the supply of labour depend not on the real wage rate, but on the money wage rate. Here a doubling of the quantity of money will depress the real wage rate via the increase in the price level. The employers, who do not suffer from money illusion and whose demand for labour is therefore a function of the real wage, will now be demanding more labour. The money wage will rise and the supply of labour will increase. The result is increased employment and a larger national output. Patinkin assumes that the increase in national output, taken by itself, will shift the supply and demand for securities to the right in such a way that the shifts offset each other. The price level will rise; but, because of the increase in national output, it will not quite double. According to Patinkin, the increase in the real cash balances will give rise to a real-balance effect, so that the demand for bonds will shift further to the right than the supply; and, consequently, the rate of interest will be lower than before the expansion of the money supply.

A further precondition for the "neoclassical" result of Patinkin's analysis is the assumption that a redistribution of real income, security holdings and cash balances has no influence on the collective behaviour of households and firms. If this assumption is dropped, the result with respect to changes in the rate of interest depends on the assumption about the effect of a change in the money supply, say, on the distribution of income. One of these possible assumptions has drawn the special attention of the neoclassical economists. If the increase in the price level which follows an expansion of the money supply is accompanied by a faster increase of certain types of money incomes (entrepreneurial incomes) and a correspondingly slower increase of others (money wages), and if the beneficiaries of the inflation have a higher propensity to save than its victims, the demand for bonds will rise and that for commodities will fall. The rate of interest will decline; national output will remain unchanged, but its composition will change in favour of investment goods.

Finally, let us drop the assumption that all the bonds held by households have been issued by firms. So long as this assumption is made, all changes in the real value of bonds caused by changes in the price level have offsetting and mutually compensating effects on the willingness of debtors and creditors to buy goods and bonds. But this is no longer true if we assume that, in addition to the securities issued by business firms, households are also holding government bonds.[4] If the real value of the government bonds rises, the demand of households for goods and bonds will be stimulated, an effect which will not be offset by a negative reaction of the debtor, the state – and vice versa if the real value of the government bonds falls. Let us now assume that the government doubles the quantity of money in order to effect certain expenditures with this additional money. The resulting rise in the price level depresses the real value of government bonds in the hands of households; and, as a consequence, these will curtail their consumption of commodities. Since no opposite reaction of the government ensues, this decline in the demand for commodities will be a net decline. By abstaining from consumption and purchasing bonds instead, the households will attempt to restore part of the decline in the real value of their security holdings. The real demand for bonds will thus contract somewhat less than the real supply; the latter will shrink by the entire amount of the fall in the real value of the government bonds, since the government does not issue any new securities although the real value of its outstanding bonds has declined. Hence the rate of interest must fall. This result, however, would not come about if the bonds were provided with a constant-purchasing-power guarantee. Only if the expansion of money by the state were brought about through open-market purchases of securities by the Central Bank would the rate of interest fall. This would occur even if the bonds carried a constant-purchasing-power clause, since in this case the quantity of bonds outstanding would decrease – a conclusion which was obtained already by Metzler.[5]

[4] If the private sector were to discount the future tax payments necessary to pay the interest on the public debt; and if it considered the present value of the future tax payments as the liability counterpart to the claims against the government incorporated in these bonds, no "wealth effect" would arise from the ownership of government bonds. In the second edition of his book Patinkin assumes that such discounting takes place only with respect to part of the government bonds held by the private sector. The assumption that bondholders discount future tax payments in this fashion seems to us quite unrealistic.

[5] In the second edition of his book, Patinkin supplemented his analysis by introducing

According to Patinkin, the system will – owing to the real-balance effect – always return to full employment as long as money wages and the price level are flexible. However, once we assume that the price level is fixed, thus eliminating the real-balance effect, an "underemployment equilibrium" becomes possible.[6] If we take such a situation as our starting point, we are led to the conclusion that an expansion of the quantity of money will no longer simply produce a proportional change in the price level with an invariant rate of interest, as in the "classical" case. Normally the expansion of the money supply will, with inflexible wages and prices, generate an increased demand for consumer goods and, as a result of the fall in the interest rate caused by the excess demand for bonds, also an increased demand for investment goods. In consequence, the national output will rise until the additional quantity of money is absorbed by the expansion not only of transaction balances, but also of speculative balances which increase on account of the fall in the rate of interest – a sequence which we need not pursue here since we are already familiar with it.

II. Critique

In the part of his book with which we are now mainly concerned, Patinkin develops his analysis on the assumption of full employment. This means that the real national output is held at a certain level, Y_0. Consequently the employment N will also be held constant at N_0, for if labour is optimally combined with the given capital stock there exists only *one* level of employment to produce the real output Y_0. The labour market equation

$$Q\left(\frac{w}{p}, K_0\right) = R\left(\frac{w}{p}\right)$$

shows that the employment level N_0 and the real income level Y_0 must be taken to mean those levels at which the real marginal product of labour is

the banking system. Money is then in part what he calls "inside money", i.e., money that comes into existence by the private sector borrowing from the banks rather than by government creation. However, for our purpose it is unnecessary to enter into discussion of this new assumption.

[6] However, according to Patinkin this expression is to be avoided as in his opinion the situation usually designated by this term is not an equilibrium situation at all.

equal to the real wage rate. Hence the assumption that Y, N and K are given implies that the real wage rate and, as a further consequence, the real marginal product of the existing capital stock must be considered as fixed from the start. This, by itself, does not mean that the interest rate is also given, since the marginal product of the capital stock in existence at the beginning of the period is not equal to the rate of interest. That rate is obtained from the supply of and demand for investment funds, the latter being determined by the expected marginal product (the marginal efficiency) of new capital goods which are produced and added to the capital stock during the period but will begin to be used only in the next period. If, however, we make the assumption, following Patinkin[7], that the new creation of capital goods is small relative to the stock of capital in existence and can hence be neglected, the marginal product of investment, or of the capital stock as augmented by the newly produced capital goods, will no longer be different from the marginal product of capital existing at the beginning of the period. The marginal product of investment (marginal efficiency of investment) is then also given in advance. The interest rate on bonds will appear simply as the result of supply and demand in the bond market, without any connection with the marginal efficiency of investment. Patinkin is, as a rule, interested primarily in aggregate effective demand and therefore does not differentiate in his system of equations between investment and consumption goods. As a result, the marginal efficiency of investment does not explicitly appear in his system; and the link between the latter and the interest rate on bonds remains quite obscure in large parts of the analysis.

This is not to say that Patinkin would want to deny the connection between the two. The demand for goods, of which the demand by firms for investment goods is a part, is in his analysis dependent also on the interest rate; thus he, too, has a link not only between the issuance of bonds and investment but also between the interest rate on bonds and the marginal efficiency of investment – a term which he frequently uses. Nevertheless the effect of investment on its marginal efficiency or, what comes to the same thing, the effect on the marginal product of the capital stock as this stock is expanded by investment remains somewhat obscure. This effect must remain obscure so long as the assumption is maintained that invest-

[7] Patinkin, *Money, Interest, and Prices*, 1st ed., p. 126; 2nd ed., p. 200.

ment is so small that its consequence can be neglected. To show the results of this neglect, let us regard a few cases in which monetary phenomena will, according to Patinkin, change the rate of interest permanently.

If money illusion prevails in the bond market, a doubling of the quantity of money will, according to Patinkin, produce in the new equilibrium situation a rate of interest which is lower than that in the old one; and while the price level will more than double, it will not rise high enough to absorb by itself the entire additional amount of money. It will be useful to compare this case with the "classical" one in which the price level doubles and the rate of interest remains unchanged.

In a first phase, both cases are the same: a doubling of the quantity of money will initially lead to an increase in the demand both for bonds and for goods. The existence of money illusion in the bond market, it must be remembered, does not signify that an expansion of the money supply will fail to increase the demand for bonds in the interim before the price level changes. Rather, the illusion means that this demand will not be affected by a change in the price level. The supply of bonds will contract in this first phase, since firms will be buying back their own bonds. The rate of interest falls and commodity prices rise. In the classical case this rise in the price level generates a negative real-balance effect in the bond market, so that the demand for bonds in real terms declines again and the supply increases until the old interest rate has been re-established; but this reaction will not occur if the money illusion prevails among participants in the bond market. The rate of interest here remains lower.

But a state of affairs in which the interest rate on bonds is lower than the marginal product of capital as expanded by current investment, cannot be an equilibrium situation. If the rate of interest is to remain at this low level, the marginal productivity of capital at the end of the period must also be lower. In the classical case no real capital formation is contemplated: any attempt to expand investment, which might be stimulated by the temporarily lower rate of interest, will "evaporate" in an increase of the price level since "forced saving" is excluded. In the case of money illusion in the bond market, if we do not want to regard the interest rate on bonds and the marginal efficiency of investment as entirely independent of each other, we have to show that the expansion of the money supply leads to (substantial) real capital formation through abstention from consumption and consequently to a fall in the marginal product of capital. Only then can the interest rate remain lower than in the initial situation. Patinkin, however, does not explicitly argue along these lines.

Let us now consider the case of money illusion in the labour market. According to Patinkin, in this situation a doubling of the quantity of money will lead, first, to an increase, although not a doubling, of the price level, second, to an increase in employment and national output – the assumption of a given Y_0 will naturally have to be dropped here – , and third, to a fall of the interest rate. If the rate of interest is to equal the marginal product of the capital stock at the end of the period, this fall in the rate can obviously not come about if investment is neglected: An increase in employment with an unchanged capital stock must lower the marginal product of labour and raise that of capital. A fall of the rate of interest can occur only if the growth in national output is accompanied by an investment which causes the capital stock to grow faster than employment. It is true that Patinkin does not take capital as given in this case. The assumption that the supply of bonds grows with the increase in Y implies that the capital stock will increase. Yet, the decisive question is whether and under what conditions the relationship of capital to labour will change. Whether the marginal product of capital will rise, fall, or stay unchanged depends on this relationship.

Let us now take a third case: A doubling of the quantity of money will be accompanied by "forced saving". Here if the beneficiaries of the inflation have a higher propensity to save than its victims, the real demand for bonds will rise, according to Patinkin, and the rate of interest will fall. The composition of the national output will change in favour of investment goods. With this statement Patinkin takes leave of the matter. This case shows especially clearly that, in Patinkin's analysis, the stress is entirely on the changes in the bond market, while for the neoclassical economists – who reached the same result with respect to the rate of interest – the most important thing, as Patinkin well knows, was the consequence of the change in the composition of the national output, i.e. neoclassical economists concentrated attention on the fact that, owing to the increase in real capital brought about by investment, the marginal product of capital falls.

Finally, let us look at the case in which households are holding government bonds and a rise in the price level due to the expansion of the money supply has the net effect of reducing real expenditures on consumer goods and bonds. In this case, according to Patinkin, the rate of interest on bonds will fall because, as was shown above, the real demand for bonds will shrink relatively less than the real supply. However, the argument cannot stop here, as nothing has yet been said about an expansion of real investment which alone could permanently lower the interest rate in the sense of the marginal product of capital. If we want to achieve an equilibrium with a rate of interest that is permanently lower than in the initial position, we shall have to bring into the analysis the reaction of entrepreneurs to the fall in the interest rate – a reaction in the form of an expansion of their investments financed by the issue of new bonds.

The critical analysis of Patinkin's approach in these several cases suffices to bring to the fore the point we are concerned with here, a point which is of course quite self-evident: Changes on the monetary side will only lead to a permanent change in the rate of interest if they affect the real variables in the system in such a way that a change in the marginal product of capital results. Of course, if we entirely dissociate the rate of interest on securities from the marginal product of capital, the former can move quite independently of the latter. But this separation can at best be granted for the short run in which investment had not yet time to react to changes in the "money rate" of interest. In any analysis covering the longer run – and the comparison of two equilibria is always such an analysis – this assumption is not allowed.

CHAPTER 15

ASSET PRICE DETERMINATION AS A THEORY OF INTEREST

A theory can be developed which explains the rate of interest on bonds by analysing the factors that determine the prices of assets. This type of theory is based not on flow- but on stock magnitudes and thus applies to a point in time. It can be developed as a macroeconomic or as a microeconomic theory. In the macroeconomic version we confront the total stock of each of the various types of assets with the aggregate demand for that stock, taking into account the interdependence of all markets. In a microeconomic approach, on the other hand, we must solve the problem of the choice of a portfolio of assets by individuals and firms, as a first step towards the construction of a theory of interest. However, here we shall not deal with the problem of portfolio choice; this subject will be taken up, in so far as it is necessary for the construction of the positive theory, in the fifth part of this book.

The macroeconomic theory of asset price determination has been developed in particular by Ralph Turvey.[1] Let us begin with the simplest case in which the assets consist entirely of money and of consols issued by the "monetary sector" (the banking system and the state) and held by the private sector.[2] Let the price of the securities be designated by H and the quantity outstanding at any moment by N, the unit of consols being defined as the claim for one unit of money per year in perpetuity. The supply of bonds in value terms (the value of the stock of bonds outstanding), S, will then be

$$S = NH \tag{1}$$

The demand for bonds in terms of value, D_n, is, according to Turvey, dependent on wealth, W, and the bond price, so that $D_n = \phi(W, H)$.

[1] R. Turvey, *Interest Rates and Asset Prices* (London, 1960).

[2] In his model Turvey leaves out securities issued and held within the private sector. His justification for this (in Ch. V) cannot be discussed here.

Turvey assumes that this function is linear, and writes

$$D_n = XH = cW + dH \tag{2}$$

where X designates the number of bonds demanded; c and d are coefficients; c is positive and smaller than unity, while d can, according to Turvey, be positive or negative. The second term on the right-hand side of the equation, dH, represents that part of the demand for securities in value terms which is independent of wealth and is a function of the bond price alone. Taken by itself, this part of the demand can be written $D = H\psi(H)$, where $\psi(H)$ represents the demand in terms of the number of bonds as a function of the price. If $\psi(H)$ is assumed to be equal to a constant positive magnitude d, it is implied that the demand in terms of the number of bonds is perfectly inelastic at all prices. Since the wealth of the individuals, W, is composed of the existing quantity of money M and the stock of bonds in terms of value, i.e.

$$W = M + NH \tag{3}$$

we can also write equation (2) in another form:

$$D_n = cM + cNH + dH \tag{2a}$$

The demand D_n has to equal the aggregate supply of securities S.

In Figure 28 this demand function and its components have been drawn, together with the supply function $S = NH$. The resulting price is AH_0. A positive value for d has been assumed in the diagram. Along the line

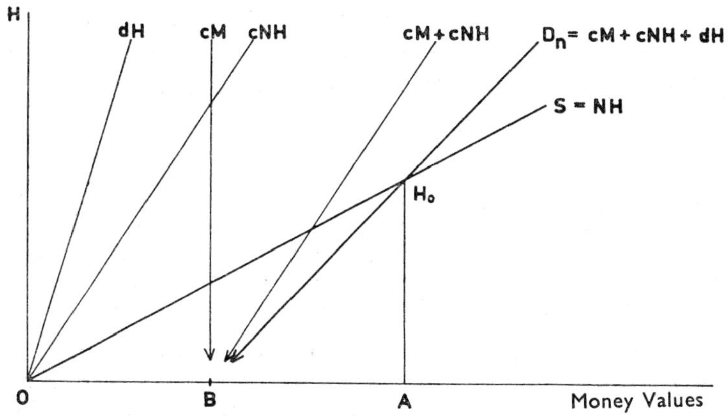

Fig. 28.

$cM + cNH$ the share of the value of bonds in total wealth is constant and equal to c, but the same is not true along the demand line D_n. The *ex post* share of bonds in total wealth is larger than c if d is positive.[3]

The bond price H will rise if, with a given supply schedule $S = NH$, the owners of wealth decide to hold a larger share of their wealth than hitherto in the form of bonds, or if the quantity of money M increases; in both cases the demand schedule D_n will shift to the right. The price will also rise if N declines; in this case both the supply and the demand curve will become steeper (the latter because of its cNH component), but, as can be shown, in such a manner that H will rise. The same results can also be read off the formula used by Turvey, which can be obtained from equations (1) and (2a) if in equilibrium aggregate demand is equated to aggregate supply:

$$H = \frac{cM}{(1 - c)N - d}$$

So far our results are rather obvious. Starting from the premise that supply and demand determine the price of bonds, and holding the supply fixed, we obtain, through an analysis of the factors determining demand, the causes for possible price changes, just as in any other supply-and-demand analysis. It should be noted that Turvey abstains from an analysis of the causes determining changes on the supply side; this is a point we shall return to later.

Let us now introduce real assets. Let the aggregate income from real assets be R units of money per year, and let the value of the right to an income from real assets of one money unit per year be Q; the aggregate value of real assets then is RQ, and the wealth of asset owners

$$W = M + NH + RQ \qquad (4)$$

[3] It should be explicitly noted that the demand function D_n is, in fact, impossible. The component dH of this function cannot be a straight line over its entire length; like any total expenditure curve, the curve showing the *value* of the securities demanded by an individual as a function of their price must from a certain point on slope backwards. Turvey himself says that his linear functions are only approximations, valid only for small changes (p. 46).

The lines which contain cM as a component have in Figure 28 not been drawn all the way to point B (whose distance from the origin is equal to cM) because at a bond price of zero it is impossible to hold securities to the value of cM. A bond price of zero, which would imply an infinite rate of return, is in any case an absurdity.

Retaining his assumption of a linear function, Turvey now writes the demand function for bonds (measured in terms of value) as follows:

$$D_n = cW + dH + eQ + fY \tag{5}$$

where Y represents income. The first two terms on the right-hand side of the equation we already know; we only have to note that W is now, as can be seen from equation (4), composed of three components instead of two. The coefficient e reflects the influence of the price Q on the demand (in value terms) for consols; e is positive, so that an increase in Q raises the demand for bonds. The last term on the right-hand side of equation (5), fY, has been introduced because the quantity of money M contains a component of transaction money; as income increases, some of this money will flow from the financial sphere into the transaction sphere, and the demand (in value terms) for consols will be depressed. Hence f is negative. Turvey further assumes that R, the yield of real assets, rises and falls together with Y. The supply of bonds is NH, as before.

If we substitute equation (4) into equation (5), we can draw the demand for bonds in value terms, D_n, as a function of the bond price H on the assumption that all other variables stay unchanged, just as we did in the simpler case above. The D_n-curve will look exactly like that in Figure 28, except that the distance OB, which comprises all terms that do not contain H and which in Figure 28 was equal to cM, will here be equal to $[cM + (cR + e)Q + fY]$.[4] Since the demand curve D_n cuts the supply curve S from below, any shift of this demand curve to the right is equivalent to an increase in H, and any shift to the left to a fall in H. It can be shown that H will fall (the rate of interest will rise) if any of the following events occurs:

(a) N increases. Both the supply and the demand curves will then be less steep, and it can be shown that their new point of intersection will be at a lower H.

(b) M or R (with a constant Q) contract, or Y increases; in all of these cases the distance OB will be shortened. A contraction of M or R signifies less wealth and hence a smaller demand for securities. The effect of an expansion of income works, as already noted, through an increased demand for transaction money. However, R and Y will as a rule change

[4] Our observations in note 3 apply here also.

simultaneously and in the same direction, thus generating opposite pressures with respect to H; the net effect on H remains indeterminate in that case.

(c) The coefficients c, e and f become smaller. A decline of c indicates the desire to diminish the share of bond holdings in total wealth. A decline of e signifies that the influence of Q on the demand for bonds has diminished, which is equivalent to saying that with a given Q the demand for other assets has risen. A decline of f (e.g., from -0.10 to -0.12; hence an increase in the absolute magnitude of f) means that more transaction money is used at a given level of Y; this diminishes the demand for bonds.

(d) Q declines. In that case, too, the distance OB in Figure 28 will be shortened. The increase of the rate of return on a unit of real assets leads to a sale of bonds in order to invest in real capital; at the same time the fall in Q signifies a contraction of wealth which also causes a fall in the demand for bonds.

We have hitherto disregarded the fact that Q and H are not independent of each other. They have to be determined simultaneously. For this purpose we need one more equation. We have the choice between a demand-and-supply equation for real assets and a demand-and-supply equation for money. It does not matter which we choose since the demand for the omitted component of wealth always emerges as the difference between the value of total wealth, W, and the demand for bonds plus either the demand foı real assets or the demand for money at the equilibrium prices H and Q. Turvey selects the money equation. On his assumption of linear functions the demand for money D_m has the same form as the demand for bonds, namely

$$D_m = aW + bH + kQ + jY \tag{6}$$

where all coefficients are positive. If W, H, Q, or Y increase, the demand for money increases. This aggregate demand for money must in equilibrium be equal to the existing quantity of money M.

Instead of the money equation let us choose the real assets equation. The demand for real assets, D_r, can be expressed in analogy to the demand for bonds as follows:

$$D_r = gW + lH + mQ + pY \tag{7}$$

We equate the demand D_r to the supply RQ, and thus obtain for the determination of H and Q the following two equations:

$$c(M + NH + RQ) + dH + eQ + fY = NH \tag{8}$$

$$g(M + NH + RQ) + lH + mQ + pY = RQ \tag{9}$$

The third equation, the money equation which is to be obtained from the above-mentioned difference, can then be written:

$$[1 - (c + g)](M + NH + RQ) - (d + l)H - (e + m)Q - (f + p)Y = M \tag{10}$$

The sum of the coefficients of $W(W = M + NH + RQ)$ in the three equations is equal to one, and the sum of the coefficients of H, Q, and Y equals zero.

Everything said above under (a) to (c) in connection with equation (5) about the factors whose changes produce a change in the bond price H applies here also, except that now a simultaneous change will as a ıule also occur in the asset price Q. For instance, if the coefficient c (i.e., the portion of wealth which owners wish to hold in the form of bonds) should rise, and if this were to happen entirely or in part at the expense of the share held in real assets, H would rise and Q would fall; if the quantity of money were to increase while c and g stay unchanged, both H and Q would rise. Thus one can derive for each change in one of the independent variables or their coefficients the corresponding effect on H and Q.

Turvey obtains his results by solving his money equation and the bond equation for H and Q, an approach that yields two extraordinarily involved expressions which contribute no other insights than those already mentioned.[5]

Since Q is the price of the right to an annual income of one money unit from real assets and H the price of the corresponding right in the case of bonds, and since the problem of risk is not brought into Turvey's analysis,

[5] Besides, the expression for H given by Turvey on p. 42 is unfortunately incorrect. The correct expression would be:

$$H = \frac{M[(1 - a)(cR + e) + c(aR + k)] - Y[j(cR + e) - f(aR + k)]}{(N - cN - d)(aR + k) + (aN + b)(cR + e)}$$

The numerator of the expression for Q on p. 45 is also incorrect.

one should expect that Q and H would be equal, as the unit of real assets and the unit of bonds defined in this manner are the same "good" if risk is neglected. If Turvey nevertheless does not obtain this result, it is due to his coefficients which indicate that wealth owners do not consider real and financial assets to be equivalent. An increase of the asset price Q will generate a tendency to sell off real assets and to purchase bonds instead, but the desire to hold real assets and bonds in a definite relationship (of g and c, respectively) to total wealth will act as a brake on the switch into a larger bond portfolio. One could view this restraint as an effect of the risk factor – as a desire to avoid putting all one's eggs into one basket. If g were smaller than c, the difference would reflect the desire to reduce risk by holding the larger share of one's wealth in the form of bonds rather than in real assets.

The fact that the coefficients of H and Q – d and m – are different (which indicates that the reaction of the demand for bonds to a change in the bond price H is different from the reaction of the demand for real assets to a change of equal magnitude in the asset price Q) also serves to show that bonds and real assets are not perfect substitutes. But Turvey does not give an analysis of the influence of the risk factor on the composition of assets and thus on the rate of return on bonds and real assets.

Furthermore, it should be clear that we cannot get very far towards a solution of the interest problem with this type of stock analysis, which neglects the effects of shifts between assets on flow magnitudes. For instance, this stock analysis disregards the fact that an increase in the yield on existing real assets, and thus an increase in R[6], will, if the rate of interest on bonds initially remains unchanged (no change in H), lead to an expansion of the issue of bonds by business firms to finance an expansion of their real capital stock. In abstracting from this effect we neglect a relationship which hitherto has always stood at the centre of the theory of interest – namely, the connection between the rate of interest and the marginal efficiency of investment. We conclude, then, that an analysis only in terms of stocks, neglecting, as it does, the process of investment, cannot provide us with a satisfactory theory of interest.

[6] If R measures the number of units of real capital, each of which brings a yield of one unit of money per period, an increase in the internal rate of return of a firm – let us say, a doubling – must find reflection in a doubling of R, not in an increase of Q.

CHAPTER 16

CONCLUSIONS

Keynes and his successors, like the group of authors discussed in the second part of this book, developed their theory on the assumption of an expanding economy in which saving and investment are taking place. They determine the rate of interest in a changing economy for a unit period, or rather for a point in time. To this extent they merely form a sub-group of the authors dealt with in the second part. They are treated separately because, at first glance, they seem to consider the interest rate an exclusively monetary phenomenon.

However, a closer analysis of the discussion centering on Keynes showed that, if one assumes flexible money wage rates as economists generally did prior to Keynes, the rate of interest is, except for the case mentioned below, determined solely by the real factors in the system. This result is identical to that obtained by all earlier theorists. In this statement, we naturally disregard phenomena arising during the transition from a system with a given quantity of money and liquidity preference to another system in which these two variables are different.

An essentially new result emerges, however, even for the case of flexible money wages, if we start from the assumption that the equilibrium rate of interest would, to achieve full employment, have to fall below the level under which the interest rate cannot fall. In such a situation, a fall of the money wage rate could not lead to a full-employment equilibrium except if we make the assumption that real saving depends not only on real income, but also on real wealth. In other words, we have to grant that the monetary factor can exert an influence on the rate of interest by way of its influence on saving. This possibility had already been admitted by Wicksell and others, although they reasoned along different lines. According to these authors "forced saving" during an inflation, because it has as its counterpart an addition to the real capital stock, can permanently lower the rate of interest. The discussion of Patinkin's analysis has now shown quite generally that the monetary factor has an influence on the rate of interest only in so far as it changes real variables in the system.

The situation becomes notably different if we assume money wage rates to be rigid. As soon as this assumption is made, it appears that the monetary factor – even without the operation of the Pigou effect – influences indeed not only employment and national income but also the rate of interest. But even here it is not true that the monetary factor – quantity of money and liquidity preference – alone determines the rate of interest. Even on this new assumption, the "productivity" of capital (the marginal efficiency of investment) and the rate of saving are determinants of the rate of interest alongside the monetary factor. Only in the extreme case, when the interest rate has dropped to its minimum level, is this statement no longer true.

Keynes and his followers developed their theory of interest in the context of an analysis, the main purpose of which was to explain, not the interest rate, but income and employment. It is understandable, therefore, that these authors did not engage in a thorough examination of the investment process, such as the first group of interest theorists had attempted. These authors were content with using the crude and inadequate tool of the marginal efficiency of investment which, as was shown earlier, suffers from important deficiencies. Nothing, however, stands in the way of incorporating the results of the more refined analysis of the investment process, undertaken by the first group of theorists, into the theory of Keynes and his followers.

The entire debate about the equivalence of liquidity preference theory and loanable funds theory seems to be one of those intensive discussions on a problem of formal logic, not rare in theoretical economics, which does not really deserve the efforts devoted to it since it does not, and cannot, give any material new insights into the problem of the interest rate. One can only hope (and perhaps even expect) that this topic ceases to fill the columns of our periodicals.

PART FOUR

THE TERM STRUCTURE OF INTEREST RATES

Our presentation of the various theories of the term structure of interest rates will be organized not by author but, rather, according to the type of the theory. We begin with the best known one according to which the long-term interest rate is an average of the expected short-term rates. By bringing in the required qualifications, we can subsume under this theory a very large part of the contributions to the problem of the term structure of interest rates. In Chapter 18 we shall deal with two further attempts to construct theories of the rate structure, and in Chapter 19 we shall consider the question of the "basic rate", – i.e., which of the many interest rates the theory of interest should primarily determine so as to give the whole structure a peg. We shall omit a discussion of the valuable attempts to verify some of the theories, even though we have followed them with much interest and were pleased to see that one author believes he is able to refute the most widely accepted theory by appealing to the empirical evidence[1], while another thinks that the facts support it[2] and a third claims that the same empirical material that was used by the first supports rather than refutes this theory.[3]

[1] J. M. Culbertson, 'The Term Structure of Interest Rates', *Quarterly Journal of Economics*, **71** (1957) 485–517.
[2] D. Meiselman, *The Term Structure of Interest Rates* (Englewood Cliffs, N. J., 1962).
[3] J. B. Michaelsen, 'The Term Structure of Interest Rates: Comment', *Quarterly Journal of Economics*, **77** (1963) 166–174.

CHAPTER 17

THE EXPECTATION THEORY OF THE TERM STRUCTURE OF INTEREST RATES

Already Irving Fisher, as we saw, viewed the long-term rate as an average of the short-term rates which are expected to prevail during the period for which a long-term loan is granted. He was the first to develop what we here call the "expectation theory" of the term structure of interest rates.[4] In expounding this theory, let us first assume perfect foresight and neglect the costs which arise if an investor shifts from short maturities to longer ones or vice versa. In this case competition will equalize the yield on all investments undertaken for equal periods, regardless of what form they take – i.e., whether we are dealing with a short-term investment repeated several times, or with a single long-term investment, or with several short-term investments succeeded by a longer-term one, and so on. If the condition of equal yields on all possible configurations of investments over the same time span is not fulfilled, profitable arbitrage operations can and will be carried out with the result that yields will be equalized. The sum into which a dollar grows if invested for n years at the long-term rate R_n must then be equal to the sum into which it would grow if it were invested several times in succession at the short-term rates $r_1, r_2 \ldots r_n$, or:

$$(1 + R_n)^n = (1 + r_1)(1 + r_2)\ldots(1 + r_n)$$

From this we can obtain the formulae for the longer rates (which were

[4] The more recent representatives of this theory are: J. R. Hicks, *Value and Capital* (2nd ed., Oxford, 1946), chs. 11–13; F. A. Lutz, 'The Structure of Interest Rates', *Quarterly Journal of Economics*, **55** (1940–1941) 36–63; reprinted in *Readings in the Theory of Income Distribution* (Philadelphia-Toronto, 1946), pp. 499–529; J. W. Conard, *An Introduction to the Theory of Interest* (Berkeley and Los Angeles, Calif., 1959), pp. 287–367; D. Meiselman, *The Term Structure of Interest Rates* (Englewood Cliffs, N.J., 1962); J. B. Michaelsen, 'The Term Structure of Interest Rates: Comment', *Quarterly Journal of Economics*, **77** (1963) 166–174.

already known to Irving Fisher)[5]:

$$R_2 = \sqrt[2]{(1 + r_1)(1 + r_2)} - 1$$
$$R_3 = \sqrt[3]{(1 + r_1)(1 + r_2)(1 + r_3)} - 1$$
$$\vdots$$
$$R_n = \sqrt[n]{(1 + r_1)(1 + r_2)\dots(1 + r_n)} - 1$$

It is through the variation in the price of the bonds outstanding that yields calculated for the same period will be equalized for bonds with different terms to maturity. If, for instance, the short-term rates are $r_1 = 5\%$, $r_2 = 6\%$, $r_3 = 8\%$, the price of a five per cent bond redeemable after three years with a nominal value of 100 will be 96.6, so that the capital gain of 3.4 plus the annual interest payments of 5 will together constitute a yield equal to the return from the three successive short rates.

With the help of the above formulae we can also calculate, from the existing long rates, the expected short rate for each future period. The short-term rate for the third period, for instance, is obtained from the formula

$$1 + r_3 = \frac{(1 + R_3)^3}{(1 + R_2)^2}$$

If someone borrows today by selling a two-year bond, and at the same time buys a three-year bond, he can already today insure that in the third period he will obtain the rate of return expected for that period.

From the view of the long rate as an average of the expected short rates the following conclusions about the term structure of interest rates result:

1. If no changes in the short rate are expected, all longer rates will be equal to the short rate.

2. If the current short-term rate is lower than the average of this rate and the successive short rates expected to prevail up to the maturity of a long-term bond, the corresponding long rate will be above the current short rate. If the expected short rate of each "last" period is above the average of the short rates of the preceding periods (i.e., if r_2 is higher than r_1, r_3 higher than the average of r_1 and r_2 ..., and r_n higher than the average

[5] The formulae rest on the assumption that all interest payments are made at the end of the period.

of r_1 to r_{n-1}), we obtain interest rates which increase with increasing terms to maturity. If it is expected that the short rates will stay unchanged from a certain period onward, the curve showing bond rates as a function of the term to maturity will eventually flatten out.

3. The long rate will lie below the current short rate if the average of the current and expected future short rates lies below the current short rate. Again, if the expected short rate of each "last" period is below the average of the preceding short rates, the long rates will fall with increasing terms to maturity. Here, too, the curve showing the interest rates as a function of the term to maturity will flatten out if expectations are that the short rate will – as it inevitably must – cease to fall from some future period onward.

4. In principle, with sufficiently differentiated expectations, any structure of interest rates is possible. The rates might initially rise with the term to maturity and then fall from a certain maturity on, or vice versa, or they might first rise, then fall, then rise again, and so on.

With respect to the movement of rates over time, two conclusions can be drawn from the expectation theory of the term structure of interest rates.

1. The long rate will fluctuate less than the short rate. Let us for simplicity's sake (as an approximation)[6] take the long rate as the arithmetic average of the expected short rates. Then, if the interest rate on a long-term bond redeemable after n unit periods is to change by the same amount from the first to the second period as the short rate, the following equation will have to hold:

$$r_1 - r_2 = \frac{r_1 + r_2 + \cdots + r_n}{n} - \frac{r_2 + r_3 + \cdots + r_{n+1}}{n}$$

or

$$n(r_1 - r_2) = r_1 - r_{n+1}$$

where r_{n+1} is the short rate expected for the period $n+1$ which will have to be drawn into the analysis if we want to compare the movement of the short rate with that of the rate on a bond whose term to maturity, after the passage of the first period, is again n unit periods. The formula shows that if the long and the short rate are to change by the same amount

[6] A calculation with the correct average according to Fisher's formula leads to the same result.

from the first to the second period, the difference between the short rate r_1 (which after the first period belongs to the past) and the newly added expected short rate r_{n+1} must be n times as large as the difference between r_1 and r_2. This is the more improbable, the longer is the term to maturity of the bond, and for very long terms it is practically impossible. Hence long rates fluctuate less than short rates.

2. If $r_{n+1} > r_1$, the long rate for n unit periods will rise from period 1 to period 2, and if $r_{n+1} < r_1$, it will fall. The short rate r_2 can in both cases rise above or fall below the short rate r_1 – i.e., the long and the short rate can over time move in the same as well as in opposite directions.[7] There is no reason to believe that the one event should happen more often than the other.

If we want to bring this theory closer to reality, we must first of all drop the assumption that the act of investing in securities causes neither cost nor trouble. For Hicks, the cost and trouble of investing play a fundamental role since they serve to explain the level of the short-term rate of interest. Hicks' line of thought is as follows:

Let us take a unit period, the Hicksian "week". In Hicks' model all transactions take place on "Monday", and during the rest of the week the market is closed, to be reopened only on the following Monday. Now the question arises, what is to prevent the owners of cash balances on Monday evening from putting all their money into bills with a term of one week if they consider these bills as perfectly safe? The answer is clear: the only impediment would be the cost and trouble involved in acquiring the bills. Hence the short-term rate of interest will be determined by the cost and trouble arising for the marginal lender or, that is to say, the marginal buyer of short-term bills. However, if *everyone* in the economy were to regard such bills as perfectly safe, the exchange of bills for money or money for bills would be unnecessary as the bills themselves would become money. The cost and trouble of obtaining bills would be eliminated, and the short-term rate of interest would necessarily be equal to zero.

This theory is unobjectionable if we interpret cost and trouble in a

[7] If we take four periods ($n = 4$) and assume the short rates for the successive periods to be 3, 2, 4, and 5 per cent, and put the rate for the additional period $n + 1$ at 7 per cent, then the short rate falls from period 1 to period 2 by 1 per cent (from 3 per cent to 2 per cent) while the long rate rises by 1 per cent (namely, on the basis of our approximation formula, from 3.5 to 4.5 per cent).

somewhat unusual fashion. It might be pointed out in this connection that also in other theories of interest the rate of interest just compensates the marginal lender for his cost and trouble, if "cost and trouble" are so defined as to refer to his time preference provided the latter is a greater obstacle to his lending than "the cost and trouble of investing" in the narrow sense of these words. A theory is formally correct but is not very penetrating if it merely states that on the demand side the borrowers will issue bills in accordance with their investment needs, and that on the supply side the lenders will offer loanable funds in accordance with their "cost and trouble" in the broader sense of the term with the result that the rate of interest just "compensates" the last lender.

However, one cannot help feeling that this is not the interpretation Hicks had in mind; his presentation reads as if he were thinking only of the cost and trouble involved in the act of exchanging money for claims. But then there is no reason why the interest rate could not rise above this limit. Depending on the demand situation – which Hicks does not analyse in this context – it should be quite possible for the interest rate to reach a level which exceeds the "cost and trouble" of the marginal lender, a level which is necessary to overcome the greater obstacle of his time preference. Moreover, it would certainly be difficult to explain the empirically observable strong fluctuations of the short rate by reference to changes in the cost and trouble caused by the technical act of transforming money into short-term claims.

Finally, we can scarcely subscribe to Hicks' contention that the short-term rate would be zero if bills, like money, were generally accepted, a thesis which is supposed to support the theory that the cost and trouble of exchanging money for claims alone can explain the short-term interest rate. Under this assumption each entrepreneur could himself create money; uncontrolled inflation would be likely to result which would rapidly lead to the repudiation of such "money". Hence we conclude that the cost and trouble of investing money cannot be the sole determinant of the short-term rate of interest. And even if it were, we would still be left with the task of explaining how this factor influences the structure of interest rates. That it has such an influence is obvious. Shifting between the bond markets for different maturities is impeded by the fact that it gives rise to "cost and trouble", so that the term structure of interest rates will be different from what it would be if there were no such costs. There is, however, little to be found on this problem in the literature[8]; and since we shall be devoting our attention to it in the fifth part of this book, we shall by-pass it here.

The second assumption which has to be dropped if the expectation theory of the term structure of interest rates is to be brought closer to reality is that of perfect foresight. If the future is uncertain, the individual investor, before he makes the decision which maturity to choose for his investment, will weigh the expected yield against the risk that his expectations will not come true. We shall analyse this problem in some detail in the fifth part of this book. For what follows here it suffices to know that, as a rule, a higher risk will have to be compensated by the expectation of a higher yield if the investment is to be taken into consideration at all. Just for this reason Hicks came to the conclusion, first, that under uncertainty the long rate would lie above the average of the short rates expected over the corresponding period, even if the participants in the market considered it most probable that the short rate will remain what it is; and, second, that this difference would be the larger, the longer the period to which the long rate refers. He obtained this result because he assumed that in the market for loan capital the demand for long-term loans predominates on the demand side[9], while the suppliers in general prefer to lend short with the result that lenders can be induced to invest their money for longer periods only by being offered higher rates which offset the risk of a capital loss associated with longer terms to maturity. However, Hicks' conclusion does not necessarily follow. Owners of wealth who can invest their money for longer periods will obtain a safe return for the whole period if they invest in a bond with a corresponding term to maturity, although they will run the risk of a capital loss if they should have to sell this bond before it is due for redemption. If they invest in the short-term market, they will not run a risk on capital account, but they will run a risk on interest account as the short rate may change over time. Hence the total yield will be uncertain here also. We can, therefore, not state unequivocally that the risk factor will induce investors to

[8] The most extensive treatment of this question is to be found in F. A. Lutz, 'The Structure of Interest Rates', *Quarterly Journal of Economics*, **55** (1940–1941) 36–63; reprinted in *Readings in the Theory of Income Distribution* (Philadelphia-Toronto, 1946), pp. 499–529.

[9] In Hicks' expression, there exists a "constitutional weakness" on the demand side in favour of long-term loan capital (Hicks, *Value and Capital*, p. 146).

lend short if the short rate is equal to the long rate. What the effect of the risk factor on the term structure of interest rates will be cannot be determined *a priori*.[10]

Apart from the introduction of the risk factor, the approximation of the theory under discussion to reality requires two further qualifications. The first is designed to take account of the fact that the participants in the market do not, by any means, all have the same expectations. As this point has received little attention in the literature and is dealt with in greater detail in the fifth part of this book, we shall omit discussion of this problem here. Let us only observe that the solution proposed by Dorrance is not satisfactory. He claims that "it seems reasonable to consider that the conflicting views in the market regarding the expected changes in interest rates, and the strength with which these views are held, may be combined into something like a weighted average, which can be given a series of numerical values measuring the interest rates that are expected to prevail in the future".[11] Instead of using weighted averages we have to rank the market participants according to their expectations, modified by their evaluation of the risk and their attitude towards it, and must then work with the marginal lender (or borrower) in the various markets in a manner which will be explained in detail in the fifth part of this book.[12]

The need for the second qualification can best be demonstrated by referring to a complaint which is often raised against the expectation theory of the term structure of interest rates. This theory presupposes, it is claimed, that the course of the short rates is forecast for a very long period, and in the case of perpetuities even for all future times. This point was made most forcefully by Luckett: "We are thus treated to the spectacle of an individual standing on the eve of World War II, atomic bombs, the cold war, the postwar inflations, the Employment Act of 1946, *et hoc genus omne*, trying to decide what short-term rates will be fifteen to twenty

[10] On this point, see F. A. Lutz, *Quarterly Journal of Economics*, **55** (1940–1941) 46 ff.; *Readings in the Theory of Income Distribution*, p. 510 ff. D. Meiselman, *The Term Structure of Interest Rates* (Englewood Cliffs, N.J., 1962), p. 13 ff. However, see also *infra*, p. 256.

[11] G. S. Dorrance, 'The Term Structure of Interest Rates', *International Monetary Fund Staff Papers*, **10** (1963) 283.

[12] This approach was already used in F. A. Lutz, *Quarterly Journal of Economics*, **55** (1940–1941) 51 ff.; *Readings in the Theory of Income Distribution*, p. 515 ff.

years in the future."[13] Such an assumption would obviously be absurd. However, most adherents of the expectation theory cannot be reproached on this score, as they have worked in one form or another with the assumption that the market participants use short periods as the basis for their calculations.[14] To be sure, we can then no longer work with the expected short rates alone, but must introduce the bond prices expected by the participants in the market for the end of their (short) time horizon. To object to this procedure on the ground that these prices are themselves determined by the short rates expected for still later periods would be quite unrealistic, as no one takes these distant short rates into consideration at the present.

A further point is even more important. Let us begin with the observation that "an investor's personal expectations about the future course of short rates do not necessarily commit him as to his expectations about the long rate, since the latter depends, not on what *he* thinks about the future short rates, but what the 'market', i.e. other people, think about them. The individual investor, therefore, may quite reasonably form an opinion about the future long rate which is inconsistent with his opinion about future short rates".[15] Luckett has quite properly shown that if we follow this reasoning we must give up the expectation theory. He takes a case in which a large majority or even all of the participants in the market expect that the long rate will rise but that the short rate will stay unchanged. A general shift out of the long market and into the short market will ensue, with the consequence of a rise in the long rate and a fall in the short rate; clearly, the resulting term structure of interest rates cannot be explained by reference to the expectations about the future short rates.

Would it perhaps help matters to base the theory on the expected behaviour of the *long* rate? Dorrance has pointed out[16] that a second variant of the expectation theory exists which starts out from the expectations about the behaviour of the long rate and reasons from there to the

[13] D. G. Luckett, 'Professor Lutz and the Structure of Interest Rates', *Quarterly Journal of Economics*, **73** (1959) 141.

[14] This assumption was also introduced as one of the qualifications in the paper attacked by Luckett, namely F. A. Lutz, *Quarterly Journal of Economics*, **55** (1940–1941) 48 ff.; *Readings in the Theory of Income Distribution*, p. 512 ff.

[15] F. A. Lutz, *Quarterly Journal of Economics*, **55** (1940–1941) 50; *Readings in the Theory of Income Distribution*, p. 514.

[16] G. S. Dorrance, *International Monetary Fund Staff Papers*, **10** (1963) 275.

short rate – a variant which, however, has not received the same attention as the first version, probably because it was thought that the two expressed basically one and the same thing. This second variant finds clear expression in Hicks' statement, cited by Dorrance, that "in stable conditions, when the long rate is expected to remain steady, the short rate will lie below it to the extent of the normal risk-premium; when the long rate is expected to rise, the short rate will lie below it still further; it is only when the long rate is expected to fall that the short rate may lie above the long rate".[17]

This second variant of the expectation theory is, according to Hicks, "perfectly consistent"[18] with the first variant. This can easily be shown: He, who expects that the long rate will rise, anticipates a loss on capital account; if the yield in the long market is to be the same as in the short, the rate of interest on long-term securities must be high enough to make the interest less the capital loss equal to the interest obtainable in the short-term market. The short rate thus lies below the long rate if the participants in the market expect the long rate to rise. The reverse will be true if they expect the long rate to fall. This conclusion rests on the same type of reasoning as the first variant of the expectation theory – namely, that arbitrage operations will bring it about that all types of investment will over the same time span carry the same yield. If one assumes perfect foresight – so that the expected long rate is nothing other than the average of the successive short rates expected over the time span under consideration – the two approaches will yield the same result. Hence they are indeed consistent.

This second variant of the expectation theory does, however, have great advantages. In the first place, it is much more realistic since speculators in long-term bonds are concerned with the prices of these bonds in the relatively near future and not with short rates over a long period ahead. By assuming that a participant in the market has expectations about the price of the long-term bond at the date when the short-term security falls due, we get along with the simple comparison of the current short-term interest with the yield on the longer-term bond (interest plus change in capital value) expected for the same time span. The positive theory in the fifth part of this book will be developed along these lines.

[17] J. R. Hicks, *Value and Capital*, pp. 151–152.
[18] J. R. Hicks, *Value and Capital*, p. 152.

CHAPTER 18

TWO FURTHER THEORIES

A novel theory, which takes as its starting point the assumption that participants in the bond market have neither a preference for nor an aversion to risk, has been presented by Malkiel.[1] Its basic notions can best be made clear with the help of an example.

If a bond with a face value of 100, a coupon rate of 4 dollars per year and a term to maturity of 4 years is to yield 5 per cent to maturity, its price[2] must be 96.41; if it is to yield 3 per cent, the price must be 103.74. The rise in price accompanying a fall of the rate of interest from 4 to 3 per cent is somewhat, but not very much, larger than the fall in price accompanying an increase of the interest rate from 4 to 5 per cent. If the 4 per cent bond were a perpetuity, however, the prices corresponding to a rise or fall of the interest rate by one per cent would be 80 and 133, respectively; the increase above par is much larger than the fall below par. This is the fact on which Malkiel's conclusions are based.

Let us assume that the empirically given range of fluctuations of the rate of interest runs from 2 to 6 per cent; let us further assume that all bonds with a par value of 100 are provided with a coupon rate of 4 dollars per year, whatever their terms to maturity; and that the interest rate has by intervention "from above" been held fixed at 4 per cent. This intervention shall now cease. The participants in the market are assumed to assign equal probabilities (of one half) to two possible outcomes, namely that the interest rate will either rise to 5 per cent or fall to 3 per cent.[3] If now the "collective investor" – i.e., the community of the individual investors, each of whom has the same opinion about the future of the interest rates –

[1] B. G. Malkiel, 'Expectations, Bond Prices, and the Term Structure of Interest Rates', *Quarterly Journal of Economics*, **76** (1962) 197–218.

[2] Assuming semi-annual interest payments.

[3] In one of his examples Malkiel also assumes that the range of fluctuations taken into account by market participants is not identical with the extreme range of empirical fluctuations.

attempts to equalize the possible capital loss and the possible capital gain, the price of bonds which at this moment have a term to maturity of four years will have to rise to $(96.41+103.74)/2=100.075$, and the price of consols to $(80+133)/2=106.5$. These two prices constitute the mid-points between the prices corresponding to interest rates of 5 or 3 per cent respectively. With a coupon rate of 4 dollars, these prices in turn imply an effective rate (yield to maturity) on four-year bonds of 3.8 per cent and on consols of 3.75 per cent. Hence we obtain a series of rates which fall with increasing terms to maturity. Thus, if changes in the interest rate by one per cent upwards or downwards are assigned the same probability of one half, the rate on a long-term bond comes to lie below that on a short-term bond; moreover, all rates except the very shortest will lie below the initial rate of 4 per cent.

If in the initial position we had assumed an interest rate which was closer to the lower limit of the empirical range of fluctuations, and/or if the probability that the rate would fall had been given a lower value than the probability that it would rise by an equal or larger amount, we could have obtained a series of rates that increased with increasing terms to maturity.[4] It should also be noted that the resulting interest rates depend upon the width of the range of fluctuations entering into the calculations. If in our example we had figured with a fluctuation of only one half of one per cent in either direction, the effective rate which would have emerged after the adjustment would have been higher on both the four-year bonds and the consols.

The result obtained by Malkiel seems peculiar as there appears to be no reason why an investor with neither preference for nor aversion to risk – for whom, accordingly, the two equal chances that the bond will rise or fall in value by a given amount are mutually offsetting – should be content with a rate of return of 3.75 per cent on consols or of 3.8 per cent on a four-year bond if he can obtain 4 per cent on a one-year bond.

Instead of criticizing at length Malkiel's assumptions which led him to this conclusion, we prefer to state briefly – leaving the detailed analysis for the fifth part of this book – which assumptions constitute a useful point of departure, and what follows from them.

Let us assume that an investor has a time horizon of one short period.

[4] As Malkiel shows, there would be a slight fall in the rates at the end of the series – i.e., in the extremely long rates.

He has the choice between bonds of different maturities. He will choose the maturity which promises to maximize his yield consisting of the interest payment plus capital gain or minus capital loss expected for the end of the period. Let us assume further that the rate of interest on all maturities had been stabilized, as in the above example, at 4 per cent. The interest rate will now be allowed to move freely. If all bond holders, whom we suppose to have neither a preference for nor an aversion to risk, are of the opinion that bond prices may with equal probability rise or fall by the same amount, then interest rates will not change at all. They will all remain at 4 per cent. If investors believe that the prices of long-term bonds are more likely to rise by a given amount than they are to fall by that amount, they will acquire long-term bonds as Malkiel says; the prices of short-term bonds will then fall, i.e., the short-term rate will rise and the long-term rate will fall. This process will continue until the short-term interest for the period is equal to the interest plus the "expected" capital gain on the longer-term securities. For details, and in particular for the definition of "expected" in this context, we have to ask the reader to wait until the fifth part of this book.

Let us now turn to another theory which might be called the "theory of risk avoidance".

If a lender knows exactly how long his money will be available for investment, he can select the maturity date of the claim in such a way that he runs neither an income risk nor a capital risk. If he chooses a maturity date earlier than the point in time at which he needs cash, he will not run the risk of a capital loss since he can always invest his money a second time for the "correct" date, but he runs an income risk since the rate of interest obtainable on the second investment may be lower. If, on the other hand, he selects a maturity date later than the date on which he needs his money, his income from the investment will be certain, but not the capital value. Only the coincidence of the maturity date of the claim and the date of his need for cash will insure him simultaneously against both types of risk – that is, insure him against what we shall call yield risk (yield = interest plus capital gain or minus capital loss).

If we assumed the relevant dates to be known and all participants in the market to be intent exclusively on avoiding any risk, the capital market would consist of a great number of tightly sealed compartments, one for each maturity date, in which the supply of and demand for bonds of each given maturity would determine the interest rate on these bonds irrespective of what happened in the other compartments. The term structure of interest rates would then be determined exclusively by the maturity structure in which debtors wanted to borrow money on the one hand, and on the other hand by the maturity structure in which owners of funds wanted to invest their money. If on the demand side the demand for long-term capital were to predominate and on the supply side the offer of short-term money, the long rates would come to lie above the short rates, and vice versa in the opposite case. Under the "expectation theory", by contrast, the maturity structure of claims or debts has no influence at all on the term structure of interest rates as long as perfect foresight or at least the absence of risk aversion is assumed.

It was Culbertson who more than anybody else stressed the maturity structure of debts as an important – although not the only – factor determining the term structure of interest rates.[5] On this theory the rate structure can be influenced to a significant degree by the debt management policies of the government, as for instance when it shifts from short-term into long-term debt or vice versa. Changes in the economic structure also influence the structure of interest rates, since the length of time for which debts are incurred changes with the purpose for which borrowing is effected. Accordingly, Culbertson points out that "shifts in business and financial developments tend to be reflected in changes in the maturity structure of borrowing. Business inventory developments and securities speculation are reflected in changes in short-term borrowing; changes in automobile sales affect extensions of the intermediate-term credit commonly used in this area; changes in sales of new houses, in business fixed investment, in state and local government construction are reflected in demands for new long-term credit".[6]

Only in the rarest cases, however, is it known in advance exactly when the lender needs his money again. According to Culbertson it is this fact which makes the liquidity of investment significant for the structure of

[5] J. M. Culbertson, 'The Term Structure of Interest Rates', *Quarterly Journal of Economics*, **71** (1957) 485–517. This paper brings out the essence of the theory much better than Culbertson's later essay, 'The Interest Rate Structure: Towards Completion of the Classical System', in *The Theory of Interest Rates*, Proceedings of a Conference held by the International Economic Association, edited by F. H. Hahn and F. P. R. Brechling (London, 1965).

[6] J. M. Culbertson, *Quarterly Journal of Economics*, **71** (1957) 503.

interest rates, liquidity being defined as the possibility to turn the investment into money "on short notice on definite and favourable terms".[7] Short-term claims, which automatically turn into money in the near future or cause only small losses if they have to be sold prematurely, are therefore more liquid than those with a longer term to maturity. Hence investors will prefer to lend their money on short term whenever they do not know when they will need it again. If the supply of short-term debt instruments in the system is not large enough to satisfy this need for liquidity of the investors at a rate of interest equal to the long-term rate, the short rate will lie below the long rate. Since the supply of short-term securities by private debtors is as a rule relatively limited – long-term investments will in general not be financed with short-term credit –, the natural outcome is a short-term rate of interest below the long rate. "Average yields on short-term debt lower than those on long-term debt can be explained, therefore, as representing the market's marginal evaluation of the superior liquidity of existing short-term debt."[8] Speculation and the consequent arbitrage operations between markets are not granted a significant influence on the rate structure by Culbertson. The "expectation theory" of the term structure of interest rates has been replaced by a "theory of risk avoidance".

Let us for the moment accept the extreme point of view that lenders and borrowers are indeed dominated only by the desire to avoid risk, or at least to reduce it as far as possible. Even then we cannot agree with Culbertson's conclusions. It does not at all follow from this assumption that lenders will prefer short-term investments whenever they cannot accurately foresee when they will need their funds again; for with short investments they can only avoid a capital risk, but not an income risk as the interest rate may have changed when the reinvestment has to be effected. The desire to reduce the total yield risk – that is, interest risk and capital risk together – thus might very well cause the lender to select longer-term investments. Apart from this point, however, it seems absurd to assume that an investor would select the maturity with the smallest total yield risk without comparing risks with yields, i.e., to assume that he would attempt to avoid risk "at any price". But once we admit that the investor might possibly choose the more risky of two investments because

[7] J. M. Culbertson, *Quarterly Journal of Economics*, **71** (1957) 491.
[8] J. M. Culbertson, *Quarterly Journal of Economics*, **71** (1957) 489.

it also promises a greater yield, we have taken a decisive step back towards the expectation theory treated in the previous chapter.

Even if we were to adhere completely to this latter theory, we would not need to assume that all investors are prepared to shift, without any hesitation, all the way from the short to the long end of the market whenever such shifts seem profitable.[9] Banks hold only relatively short-term securities because their liabilities are short-term. But they "speculate" and thus influence the rate structure whenever, within the limits of this "short" sector of the capital market, they change the maturity structure of their portfolios. An analogous statement can be made about institutional investors at the other end of the market, insurance companies for instance, whose portfolios typically consist of long-term securities. Between these two groups other institutional investors, security dealers, and individuals speculating in the market see to it that arbitrage operations provide a continuous link from the short-term market all the way to the market for long-term investments. The fact that different groups of participants in the market concentrate on different and relatively narrow sectors of the market thus does not lead to a mutual insulation of these sectors since the sectors themselves overlap.

[9] For the following see D. Meiselman, *The Term Structure of Interest Rates* (Englewood Cliffs, N.J., 1962), p. 53; G. S. Dorrance, 'The Term Structure of Interest Rates', *International Monetary Fund Staff Papers*, **10** (1963) 279 ff.

CHAPTER 19

THE "BASIC RATE" OF THE TERM STRUCTURE OF INTEREST RATES

Occasionally the notion finds expression that one out of the many interest rates should be considered as the base of the rate structure, as *the* rate of interest which a theory of interest should explain above all others. As the theories of the structure of rates say nothing about the absolute level of the rates, it seems indeed necessary, if the structure is to be given a peg, to single out one of them as the "basic rate" and to determine its level, whereupon the others can be grouped around it in accordance with, say, the "expectation theory". The question of the "basic rate" of the interest structure is, according to some authors, identical with the other question, which of the many existing interest rates is being explained by the theories that assume only a single rate of interest.

The answer to this latter question is easy to give in the case of the theories treated in the first part of this book which assume a stationary state of the economy. On the assumption of a stationary economy the problem simply does not exist since then the short and the long rates are equal or, putting it differently, since there will indeed be only *one* rate. Hence it is only in a dynamic economy that we can be faced with the problem of the base of the rate structure.

According to the expectation theory, with perfect foresight the rate of return on bonds of all maturities in each short period will, in a dynamic economy, be identical with and equal to the short rate in that period. According to Conard, it is this rate, and thus the short rate, which theories of *the* interest rate attempt to determine.[1] He comes to his conclusion that the short rate is the basic rate because interest theories, according to him, must be developed for short time spans within which the interest rate does not change, or at least does not change significantly. Hicks, as we know, also decided in favour of the short rate. Yet, there can be little doubt that

[1] J. W. Conard, *An Introduction to the Theory of Interest* (Berkeley and Los Angeles, Calif., 1959).

most of the theorists who attempted to explain *the* rate of interest had the long-term rate in mind.

The question about the base of the rate structure should never have been raised. No one interest rate can be assigned priority over the other rates. Once several rates are assumed, they will all have to be determined simultaneously. The approach of Erik Lindahl may serve as an illustration.[2]

Lindahl divides the future into small unit periods and assumes that changes in the determinants of prices always occur at the points of transition from one short period to the next. He starts with the assumption of perfect foresight (we shall limit ourselves to this case) and further assumes that at the end of the entire time span under consideration a stationary state will have been reached.

Lindahl's model assumes the existence at the start of a stock of real capital goods of an arbitrary composition, whose services are treated as "original" factors of production if they are used in the first unit period and as "saved up" services if they are used in later unit periods. The production of new capital goods and the prices of these goods do not appear directly in the model. Capital goods are viewed, following Wicksell, as saved up "original" services which are on the way to becoming consumer goods. Consumption plans are made at the beginning of the time span for all future unit periods, and the same is true for investment plans – i.e., for plans determining how many service units will be used in each period in the production of consumption goods which become available only in later unit periods. The investment periods of these services are considered variable, but entrepreneurs know exactly when these services can be made to ripen into consumer goods. Investment and consumption plans are coordinated from the beginning for each future unit period by the equilibrium prices and interest rates which, on the basis of the assumed data, follow from the perfectly flexible price mechanism of the system.

In this model Lindahl determines for each unit period the following unknowns: 1. the quantities of the consumer goods demanded in each period; 2. their prices; 3. the quantities supplied in each period of the "original" productive services; 4. their prices; 5. the quantities of the various "original" productive services which in each period are used in the production of the various consumer goods that become available in the same

[2] E. Lindahl, *Studies in the Theory of Money and Capital* (London, 1939), p. 318 ff.

period or in later periods; 6. the rate of interest for the current and the future short unit periods.

In order to determine these variables, Lindahl sets up a system of several groups of equations. The *first* group expresses the supply of each productive service in each period as a function of the prices of all productive services and consumer goods and of the interest rates prevailing in the current and succeeding periods. The *second* group expresses the same functional relationship for the demand for each consumer good in each period. The *third* group serves to determine the technical coefficients in the production of consumer goods in each period. These coefficients can be considered functions of the prices of productive services available in each period. Part of these services are "original", and part are "saved up" from earlier periods. The prices of the latter must be taken as equal to their original prices plus the interest accrued during the time of their investment. The technical coefficients thus are functions of the prices of all "original" productive services and of the interest rate during this period and all preceding periods. Since perfect foresight does not preclude technical inventions, it is possible that these functions, and thus the technical coefficients, are different in each new period. The *fourth* group of equations equates the price of each consumer good in each period with the costs of production of this good, the costs consisting of the costs of the "original" productive services used up in the production of the good plus the accrued interest. A *fifth* group, finally, equates the aggregate demand for the "original" productive services in each period with the aggregate supply. If all prices are expressed in terms of a single consumer good chosen as the *numéraire*, these equations suffice to determine the unknowns mentioned above. We shall not here reproduce the entire complicated system of equations.

At first sight this model seems to have only one rate of interest in each unit period, namely the short rate. But Lindahl, like Fisher, considers the longer rates as averages of the expected short rates.[3] If we limit ourselves, as is usual, to a single period, namely the first short unit period in Lindahl's model, then we will have for this period an entire family of interest rates, one for each term to maturity. The longer rates are all determined simultaneously since the short rates for all future periods, from which the long

[3] E. Lindahl, *Studies in the Theory of Money and Capital*, p. 187 ff.

rates are derived, are determined simultaneously. One cannot say that the short rate for the first unit period is the "base" for the short rates of all future periods, and by the same token one cannot say that it is the "base" for the longer rates valid in the first period.

Short and long rates thus have to be determined simultaneously, whether we limit the analysis to a single short period or whether, like Lindahl, we consider a succession of short periods and treat the long rates in each period as an average of equilibrium rates in the relevant future short periods. Lindahl's model is vastly more complicated than a model that is restricted to one short unit period; but it does have the advantage that the term structure of interest rates in any given short period is not determined with the help of more or less nebulous expectations about future short rates or about future bond prices, but rather on the basis of the real data of the economic system which determine the short rates also for the future.

PART FIVE

THE POSITIVE THEORY OF INTEREST

In the last part of this book we shall, to use Böhm-Bawerk's expression, turn to the "positive" theory of interest. We shall initially keep within the limits of partial equilibrium analysis, restricting ourselves to the money and capital market. By slowly expanding our assumptions, we shall gradually bring the theory closer to reality. Only in the final chapter shall we consider the determination of the interest rate in the framework of a general equilibrium analysis – an undertaking which, however, forces us back into starkly simplifying assumptions. We shall not attempt to construct a dynamic model showing how the interest rate changes over time, nor shall we analyse the relationship between the growth rate of the economy and the rate of interest.[1]

[1] On this subject see, for example, C. C. von Weizsäcker, *Wachstum, Zins und optimale Investitionsquote* (Tübingen, 1962); L. M. Koyck and Maria J. 't Hooft-Welvaars, 'Economic Growth, Marginal Productivity of Capital, and the Rate of Interest', and Amartya Kumar Sen, 'The Money Rate of Interest in the Pure Theory of Growth', both in *The Theory of Interest Rates*, Proceedings of a Conference held by the International Economic Association, edited by F. H. Hahn and F. P. R. Brechling (London, 1965).

CHAPTER 20

THE MARKET FOR MONEY AND CAPITAL: ONLY ONE RATE OF INTEREST

Let us approach our problem in a series of steps, beginning with the following three assumptions: 1. An individual considering possible uses for his money has only the choice between holding cash or investing in long-term bonds, which we shall take to be perpetual bonds or consols. We thus neglect the possibility of investing in bonds of short maturity or in real capital. The first limitation will be dropped in the next chapter, and the relationship between the rate of interest and the yield on real capital will be dealt with when we make the assumption that the real assets can be expanded – that is, when we depart from the initial approach of analysing matters at a single point of time. 2. We assume single-valued expectations, which means that investors feel certain that the expected yields on securities will actually be realised. This assumption will be dropped in the second section of this chapter. 3. We neglect the cost and trouble involved in the purchase and sale of securities. This assumption, too, will be dropped in the second section of the present chapter.

I. Stock Analysis

Let a unit of money invested in consols earn interest of R_0. At the end of the unit period – that is, at the point of time t_1 – a bond which at the moment t_0 costs one unit of money will have the value of R_0/R_1, where R_1 stands for the long-term interest rate expected for time t_1. The expected capital gain thus is $(R_0/R_1)-1$, an expression which signifies a capital loss if it is negative. Hence the entire yield on a unit of money invested in consols is equal to $R_0+(R_0/R_1)-1$. For instance, if the coupon rate is 4 dollars and the price of the bond is 80, then $R_0=0.05$ dollars. If $R_1=4\%$, the total yield on a dollar for the period will be equal to $0.05+(0.05/0.04)-1=0.3$ dollars.[2] The purchase or holding of such a

[2] R_0 stands either for a return expressed in units of money, such as 0.03 dollars, or for

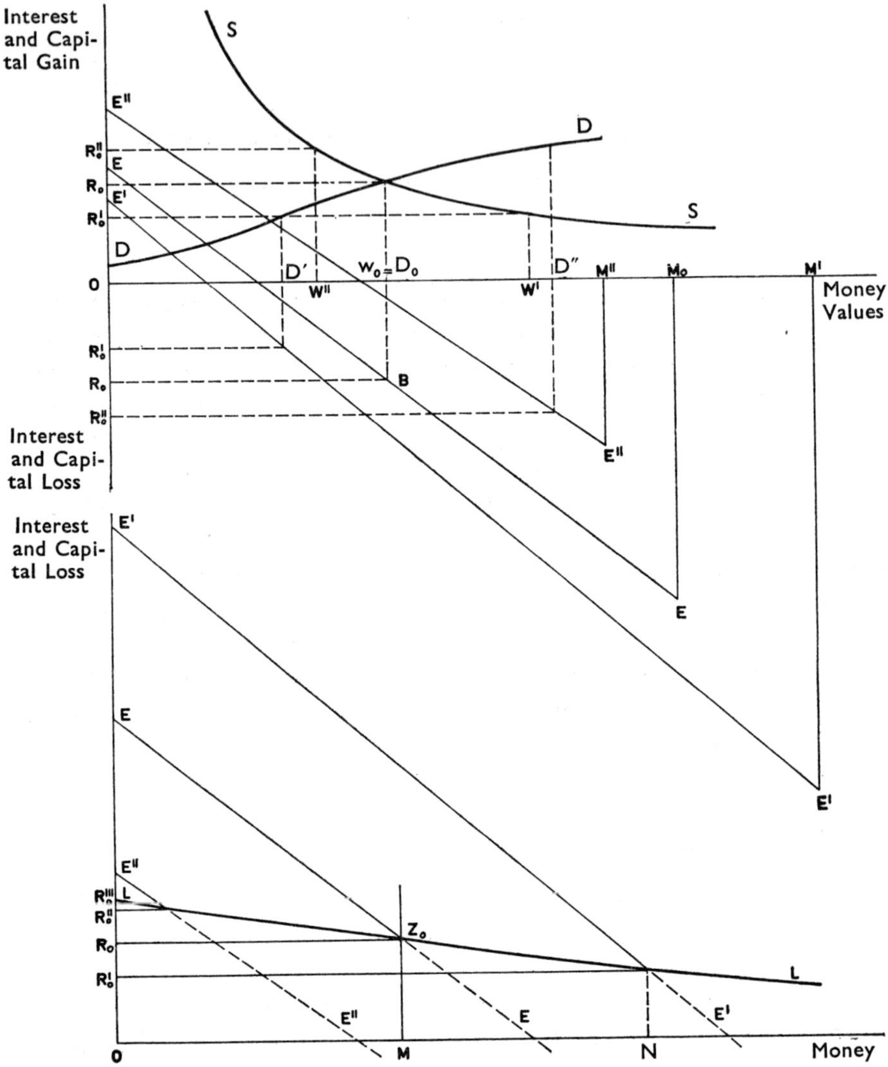

Fig. 29.

an interest rate, such as 0.03 (3 per cent). In the first case we shall speak of "interest" and in the second of "interest rate". Similarly, $R_0 + (R_0/R_1) - 1$ can be considered a return (yield) expressed in units of money, or a percentage rate of return. In the first case we shall speak of the "yield on the bond", in the second of the "effective rate of return" or simply "effective rate".

security will be profitable as long as $(R_0/R_1)-1$ is positive or, if it is negative, as long as it is, in absolute terms, smaller than R_0.

In the lower diagram of Figure 29 we measure on the vertical axis the expected capital loss on a unit of money, $1-(R_0/R_1)$, as well as R_0. On the horizontal axis we measure cash holdings. All market participants who, at interest of R_0, expect a negative yield on the bond will wish to hold their entire funds in the form of cash. We array them in sequence, beginning with the funds of the investor who expects the biggest capital loss, followed by the funds of the second greatest "pessimist", etc. The resulting *EE*-curve – which actually should have the shape of a step function, but has for simplicity's sake been drawn as a continuous straight line – falls towards the right and cuts the interest-horizontal R_0 at the point Z_0. At this interest rate the demand for speculative cash balances will be *OM*.

If we could assume that the expected capital losses were independent of the existing rate of interest, the *EE*-curve would be the liquidity preference curve, showing the amount of cash that would be held at each interest rate. But such an assumption would be just as, or even more, unreasonable than the one frequently made in the literature, namely that the interest rate R_1 expected by each individual is independent of the existing rate. This latter assumption would mean that an individual who expects an interest rate R_1 of 3 per cent will have this expectation regardless of whether the existing rate is one or eight per cent. On the other hand, an assumption that expected capital losses are independent of the existing interest rate would mean that the expected rate would indeed change with changes in the existing rate, but in a most unreasonable manner. If someone expects a capital loss, he anticipates the expected rate R_1 to be higher than the existing rate R_0. The assumption that the anticipated capital loss is to remain the same implies therefore that he expects the future rate to lie above the existing rate, whether the latter is one or eight per cent. This will not do. We can thus work neither with the one nor with the other assumption.

For these reasons we have to assign a different curve of expected changes in the bond price (or of expected capital losses) to each existing rate of interest, and these curves have to be related in such a manner that at a higher existing rate the expected capital losses as well as the number of individuals expecting capital losses will be smaller. Accordingly, the demand for cash balances will be smaller at higher interest rates, and the expectation curve (the *EE*-curve) will, with a rising interest rate, shift leftwards. Thus the $E''E''$-curve in the lower part of Figure 29 is based on an interest rate R_0'' which is higher than the rate R_0 associated with the *EE*-curve. The demand curve for speculative cash balances is given by the *LL*-curve, i.e., the line which connects the points of intersection of the expectation curves with the corresponding interest-horizontals. At an interest rate of R_0''' no one expects a capital loss exceeding R_0'''.

Let us now assume that a certain volume of speculative cash balances exists, equal to *OM* in the lower part of Figure 29. Together with the *LL*-curve this money supply yields the interest rate R_0. It should be noted that implicitly we are assuming that the quantity of money used for transaction purposes is independent of the interest rate – an assumption which, strictly speaking, is not justified even for a very short period.

Let a certain quantity of money, consisting of cash and sight or demand deposits, be in the hands of households and firms at time t_0. That part of this money which these units spend in the coming period on goods and services we shall call transaction money, the rest speculative money. If we want to be very precise, we should assume, like Hicks[3] and Patinkin[4], that all transactions are effected on "Monday", so that in each short period the money is turned over only once. Let us now assume that at a lower interest rate expenditures on consumer and investment goods during each short period will be greater than would be the case at a higher rate, in so far as households will be saving less at a lower rate and entrepreneurs will invest more. But once the quantity of transaction money has thus been made dependent on the interest rate, one can no longer take the quantity of speculative money as given. This is taken into account in Figure 30. The entire existing quantity of money is there represented by OO'. The curve *TT*, read from the origin, shows how much money will be used for the purchase of goods and services during the period from t_0 to t_1 at different rates of interest, always assuming the corresponding equilibrium price level in the market for goods and serv-

[3] J. R. Hicks, *Value and Capital* (2nd ed., Oxford, 1946), chapter 9.
[4] Don Patinkin, *Money, Interest, and Prices* (1st ed., Evanston, Ill., and White Plains, N.Y., 1956; 2nd ed., New York, 1965).

ices.[5] The *LL*-curve is the demand curve for speculative balances already known to us; it has to be read from O' rather than from the origin O. The interest rate will be MZ, the transaction balances OM, and the speculative balances $O'M$.

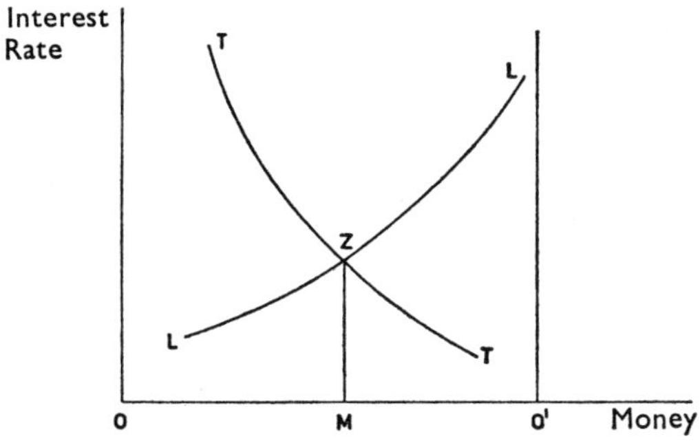

Fig. 30.

However, in order not to complicate the presentation more than necessary, we shall for the time being neglect the influence that the functional relationship between the rate of interest and the volume of transaction money exerts on the quantity of speculative balances, even in the short period. Hence we consider the latter to be given.

Instead of starting out from the quantity of money and the demand for money, it should be possible to operate with the quantity of securities outstanding and the demand for securities. Since we are interested in determining the rate of interest, this would have the advantage of being the more natural approach. Each of the two approaches, of course, implies the other; and both must lead to the same result. In order to clarify these relationships we have added to the lower diagram in Figure 29, which has already been discussed, an upper one which illustrates this second method of determining the interest rate.

On the x-axis we measure money values, and on the y-axis the interest rate; the latter is measured off on the y-axis in both directions from the origin O. On the same axis we also measure expected capital gains per unit of money (upward from the origin) and expected capital losses per unit of money (downward). The value K of the outstanding consols is shown as a function of the interest rate by the rectangular hyperbola SS. It represents

[5] Cf. p. 179ff.

the equation $K = C/R_0$, where C stands for the sum of all interest payments per unit period. We now again draw expectation curves, for the reasons already discussed a separate one for each interest rate. Thus the line EE is associated with the interest rate R_0 and the line $E''E''$ with the rate R_0''. Since all participants in the market who expect either a capital gain or a capital loss smaller than the interest will want to hold bonds, the distance (situated below the x-axis) R_0B, equal to OD_0, represents the value of the bonds which participants wish to hold at the interest rate R_0; correspondingly, the distances OD' and OD'' represent the value of bonds demanded at the interest rates R_0' and R_0'' respectively. By plotting these distances against the corresponding interest rates as measured upwards from the origin, we obtain the curve DD which shows the value of bonds that participants wish to hold at different rates of interest. Let us for a moment assume the interest rate is R_0'. At this rate the market participants wish to hold bonds to the value of OD'. The value of the outstanding consols, however, is OW'; hence consols to the value of $D'W'$ will be offered on the market. This drives down the price of consols, thereby raising the interest rate, until at a rate of R_0 an equilibrium is reached at which everyone wishing to hold bonds is provided with them.

To the value of bonds OW_0 we add the quantity of speculative money, assumed to be given, namely W_0M_0 which is equal to OM in the lower diagram of Figure 29. The distance OM_0 then represents the value, at the interest rate R_0, of all assets existing in the market (cash plus consols). The EE-line below the x-axis, as extended beyond B to the intersection with the vertical line through M_0, is nothing other than the expectation curve EE in the lower diagram "put on its head". It shows that the given quantity of money W_0M_0 will be held by all those who expect capital losses exceeding the interest R_0. Analogous statements can be made for the other interest rates. At the rate R_0', for example, the value of the consols is OW' and the value of all assets OM'. The expectation curve $E'E'$ shows that the market participants wish to hold OD' in bonds and $D'M'$ ($=ON$ in the lower diagram) in cash balances. The liquidity preference curve in the lower diagram can thus be considered as constructed with the help of the expectation curves in the upper graph, these having been turned upside down and the corresponding vertical lines all going through the origin of the diagram.

If the demand curve for consols, DD in the upper diagram, is shown as rising to the right, this is due to the fact that the demand is here viewed not as a function of the price of consols but as a function of the interest rate on consols. We could also interpret this curve as a supply curve of money for consols, but in that case the bondholders retaining consols which they already own would also have to be considered "suppliers" of funds.

In equilibrium the condition has to be satisfied that all who, at the equilibrium interest rate, want to hold money are in the possession of cash and all who want to hold bonds are in the possession of bonds. The "last" one still holding cash and the "first" one already holding bonds have to be indifferent between cash and bonds. This presumes that they have the same expectation with respect to R_1. For both, the equation holds true that $R_0+(R_0/R_1)-1=0$ or that $R_0=1-(R_0/R_1)$, i.e. that the interest just balances the expected capital loss.

Since it is considerably simpler to work with the demand for money and the quantity of money, rather than with the demand for securities and the quantity of securities outstanding, we shall in what follows always use the former approach. In the next few sections we shall assume that at the beginning of the period under consideration an equilibrium of the kind shown in Figure 29 for the interest rate R_0 exists. At that moment, the supply of cash will be in the hands of those participants in the market having suitably pessimistic expectations, while the others will be holding the bonds outstanding. The equilibrium rate of interest maintains the balance between the two groups in the sense that no transactions in securities or money will occur as long as none of the data in the system are changed.

II. Trouble, Cost, and Uncertain Expectations

In this section we shall drop the assumptions that transactions in securities involve neither cost nor trouble, and that expectations are held with certainty.

Let us first deal with the factor "cost and trouble", retaining for the moment the assumption of single-valued expectations. Assume the money cost of security transactions to be a given percentage rate c of the investible funds G; hence it amounts to cG. We furthermore assume that the total yield of the investment must be at least equal to $\bar{S}$, if the investment is to compensate for the trouble which we assume to be independent of the volume of investible funds. In equilibrium it must then be true for all holders of cash that

$$G\left(R_0 + \frac{R_0}{R_1} - 1\right) \leq \bar{S} + cG$$

where, of course, $\bar{S}$ and G are different – or at least can be different – for each participant in the market.

In Figure 31 let $\bar{S}$ be represented by the distance OS on the y-axis. On the x-axis we measure investment. The line $\bar{S}+cG$ represents the cost and trouble associated with different volumes of investment, and the line $g=G[R_0+(R_0/R_1)-1]$ the money yield on the same investments. If an investor has less money available for investment than $G=ON$, the investment will not be worth the effort; if he has more to invest, it will be worthwhile to invest the entire amount. With a higher effective rate of return on securities, the yield curve will be steeper – for instance, like the g'-curve in Figure 31 – and the investment of smaller sums will also pay off; thus in our example the necessary minimum reduces to $G=ON'$, which is smaller than ON.

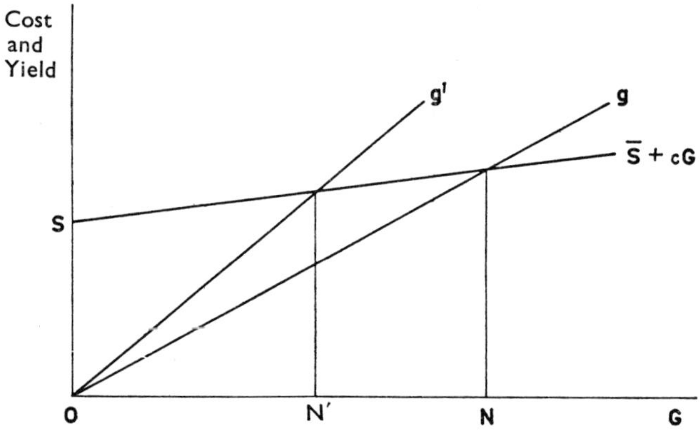

Fig. 31.

Conversely, someone already holding securities will sell them only if the expected future loss exceeds the cost and the trouble (measured in money terms) of disinvesting. In equilibrium, the following equation must hold for the owners of consols:

$$G\left(R_0 + \frac{R_0}{R_1} - 1\right) \geq -(\bar{S} + cG)$$

The expression $(\bar{S}+cG)$ must be given a negative sign; the expected yield on securities can be negative without yet causing a shift into cash, provided the yield remains larger than the cost and trouble. If the entire cost of disinvesting is equal to -3 and the expected loss is equal to -2, the owner of consols will still not sell; he will do so only if the expected yield falls to -3 or less.

We should not slide over the fact that our taking into account the cost and trouble of investing and disinvesting introduces a problem which we have previously neglected. If cost and trouble are neglected, it is quite proper to limit the time horizon of the individuals to the short period t_0 to t_1 as was done in our formula for the expected bond yield $[R_0+(R_0/R_1)-1]$. Since an individual can rearrange his holdings at the beginning of each new short period without incurring any cost, any behaviour pattern which is optimum in each short period will also be optimum over a longer period. But if we take the cost and trouble of bond purchases and sales into account, the time horizon itself becomes a problem since these costs will be the less significant, the longer the security is held. Hence it is quite possible that an investor taking into account only the period t_0 to t_1 would come to the conclusion that he should keep his funds in the form of cash, while if he were to expand his time horizon to t_2 he would find the purchase of securities more advantageous. However, if we were to take account of this complication, our presentation would have to consider the expected interest rates for t_2, t_3, etc.; and it would become exceedingly involved. To avoid such complexities, we shall continue to work with a short unit period.

Let us now drop the assumption of perfect foresight. Then each investor will have to weigh the utility of the probable yield on bonds against the utility of the greater liquidity obtained by holding cash rather than bonds. This is a problem of portfolio selection, a subject around which a subtle literature has arisen in the last few years.[6] Some relatively simple considerations, however, will suffice to bring to the fore those aspects which are significant for our purpose.

[6] H. Markowitz, 'Portfolio Selection', *The Journal of Finance*, **7** (1952) 77–91, reprinted as a Cowles Commission Paper, New Series, No. 60. H. Markowitz, *Portfolio Selection, Efficient Diversification of Investments*, Cowles Foundation Monograph No. 16 (New York-London, 1959). J. Tobin, 'Liquidity Preference as Behavior Towards Risk', *Review of Economic Studies,* **25** (1957–1958) 65–86. J. Tobin, 'The Theory of

The liquidity of cash balances consists of three components: (1) the safety of cash – i.e., the fact that the holding of cash, in contrast to the holding of securities, is not associated with a danger of loss[7]; (2) the immediate usability of cash, as contrasted with securities which first have to be sold before the funds invested in them can be used for other purposes; and (3) the fact that the holding of cash obviates the cost and trouble of investing and disinvesting. The influence of the latter element on cash holdings we have already analysed; henceforth we shall disregard it. In order to investigate the effect of uncertainty on cash holdings in isolation, we shall also neglect the second component of the liquidity of cash balances. Accordingly, the advantage of holding cash will be considered to lie exclusively in its safety.

Let us start our analysis with the case of an investor who, weighing at time t_0 whether he should purchase a bond, "expects" that a certain yield will have accrued by t_1. The "expected" yield is defined as the mathematical expectation of all yields considered possible; their dispersion around this "expected" value is measured by the standard deviation.

On these assumptions we can state, first of all, that the investor will put his entire funds into bonds as long as the smallest yield which he considers possible is still positive.[8] Conversely, he will hold all his funds in the form of cash if even the largest "yield" which he considers possible is negative. In what follows it will be assumed that the range of possible yields contains both positive and negative values.

Let us further assume that the investor's aversion to the risk associated with the expected yield grows as he invests more in bonds. It is indeed a common experience that a person is ready to risk more with the first five per cent of his wealth than with the second, and so on. The counterpart to this is that the marginal utility of the cash balance increases, the

---

Portfolio Selection', and Don Patinkin, 'An Indirect-Utility Approach to the Theory of Money, Assets, and Savings', both in *The Theory of Interest Rates*, Proceedings of a Conference held by the International Economic Association, edited by F. H. Hahn and F. P. R. Brechling (London, 1965). W. Fellner, *Probability and Profit* (Homewood, Ill., 1965).

[7] We assume stability of the price level.

[8] Even if we continue to neglect the cost and trouble of investing, cash holdings might nevertheless arise if we take into account the second component of the liquidity of money – namely its immediate usability. The reason for this will be clear if the analysis later in the text is applied to this case.

smaller it becomes in consequence of the holder's investment in bonds. A concrete example will best clarify these relationships. Let us assume that an investor "expects" the gross proceeds (price plus accrued interest, or $R_0 + (R_0/R_1)$) from the sale at time t_1 of a consol purchased now for one dollar to be 1.3 dollars. It is quite possible that he equates the utility of the first dollar invested in consols to the utility of more than 1.3 dollars held in cash – i.e., that he would be willing to spend more than 1.3 dollars to "buy" the expected proceeds of 1.3 dollars. This means that the investor would be ready to bank on the chance that the proceeds might ultimately be larger than 1.3 dollars. Naturally this would not be true for all investors; others, who are less ready to incur risks, will assign a utility to the first dollar invested in consols which is less than the utility of 1.3 dollars held in cash. In both cases, however, we can take it for granted that, in considering the investment of the second dollar, the amount of cash whose utility as a balance will equal the utility of the dollar invested in consols will be smaller than for the first dollar. If this relationship in the case of the first dollar was 1.4 to 1 for the gambling investor and 1.2 to 1 for the cautious one, it will perhaps be 1.3 to 1 and 1.1 to 1 in the case of the second dollar invested in consols. If we measure dollars held in cash on the y-axis and dollars invested in bonds on the x-axis, we obtain in this manner an indifference curve of the usual kind for each level of utility, i.e. curves falling towards the right and convex to the origin, each higher curve having a steeper slope for a given level of investment (but higher cash holdings) than the lower ones (Figure 32). The volume of funds available to the investor would be OF if entirely held in cash and OF' (which, of course, is equal to OF) if entirely held in bonds. The cash actually held will then be OK and the value of bonds OW.

At the point L the marginal rate of substitution between cash and bonds is equal to unity: the investor is indifferent between holding another dollar in cash or investing it in bonds. Thus the utility obtained from the last dollar held in the cash balance is here equal to the utility of the last dollar invested in bonds, due regard being given to the risk factor.

The point at which the relevant indifference curve is tangent to the 135°-line (FF' in Figure 32) depends on three factors:

1. Upon the personal attitude of the investor to risk: Of two investors expecting the same yield and the same dispersion of possible yields around it, the one with the greater aversion to risk will equate the utility of the

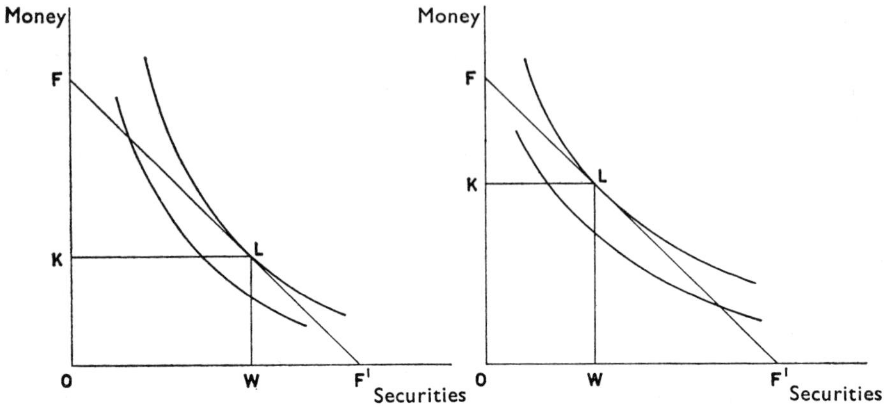

Fig. 32.

first, second, etc. dollar invested in securities to the utility of less cash than the one who is less afraid of risk. The former will have flatter indifference curves than the latter, and his point of tangency (L) will lie more to the north-west. The more risk-shy the investor is, the larger cash balances will he hold (compare the right-hand diagram in Figure 32 with the left-hand one).

2. Upon the dispersion of the possible yields around a given expected value: The larger the dispersion anticipated by the investors, the flatter the indifference curves will be (as a rule – i.e., excepting those of gamblers), and the more to the north-west will the point L come to lie – i.e., the larger will the cash balances be (compare the right-hand graph in Figure 32 with the left one).

3. Upon the level of the "expected" yield itself: Given two investors with equal dispersion of possible yields and the same attitude to risk, the entire distribution curve of the investor expecting a higher yield lies further to the right and the possibility of losses is smaller. This investor will therefore be ready to give up more cash for the first, second, etc. dollar invested in bonds than the investor expecting the lower yield; the indifference curves of the former are steeper, and he will thus be holding more bonds. The readiness to sacrifice liquidity for the sake of yield increases as the expected yield increases, all the more so as the possibility of losses decreases at the same time.

In the preceding section we saw that, on the assumptions of single-valued expectations and absence of cost and trouble, each participant in the market will hold all his funds entirely in cash or else entirely in bonds. On these assumptions a liquidity preference curve sloping downwards to the right could be constructed only if different participants had different expectations with respect to the future interest rate R_1. But once uncertainty of expectations is introduced, the liquidity preference curve will slope downward even if all participants believe unanimously that neither capital gains nor capital losses are to be expected, i.e., that R_1 will be the same as R_0. This conclusion follows from the reasoning above, namely, that everyone will be willing to sacrifice a larger amount of cash for bonds the higher the interest rate and thus the expected yield.[9]

Up to now we have assumed that the mathematical expectation (the "expected value") of the yields is taken by the investor to be positive; and we have shown that he will nevertheless hold part of his funds in the form of cash. If the mathematical expectation is negative, but the investor still reckons with the possibility of positive yields, the part of the funds held in cash will be larger without necessarily absorbing all of the funds. The very possibility that the pessimist might be "disappointed" in his expectations (i.e., the possibility that the actual outcome might be a positive yield) may, in spite of his pessimistic outlook, induce him to assign up to a certain point a higher utility to dollars invested in bonds than to dollars held in cash.

Thus we can also determine in the case of uncertainty of yields how much cash each individual market participant will hold. But if, owing to uncertain expectations, pessimists also hold bonds and optimists also hold cash, the demand curve for speculative balances can no longer be found by simply taking the points of intersection of the expectation curves with the relevant interest lines. The liquidity preference curve will now have to be constructed in the following manner.

[9] One could, of course, also claim that because higher interest rates mean larger incomes, the safety of cash will, from a certain point on, again be preferred, so that the share of cash balances in total assets will again increase. This was stressed by Tobin, who also showed that a liquidity preference curve sloping downward to the right will be obtained, under the assumption of uncertainty of security yields, even if *all* participants in the market, without exception, have the expectation that the relationship $R_1 = R_0$ will come true. J. Tobin, 'Liquidity Preference as Behavior Towards Risk', *Review of Economic Studies*, **25** (1957–1958) 65–86.

For each individual market participant we can determine in the manner shown above (Figure 32) what part of his funds he will hold in cash and what part in bonds at a given interest rate R_0 and an "expected" (by him) future rate R_1. By adding these cash balances we obtain the demand for speculative money at the given interest rate R_0.

In Figure 33 the line *EE* represents the expectation curve associated with the interest rate R_0. We measure the capital losses and gains expected by the market participants on the *y*-axis and the cumulative total of cash holdings desired by them on the *x*-axis. The *EE*-curve will be continued below the abscissa since investors expecting capital gains will now also want to hold cash balances. In order to obtain the total demand for cash at the given interest rate R_0 we have to continue the expectation curve to the gain "expected" by the last investor who will not exclusively hold bonds. From this point *E* we draw a vertical line upward to the intersection with the interest line R_0 at *L*. The demand for cash at the rate R_0 will then be equal to *OK*. At a higher rate of interest R_0' an investor who at the rate R_0 expected a capital loss will now either anticipate a smaller loss or perhaps even a gain, and those who already at the rate R_0 expected a gain will now count on a larger one. Our previous analysis of

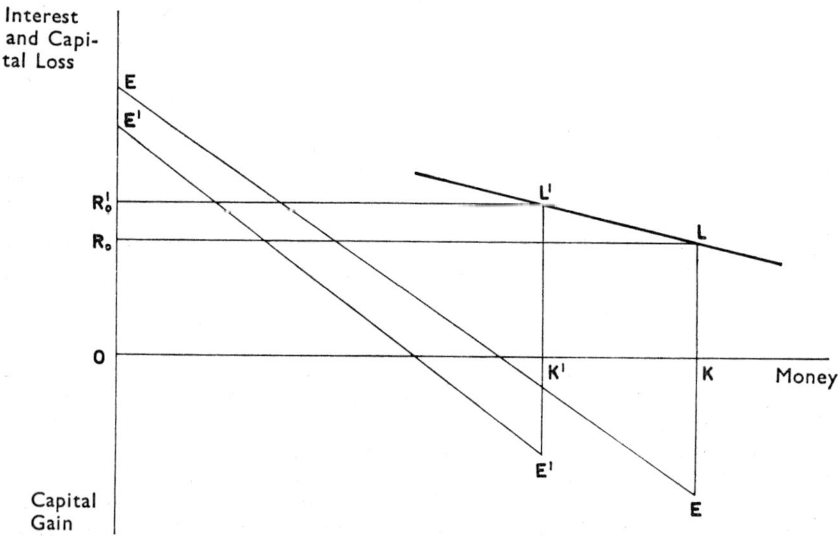

Fig. 33.

the allocation of funds between cash and bonds tells us that every investor will, under these circumstances, wish to hold less cash than at the lower interest rate. The new expectation curve $E'E'$ will lie below EE and will come to an end at a smaller total demand for cash. In Figure 33 we obtain for the interest rate R_0' a demand for cash of OK'. In this manner we construct the $L'L$-line as the demand curve for cash.

III. Flow Analysis

Let us now turn from a "stock" to a "flow" analysis and begin by examining the effect of changes that take place during a period in the number of consols outstanding and in the quantity of speculative money.

First let us introduce a new demand for long-term funds, either by the state or by entrepreneurs. To obtain the funds, new bonds in the form of consols are issued. It is an essential task of any interest theory to analyse this demand, or, at least, that part of it which stems from the business sector. However, we shall postpone this task to the next chapter where it will be tackled on the assumption that more than one rate of interest exists. In order to avoid repetitions we shall here simply assume that the demand curve – the funds demanded as a function of the interest rate – has the normal downward-sloping form. We retain the assumption that a given quantity of money which is available for investment in bonds is, at the beginning of the period, in the hands of those who have pessimistic expectations about the future bond prices. This has been discussed above.

We can now introduce the new demand by entrepreneurs (or by the government) in two ways portrayed in the two diagrams of Figure 34. For simplicity's sake we shall again use straight lines.

In the left-hand diagram the DD-curve represents the demand by entrepreneurs for long-term funds as a function of the interest rate. The LL-curve is the liquidity preference curve (single-valued expectations being assumed). The LGG-curve is the addition of these two curves. With a given quantity of speculative money OM the interest rate will be R_0'. The quantity of money OK (or $M'M$) will be transferred to the entrepreneurs and will enter into the transactions sphere. At the end of the period, or at the beginning of the next one, a quantity of speculative money of OM' will remain; and, with the unchanged liquidity preference curve LL, the stock analysis will yield the same interest rate R_0'.

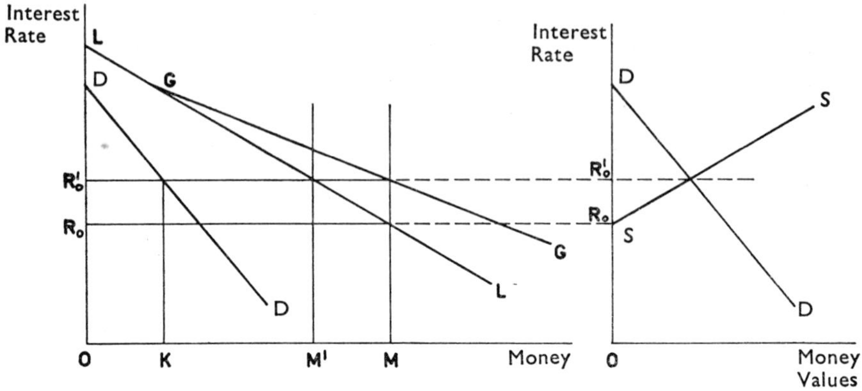

Fig. 34.

In the right half of Figure 34 the same situation is shown with the help of ordinary supply and demand curves. The *DD*-curve is the same as in the left half of the diagram; the *SS*-curve is the supply curve for funds: the *LL*-curve of the left-hand diagram measured from its point of intersection with R_0 (the equilibrium interest rate at the beginning of the period) and plotted to the right. This supply curve shows how much of the speculative money will be invested at various rates of interest. The intersection of supply and demand yields the same interest rate R_0' as in the left-hand diagram.

From the presentation in the right-hand diagram, one might gain the impression that the stock of bonds outstanding had no influence on the new interest rate, since the latter appears to be determined exclusively by the supply of funds for new long-term bonds and the corresponding demand. However, this impression would be wrong. The old bonds exert their influence on the initial interest rate R_0 in the left-hand diagram and thereby on the starting point *S* of the supply curve on the right side. This is particularly obvious if we return for a moment to the upper half of Figure 29. With a greater quantity of consols outstanding, the equilibrium rate of interest in that diagram – which corresponds to the initial rate R_0 in the left half of Figure 34 and to the starting point *S* of the *SS*-curve in the right half – would be higher.

So far we have been assuming that the supply of funds in the capital market resulted from the dishoarding of cash balances existing at the beginning of the period. We have not taken account of the possibility that current saving could be a further source of supply. Let us now introduce saving as we introduced new demand, that is, without further analysis; and let us assume that it increases with a rising rate of interest. Saving increases the quantity of "speculative money" available for investment in bonds. If we assume that the entire volume of new savings will be offered in the capital market, we will have to imagine the vertical erected over *M* in the left-hand diagram of Figure 34 replaced by a line sloping upward to the right. The interest rate would then be determined by the intersection of this line with the *LGG*-curve. Alternatively, we can confront the demand by entrepreneurs in the right half of the figure by the supply of funds offered in the capital market, shifting the supply curve to the right by the amounts which will be offered from new savings. The interest rate will again be the same as that obtained in the left-hand diagram with savings added. If then, after all transactions in the capital market have come to an end and the money has flown into the transactions sphere, we confront the residual quantity of money still available for speculative purposes with the liquidity preference curve (the *LL*-curve, which does not include the entrepreneurial demand for funds), we will again obtain the interest rate which resulted from the demand for and supply of funds during the period.

We have seen how in the current period a new demand for funds by the entrepreneurs and the government tends to raise, and new savings offered in the capital market tend to lower, the interest rate. Let us now consider a change in the interest rate caused by a change in expectations.

In Figure 35 the *LL*-curve represents the liquidity preference curve at the beginning of the period on the assumption of single-valued expectations, *OM* the quantity of speculative money, and R_0 the interest rate. Let us now postulate that every market participant expects a lower interest rate (R_1) than he did before. In the lower part of Figure 29 this would have to be shown as a downward shift of all *EE*-curves, with the consequence of a downward shift of the *LL*-curve. The new position of the liquidity preference curve is given by *L′L′* in Figure 35. The new interest rate is R_0'. Let us assume that all participants in the market, including the owners of consols, change their expectations in such a manner that the sequence in which they were arrayed before they changed their expectations remains unaltered. Then the market participants who hitherto were holders of cash will remain holders of cash. To put it in Wicksteed's term, they have merely changed their "reserve price". If this assumption is strictly fulfilled, there will not even be any transactions in bonds. Only if the market participants change their expectations in such a manner that some former holders of bonds will become pessimists and some holders of cash optimists – which, of course, is what one would in reality expect –, will bond transactions occur with the consequence that some cash holders will become bond holders and vice versa.

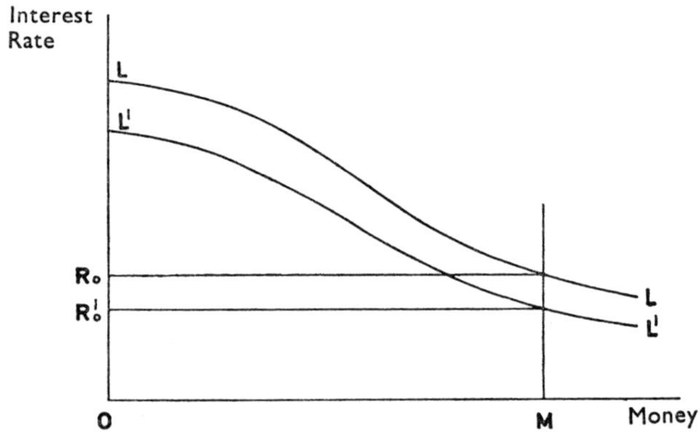

Fig. 35.

This presentation shows how the long-term interest rate can change temporarily even if the yield on real investments has not changed so as to cause a shift in the demand for investment funds. In fact, neither the small daily fluctuations nor, more importantly, the abrupt larger changes which sometimes occur in the prices of bonds (and thus in the interest rates) can be explained by changes in any one of the other factors codetermining the interest rate (such as, e.g., an increased demand for funds or a larger supply of funds). They must be attributed to changes in the liquidity preference.

The *ceteris paribus* analysis of the effect of certain factors on the interest rate should not lead us to conclude that this effect will occur whenever these factors are present. In Figure 34 the demand of entrepreneurs draws money out into the transactions sphere, so that both flow and stock analysis (as applied to the end of the period) give the result that the interest rate will rise. It must however be remembered that in reality money is also flowing from the transactions sphere, via savings, back into the money market. If these two flows are equal, the interest rate will remain unchanged. Whether a change occurs depends upon the mutual relationship of saving, liquidity preference, and the demand for funds by entrepreneurs and the government.

Three additional observations should be made. The first concerns the clarification of two seemingly contradictory statements often met in the literature. According to one of them, a higher interest rate will draw idle money out of hoards, thus reducing the speculative cash balances or, as it is sometimes put, the liquidity preference. According to the other, a reduction in the liquidity preference will lead to a fall in the interest rate. It is quite obvious that in the first statement the term "liquidity preference" refers to the absolute volume of cash balances, while the second statement refers to the liquidity preference curve. There is no contradiction between the two statements. The first refers to a movement along a given liquidity preference curve to the left, while the second deals with a shift of the entire curve to the left.

The second remark concerns the significance of the liquidity preference curve for the determination of the interest rate. In Figure 34, if we shift the demand by entrepreneurs for funds sufficiently to the right, the entire volume of speculative money will be drawn into the transaction sphere and liquidity preference would be eliminated as a factor codetermining the level of the interest rate. We would find ourselves in a situation in which all money is transaction money. It is this state which the "classics" of the theory of interest considered the normal one. In such a state the interest rate is determined exclusively by saving and the demand for funds, and the "classical" interest theories come into their own.

Our third comment is that, if we so desire, we can impute all changes in the interest rate to changes in the liquidity preference or in the quantity of speculative money. To this end, we merely have to include in the liquidity preference curve (1) the demand for money by the holders of idle cash balances and (2) the demand for funds in the capital market by entrepreneurs and the government. The interaction of the sum of these two demands with the quantity of speculative money (including the amounts saved) will always yield the interest rate; and any shift of these two curves will result in a change of the rate.

CHAPTER 21

THE MARKET FOR MONEY AND CAPITAL: SEVERAL INTEREST RATES

Let us now introduce the short-term interest rate on bills and analyse the term structure of rates at a single point of time. The bills, which yield the short rate r_0, are taken to have a period to redemption of t_0 to t_1, which is supposed to be identical with the period for which expectations are formed about the yield of consols. New decisions about the composition of assets are made only at the beginning of such periods.

I. Stock Analysis: The Term Structure of Interest Rates

We now have three markets: one for bills, one for consols, and the money market. Now an investor who is pessimistic with respect to the yield on consols need no longer hold cash, because he has the choice between cash and bills. As long as the interest rate on bills is positive, there remains only one reason to hold speculative cash balances – namely, the cost and trouble of investing which might make it unprofitable to acquire bills.

Let us begin, as we did in the preceding chapter, with an analysis in terms of stocks. At a certain moment of time the quantities of bills and of consols outstanding and the volume of speculative money are given. We now ask, what conditions have to be fulfilled so that the three markets are in equilibrium – leaving aside the problem of how this equilibrium comes about. They are three in number:

1. For all holders of cash the equilibrium condition is that neither the interest on bills nor the expected yield on consols is large enough to compensate for the cost and trouble of investing. If $\bar{S}$ again represents the amount of money required to compensate the investor for the trouble of investing and c the costs of the transaction as a percentage of the invested funds G, the entire cost and trouble will be equal to $\bar{S}+cG$. Thus for each holder of cash it must be true in equilibrium that

$$0 \geq Gr_0 - (\bar{S} + cG)$$

and

$$0 \geq G\left(R_0 + \frac{R_0}{R_1} - 1\right) - (\bar{S} + cG)$$

where $\bar{S}$ and G can be different for each investor. The equality sign applies to those who are indifferent between the markets.

The market participants who consider the short-term interest rate and the expected yield on consols too low in comparison to the cost and trouble of investing must thus be sufficient in number to absorb into their cash balances the entire quantity of speculative money. With this statement we seem to come very close to the Hicksian theory, criticized in the history-of-doctrines part of this book, that the short rate is determined by the cost and trouble of the marginal lender in the short-term market. These costs, after all, can be considered the same as the cost and trouble of the marginal participant who still holds cash. Two points must, however, be made to show why our theory should not be considered identical with that of Hicks:

a) Since the intramarginal cash holders have to prefer cash both to bills and to consols, the yield expectations with respect to consols also have an influence on the short rate. If, for instance, those who evaluate the cost and trouble of investing higher than the interest on bills are at the same time optimists with respect to the yield on consols, and hence owners of consols; and if, on the other hand, those for whom the trouble of investing is small are at the same time pessimists in their expectations about the yield on consols and hence holders of bills or cash, the short-term equilibrium rate will be lower than it would be if, with an equal distribution of funds, the "high-$\bar{S}$" fund owners were the pessimists and the "low-$\bar{S}$" ones the optimists.

b) The assumption of a given quantity of speculative money, which was made here, is essential for our equilibrium condition. As soon as we drop this assumption and let the speculative money be absorbed into the transactions sphere, the cost and trouble of investing ceases to be the rate-determining factor. The short rate can then rise above the level required to induce even the "highest-$\bar{S}$" fund holder to invest his money.

2. At the beginning of this chapter we posited that the term to maturity of bills coincides with the "expectation period" or the time horizon of investors, t_0 to t_1. Hence at the beginning of each "expectation

period" the entire stock of bills has to be renewed. We shall imagine that each holder of bills can have the old ones replaced by new bills automatically and without costs. We then have to ask: on what conditions will he hold on to these new bills? As long as the term to maturity of bills is identical with the calculation period of investors, these will never want to shift into cash since at a positive short-term interest rate the yield on bills can never be negative. A shift into consols involves cost and trouble twice – when the bills are sold and when the consols are bought –, so that in equilibrium the following is true for holders of bills:

$$Gr_0 > 0$$

and

$$Gr_0 \geq G\left(R_0 + \frac{R_0}{R_1} - 1\right) - 2(\bar{S} + cG)$$

3. The holders of consols, finally, prefer consols to cash and to bills. Since a shift into cash is accompanied by cost and trouble only once but a shift into bills twice, we have for owners of consols:

$$G\left(R_0 + \frac{R_0}{R_1} - 1\right) \geq -(\bar{S} + cG)$$

and

$$G\left(R_0 + \frac{R_0}{R_1} - 1\right) \geq Gr_0 - 2(\bar{S} + cG)$$

A shift from consols into cash can thus occur in the case of a positive short rate only if the interest is so low that it does not cover the doubled transaction costs of a shift into bills.

If we neglected the cost and trouble of investing, the condition of indifference between the market for consols and that for bills would be that $r_0 = R_0 + (R_0/R_1) - 1$; i.e., the marginal holder of consols and the marginal holder of bills would have to have the same expectations with respect to the future long rate, R_1. The introduction into the analysis of cost and trouble creates a discrepancy between the expectations as to R_1 of the marginal holders of bills and of consols. The marginal investor still holding consols expects a higher future long rate R_1, regardless of the level of R_0, than the marginal investor still holding bills, if both have the same evaluation of the trouble of investing (equal values of $\bar{S}$) and the same volume of investible funds.

These marginal conditions for equilibrium in the short-term and the long-term market can obviously be satisfied at a long rate R_0 which is either higher, lower, or equal to the short rate r_0. If we neglect cost and trouble for a moment, the conditions under which the short-term equilibrium rate may be different from the long-term rate can easily be formulated. When expectations with respect to the yield on consols are decidedly optimistic and a capital gain is expected even by the least optimistic investor who still has to hold consols in order that the entire stock finds owners, then r_0 will be higher than R_0. Since expectations of capital gains (i.e., of a fall in the long rate) are more likely the higher the present long rate is, the short rate will be most likely to stand above the long rate if the latter is relatively high – a statement which is confirmed by experience. If expectations are largely pessimistic, the short rate will lie below the long rate; and if the marginal investors in both markets expect that the long rate will not change, the long and the short rate will be equal.

If we take cost and trouble of investing into account, the formulation of the conditions under which the long rate will be equal to, above, or below the short rate becomes much more complicated. One condition for the equality of the two rates, for instance, would be that the marginal owner of bills must expect a future long rate (R_1) which is lower than R_0 by an amount which assures that the capital gain expected from his investment in consols is equal to the cost and trouble of disinvesting and reinvesting; hence

$$G\left(\frac{R_0}{R_1} - 1\right) = 2(\bar{S} + cG)$$

Furthermore, if R_0 is to be equal to r_0 the marginal owner of consols will have to expect an R_1 which is higher than R_0 by an amount assuring that the expected capital loss is just equal to the cost and trouble of shifting into bills. Since the use of these exact formulae would make the verbal presentation exceedingly complicated, and since, when expectations or other data change, the interest rates move in the same direction whether we neglect the cost and trouble of investing or take them into account, we shall in what follows abstract from them.

We still have to drop the assumption of single-valued expectations. The fund owners will then no longer hold *either* consols *or* bills *or* cash, but a mixture of the three. (The cost and trouble may, of course, prevent them from investing in securities altogether.) For the determination of the optimum mixture with uncertain expectations the same criteria are applicable as were discussed in the last chapter for the mixture of cash and consols; hence we shall not discuss them again. In equilibrium the utility deriving from the liquidity of the last money unit held in cash has to be equal to the utility of the last unit held in either of the other two forms of investment.

In this context it should be stressed that the long rate R_0 must be equal to the short rate r_0 if all participants in the market are of the opinion that R_1 will be equal to R_0 and if the cost and trouble of investing are neglected and single-valued expectations are assumed. We cannot determine, however, who will be in the short market and who in the long. If expectations are uncertain, everyone who, on his best estimate, concludes that R_1 will be equal to R_0 but who at the same time has an aversion to risk, will choose consols only if $R_0 > r_0$. He will make that choice, because he will need a compensation for the risk associated with consols. From this it follows that in spite of such "neutral" expectations about R_1 by all participants, the long rate will lie above the short rate if the risk-averters predominate, while with single-valued expectations the two rates will be equal. This conclusion is valid only, however, if we limit ourselves to a very short period.[1]

From the analysis up to this point we can draw certain preliminary conclusions:

1. On our assumption of a short time horizon, if risk-averters predominate, the long rate will come to lie above the short rate even if the market participants do not expect a change in the price of consols (and thus in the long-term interest rate). The same relation of rates will hold also in a situation where the expectations of the market participants are different (and uncertain), but the last one who still has to be induced to buy or hold consols is of the opinion that R_1 will be equal to R_0.

2. The excess of the long rate over the short rate will be greater the greater the expected increase in the long rate.

3. The long rate will lie below the short rate if even the most pessimistic

[1] Hence it does not contradict the statement made on p. 216-217.

holder of consols expects a capital gain (i.e., a fall in the long rate). This situation becomes more likely the higher the existing long rate.

We may insert a remark here relating to bonds which are not consols. Since a change in the interest rate has less influence on the capital value of bonds the shorter the maturity, it follows that the interest rates on these debt instruments will lie between the short rate and the rate on consols; if the rate on consols lies above the short rate, the rates on intermediate maturities will be rising with increasing terms to maturity, and vice versa if the long rate lies below the short rate. We thus have the three possibilities for the term structure of interest rates shown in Figure 36.

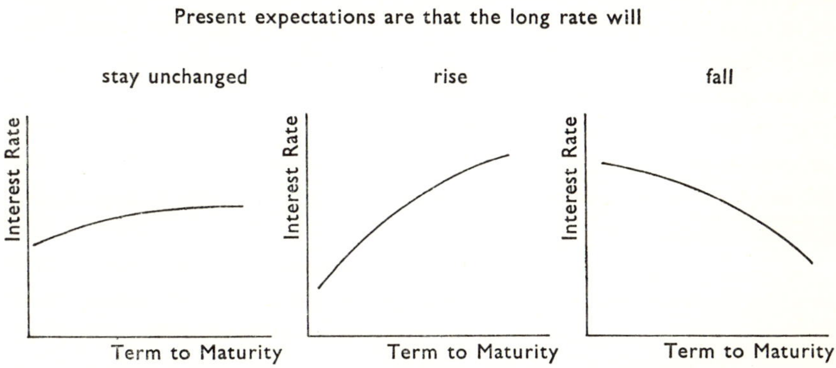

Fig. 36.

In this analysis we have attributed a level of rationality to the owners of financial assets which will rarely be found in reality. It is certainly not true that all participants in the markets for bonds are "speculators" who choose between markets on the basis of short-term yield expectations and consequently shift from one market to the other every time these expectations or some of the interest rates change. The great mass of wealth owners does not invest in bills but compares – at best – bond yields and the interest obtainable from banks and savings institutions; and only very few will give a thought to what the price of a security might be after a short period ("at the moment t_1"). Banks and financial intermediaries such as insurance companies also operate only within a limited sector of the market. Banks are almost exclusively interested in bills and bonds of relatively short maturities, while insurance companies invest primarily in long-term instruments. However, for the tendencies deduced above to prevail, it is sufficient, as we have already noted[2], that the banks, insurance companies and similar institutions, and individual speculators choose – within their respective and mutually overlapping "maturity horizons" – between securities on the basis of rational considerations.

II. Flow Analysis: Supply and Demand in the Capital Market

The existence of certain financial assets – cash, bills and consols – at a given moment in time has been the starting point of our analysis so far. We asked: what conditions would have to be satisfied for an equilibrium to exist, i.e. a situation characterized by the absence of any motivation for market participants to part with or to acquire financial assets? We could have expanded our investigation also to include real assets or capital goods; however, we prefer to discuss the relationship between the yield on real assets and interest rates in a context in which an increase in the real assets is possible. This possibility of expansion is the factor which generates the close connection between the yield on new capital goods and the interest rates.

Let us now turn to a flow analysis and consider a short period within which new investment and saving take place. We shall again assume that the long-term bonds traded in the market are of the "perpetual" type, consols; and we shall further assume that the short-term bonds, bills, have a term to maturity equal to our short period, a time span which also coincides with the period for which yield expectations are made. A short-term interest rate would, in a hidden form, also exist in an economy where consols are the only type of fixed-interest security. It could be calculated from the coupon rate and the price of the consols at the beginning and the end of the short period. Short-term borrowing would then take the form of issuing consols at the beginning and repurchasing them at the end of the current period. It is simpler, however, and at the same time more realistic to let the short rate be represented by the interest rate on a security different from consols.

Our first task is to analyse the supply of funds. In this chapter we shall neglect the role of the banking system.

In general, saving by an individual is considered to be a function of his

[2] See p. 225.

income, his wealth, and the rate of interest. Since we conduct our investigation here in the framework of a partial equilibrium analysis restricted to the capital market, we shall take income and wealth as given and concentrate on the relationship between saving and the interest rate.

According to Irving Fisher, a person will, on the assumption of a time horizon covering the two income payments at t_0 and t_1, save until his time preference – assumed to be initially lower than the interest rate for the period t_0 to t_1 – is, at the margin, equal to the interest rate. When this point is reached, the utility obtained from the last money unit invested in bonds is equal to the utility of the last money unit used for consumption (or held in cash). It is presumed in this analysis that the savings will be liquidated at the moment t_1. Conversely, if the time preference of the individual initially exceeds the interest rate, he will borrow money until the same equilibrium condition is satisfied. The same principle also applies if the time horizon of the individuals stretches over many periods. The maximization of utility from the income stream up to the horizon requires in this case – again assuming that at the end all savings are liquidated or all debts are repaid – that each individual plans his saving or borrowing in such a way that for each future short period the marginal time preference becomes equal to the interest rate of that period.[3] It does not follow from this that in each period the same amount will be saved or borrowed as would be the case if the individual had a planning horizon covering only one period (from t_0 to t_1). Suppose someone expects an income stream consisting of 120 at t_1, 80 at t_2, and 70 at t_3, and has a marginal time preference of zero if his income stream is even. Suppose further that the interest rate is zero. Then he will save 30 at t_1 and liquidate 10 of these 30 at t_2 and the remaining 20 at t_3, so that his income stream will become 90, 90, 90. If he has a planning horizon only up to t_2, he will save only 20, thus arranging for an income stream of 100 and 100. Once t_2 has arrived, he will save 15 out of the second 100 in order to assure for t_2 and t_3 (now within his planning horizon) incomes of 85 and 85.

The premise that all savings are liquidated by the end of the period defining his time horizon is, of course, quite unrealistic. However, it follows necessarily from the assumption that an income receiver maximizes the utility of his income stream. If at the moment t_n, the end of the

[3] See the Mathematical Appendix on Irving Fisher.

entire time span considered, the individual still held claims (arising from his previous savings) of a positive amount K, we would have to conclude that this accumulation is due to a utility-maximizing calculation taking into account the consumption which the accumulation will make possible in the periods following t_n. Hence we are forced to extend the time horizon beyond the moment t_n.

In equating the marginal time preference to the interest rate in each period, Fisher had in mind the short-term rate of interest valid for the period on the assumption of perfect foresight. Hence when dealing with consols we cannot compare the interest rate on consols (coupon payment divided by the price) with the marginal time preference; rather, we must use the effective rate of return on consols as calculated from the coupon payment and the price at the beginning and at the end of the period. It is this effective rate which, assuming perfect foresight, will be equal to the short-term interest rate for the period.

If we substitute subjectively certain expectations for perfect foresight, a discrepancy can arise between the short rate and the effective rate on consols for the same period. In this case the saver must for each future period compare the higher of the two with his marginal time preference.

If, in the analysis of saving, we start out from a comparison of marginal time preference with the short-term interest rate or the effective rate on consols (whichever is the higher), if we operate with single-valued expectations, and if we neglect the cost and trouble of investing, then we must assume that all savings will always be invested since the short rate is always positive. This need no longer be true if we take the cost and trouble of investing into account. The comparison will then have to be made between the marginal time preference and either the short-term interest or the short-term yield on consols (whichever is the higher), both net of the cost and trouble of investing. The consequences of introducing investment costs can be made sufficiently clear by a simple example with a time horizon covering only two successive income payments. If both the net short rate and the net effective rate of return on consols are positive, the higher of these two will be compared with the marginal time preference. Let us now, by contrast, assume that the net short rate and the net effective rate on consols are negative for a saver. Let him expect a declining income stream so that he has, therefore, initially a negative marginal time preference. On these conditions he will save, in the form of hoarding, until the marginal time preference is zero.[4] Conversely, a sufficiently high positive net short rate or net effective rate on consols will cause him to invest not only the money saved out of current income, but also the money previously held idle. The threshold at which this happens lies, for each individual, at different short rates (or effective rates of return on consols) because of the different evaluations of the factor "trouble" and because of the different magnitudes of the investible funds.

With given short and long interest rates and with given expectations about the future rates, we can thus determine the volume of saving of each individual for the present period (and for future periods). Accordingly, aggregate saving is also determined. It should be emphasized that the problem in which market a saver should invest – discussed in the preceding section – must already have been solved before the volume of his savings can be determined, since it is the highest possible return which enters into the saver's comparison with his marginal time preference. The above analysis was restricted to the case of single-valued expectations. Uncertainty about the future, as we already know, will cause the total sum of savings to be distributed between the three possible forms of investment in such a manner that the utility of the last money unit invested is equal in all three uses.

We now turn to the demand side, starting out from the individual entrepreneur who considers either expanding production or producing a new product.[5] The following problems must be solved:

1. In all cases in which the investment period of productive inputs or the durability of capital goods is variable, the investment period oı the durability has to be determined.

2. The scale of the investment has to be determined.

3. Whenever more than one interest rate exists, it has to be determined which rate is relevant for calculating the profitability of the project.

4. The manner of financing the investment project has to be decided

[4] We have here neglected the fact that the trouble of investing per unit of saved income will be the smaller, the larger the total amount of saving. Hence the net interest itself can increase from a negative value through zero to a positive value as total saving increases.

[5] The problem, which of the several products within his sectoral horizon an entrepreneur should produce, will be solved as follows: for every possible product he will carry out the calculations described in the text and then choose the product promising the largest profit.

in order to determine in which section of the capital market the entrepreneur will borrow.

The first two points involve problems treated in greatest detail by the first group of authors discussed in this book. Any complete treatment of the factors determining these two entrepreneurial decisions would require a re-investigation of the cases discussed by our first group of interest theorists. Unnecessary repetition may be avoided by restricting ourselves here to a few examples. We assume that the time horizon of the entrepreneur will conform to the investment periods of the productive inputs or to the length of life of the capital goods which he takes into account for his investment project.[6]

As our first example we take the "point input–point output" case with a variable investment period for the inputs, which is thus one of the unknowns in the problem. We illustrate the case by trees, an example of production very frequently used in capital theory. We assume single-valued expectations.

For a stationary state with only one rate of interest which remains unchanged, the solution is as follows. The investor will, for each individual tree, strive to maximize the difference between the present value of the tree and the cost of planting it. This difference will be maximized if the tree is cut at the date when the growth rate of the value of the tree divided by the value of the tree is equal to the interest rate. The scale of planting will then be determined by the rule that the discounted value of the marginal product of the inputs must be equal to the price of these inputs. We assume perfect competition in all markets, so that the wage rate and the prices of other productive inputs as well as the price of the product is given for the

[6] The question of the time horizon has been treated in detail in Friedrich and Vera Lutz, *The Theory of Investment of the Firm* (Princeton, 1951). In this book one can also find a detailed investigation of all possible investment types; the largest part of the work is a very minute elaboration of the subject matter of this section.

Considering the nature of the investment process – investment in durable goods –, we obviously cannot restrict the time horizon of the investing entrepreneur to a short period. But this would not be required even if we wanted to pursue the analogy between the supply and the demand side in the capital market to the limit. For also on the supply side we do not restrict the time horizon of individuals making a decision on saving to one short period; we merely assume that the yield calculations are periodically repeated at short intervals and that the investment of funds in the given period is based on these short-period calculations. The analogy would thus only require that in the *financing* of his investment the entrepreneur works with a short calculation period.

individual entrepreneur; and it is presumed that the marginal physical product of the inputs decreases with the expansion of production – i.e., that diseconomies of scale exist. The scale of planting determines the demand for funds; but it is clear that the determination of the scale of planting has to occur simultaneously with the determination of the optimum investment period ("lifetime" of the trees), since the discounted value of the marginal product of the productive inputs will be larger or smaller depending on the length of the growth period. Hence, it is erroneous to hold that the length of the investment period does not affect the demand for funds in the current period.

How does the solution change if we introduce more than one interest rate and if we introduce expectations about the future course of these rates? A consideration of this question necessarily starts from the proposition that the entrepreneur must earn from his investment at least the maximum rate which he could obtain by lending the same sum in the capital market. This rate is determined by the entrepreneur's expectations about the future interest rates. He will now have to proceed as follows in discounting the value of the tree at each point on its growth curve: If the long rate for the corresponding time span is higher than the average of the expected short rates over the same time span, the long rate will be chosen for discounting[7]; in the opposite case he will have to discount with the successive expected short rates or with the average rate calculable from these. With very differentiated expectations, the highest possible rate of return obtainable in the market for credit may have to be calculated from a succession of short-term and longer-term market rates of interest.[8]

The discounting of the value of the tree at each point on the growth curve with the maximum interest rate found for the corresponding period will yield the lowest present value for this lifetime. The optimum "lifetime" of the tree will be indicated by that point for which the present

[7] We deviate here from the premise that only bills and consols exist and assume that there are securities of many maturities.

[8] Strictly speaking, the calculation should be even more complicated, since for the longer-term bonds the effective rates expected for various time spans may be different from the market rates of interest for the same time spans. Whenever the former rates are higher than the latter, they should be used instead. But since in practice not even the calculations described in the text are applied, we feel free to neglect these additional complications.

value calculated in this manner is highest; the cost of planting being given in our example, this solution is identical with maximizing the difference between the present value of the gross revenue from the tree and the cost of planting it. Hence in Figure 37, where the present value of the tree calculated in this manner for the moments T_1, T_2, and T_3 (shown on the x-axis) is V_1, V_2, and V_3 (on the y-axis, measured on a logarithmic scale), the investment period selected will be OT_2. Here it is no longer possible to express the result in a simple formula stating that the rate of growth of the value of the tree divided by that value must be equal to the interest rate.[9]

The scale of investment will of course have to be determined simultaneously with the length of the growth period. The solution is in principle the same as that described for the case of a single interest rate, except that now the maximum discount rate obtained in the manner described above takes the place of the single interest rate. If we assume that the cost of planting consists exclusively of wages, planting will be continued until the value product of a worker, discounted in the above manner, is equal to

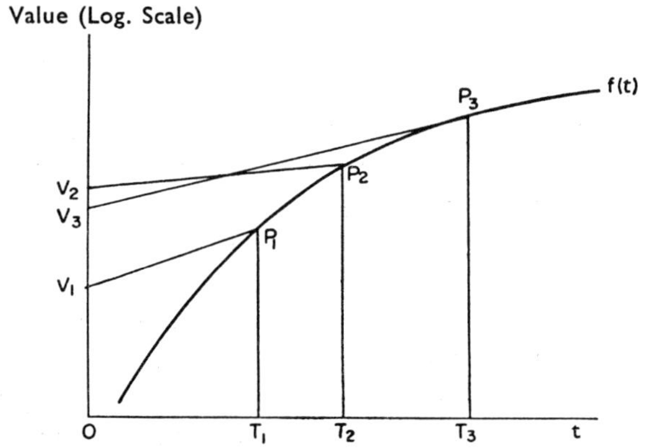

Fig. 37.

[9] It is indeed true that if, for a certain time interval, the percentage growth rate of the value of the tree were to be equal to the short-term interest rate valid for that time interval, the capitalization procedure would yield the same present value whether the investment period was extended over that time interval or not; but from this we cannot derive a criterion for the optimum period of growth. If, for instance, in the succeeding time interval the percentage growth rate were to be higher than the short rate for that interval, the extension of the growth period by this interval would again increase the present value of the tree.

his wage. The scale of planting in turn will determine the demand for funds in the current period.

It still remains to be discussed how the entrepreneur will finance his investment – i.e., in which sector of the capital market he will seek investment funds. He will, of course, select the least costly form of financing.

If we neglect the cost and trouble of financing and assume single-valued expectations, the entrepreneur will borrow in the short market whenever the short rate is lower than the effective rate on consols or lower than what he expects he would have to pay in the short period by borrowing on bonds of longer maturities. If he finds it most profitable to borrow short in the long market, he must repurchase the bonds he has issued at the end of the short period, financing this repurchase through the sale of new securities with whatever maturity seems to him most advantageous for the next period, and so on. The cost and trouble of such transactions and uncertainty about the future will of course change this result, an aspect to which we shall return later.

On the assumption of a given growth curve of the trees, given prices of the productive inputs (wage rate), and given interest rate expectations we can thus determine the volume of funds the entrepreneur will demand and the market to which he will turn in the current period.

A wage increase will reduce the scale of the investment. Whether this reduction will be associated with a reduction in the demand for funds depends on the elasticity of the curve representing the discounted marginal product of labour as a function of labour inputs. A fall in the rate at which the value product is discounted – it may occur in consequence of changed expectations, without any change in the current interest rates – will cause an expansion of investment and thus an increase in the demand for funds. An increase in productivity resulting in an upward shift of the $f(t)$-curve in Figure 37 will also increase the demand for funds.

Our second example considers an investment in durable producer goods, e.g. machines. We shall assume that they cannot be made more durable by increasing expenditures on their construction. Hence only the scale of the investment has to be decided. Under static conditions, the solution would be that the entrepreneur acquires durable goods up to the point at which the present value of the quasi-rents yielded by the good – the series of quasi-rents discounted at the prevailing rate of interest – is equal to the cost of the good. In this calculation the interest on circulating capital will have to be added to the other variable costs before the quasi-rent for each period can be obtained. This latter point makes it impossible, even with the assumption of only a single rate of interest, to summarize the solution by the statement that the entrepreneur will invest up to the point at which the internal rate of return or the marginal efficiency of investment is equal to the rate of interest, since the quasi-rents used in the calculation of the marginal efficiency can be obtained only after the deduction of an interest charge – a fact which makes the marginal efficiency itself dependent on the interest rate. (The marginal efficiency will be higher with a low and lower with a high interest rate.) Nevertheless, with a given interest rate we can determine the scale of investment with the aid of the formula that the discounted value of the quasi-rents of the last machine added must be equal to the cost of the machine.

If several interest rates exist and if the investor has single-valued expectations about the future course of these rates, he will discount each individual quasi-rent either with: (a) the rate on bonds with a term to maturity corresponding to the time that elapses between the purchase of the durable good and the emergence of the quasi-rent or with, (b), the average rate for the same time span as calculated from the optimum combination of successive shorter rates. He will choose the higher of these two discount factors so as to obtain the minimum present value of the quasi-rent.[10] The present value of the machine will then be the sum of these present values of individual quasi-rents, and the entrepreneur will invest until this present value of the machine is equal to its cost.

A fall in the rate of discount will lead to an expansion of the investment and thus to an increase in the demand for funds, and so will an increase in the quasi-rents; a reduction in the cost of the durable producer good will increase the investment in terms of units of the good, but whether the demand for funds will also grow depends on the elasticity of the curve representing the present value of quasi-rents as a function of machines used.

All types of investment can in principle be dealt with in this manner,

[10] In the calculation of the quasi-rent for each period the interest charge on the circulating capital used in this period has to be added, as we know, to the variable costs. We assume here that this charge is calculated at the short rate expected for the period in question. This, however, is an assumption made only for the sake of avoiding complications. Strictly speaking, we also have to determine for the circulating capital which interest rate should be applied.

and for all we can thus determine: 1. which interest rate or which rates will be appropriate for the calculation of the profitability of the investment; 2. how long the investment period of individual inputs will be, if it is at all variable; 3. what the scale of the investment will be and thus the amount of funds demanded in the capital market, and 4. how the investment will be financed in the current period – whence we will know on which sector of the capital market the demand will impinge.

In our example of an investment in durable producer goods, it was tacitly assumed that an antecedent problem had already been solved – the problem of selecting the type of durable producer goods in which the entrepreneur should invest. Since the selection of the type of capital good – e.g., the type of machine – also depends on the rate of interest, we shall have to pay some attention to this problem also.

In the textbook literature much use is made of isoproduct curves which show different combinations of labour and capital for a given level of output. Such isoproduct curves make little sense, since the unit of capital, which is measured on one of the axes, cannot be defined. The substitution between capital and labour as a rule means that the *type* of capital good is being changed. The normal apparatus of the theory of production evidently is not applicable to this situation, even if one works with the services of the machine instead of the machine itself, because it is not possible to measure the machines or their services in identical physical units.

Under strongly simplifying assumptions we can, however, draw a diagram which does justice to the problem. Let us assume we are dealing with machines of the same length of life which produce the same present value of gross revenue, but which differ in that all during the lifetime of the more expensive machines variable costs are lower than such costs are with the less expensive machines. We can plot the present value of the variable costs (measured on the y-axis) against the purchase price of the corresponding machines (on the x-axis) and thus obtain the l-curve in Figure 38. We also plot the expected present value of the gross revenue, which is the same for all machines; it is given by the level of the horizontal b-line.

If we draw a 45°-line down to the right from the point B which represents this level, it will be obvious that the sections of the l-curve extending beyond this line cannot come under consideration because, at all points

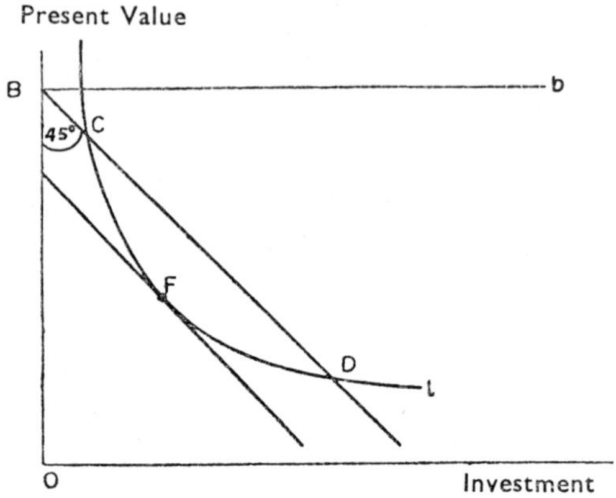

Fig. 38.

on these parts of the *l*-curve, the sum of purchase price of the machine and present value of variable costs will be higher than the present value of gross revenue. Thus we need to choose only between the combinations from *C* to *D*. If we now shift the 45°-line to the left until it is tangent to the *l*-curve (at *F*), we will have the optimum combination of "capital" and variable costs at this point of tangency. At point *F*, the substitution of a more expensive machine will cause just as much additional investment outlays as is saved in terms of the present value of variable costs.

If the discount rate is lowered, both the *b*-horizontal and the *l*-curve will shift upwards; the latter will shift by a constant percentage, thus becoming steeper. It can easily be seen that a change such as this will now yield a more capital-intensive method of production – i.e., that a higher-priced machine will now be profitable. In reality, of course, there will be no such continuous transitions between different types of machines, but the tendency described will undoubtedly assert itself.

We shall refrain from analysing the same investment examples once again under the assumption of uncertainty of expectations. In the case of durable goods this would affect both the expectations about the quasi-rents (via expectations about product prices and future variable costs) and the expectations about future interest rates. It should be emphasized, however, that it is this uncertainty about the future which prevents entrepreneurs from applying such subtle calculations and capitalization methods as those outlined here. They will as a rule deal with the uncertainty factor either by discounting the "expected" values of the future quasi-rents with an interest rate that is sufficiently higher than the market rate to compensate them for their risk, or, more frequently, by calculating the profitability of their investment on the assumption of a lifetime of the capital good much shorter than that which would be technically warranted. The entrepreneur will consider an investment advantageous, for instance, if he can recoup the capital invested in the machines within a few – three or four – years; and in the face of uncertainty about future interest rates, he will as a rule finance his investment in the market where loans are at least no shorter than the lifetime of the machine which he intends to purchase. The cost and trouble of borrowing work in the same direction. Only if he believes that long-term funds will be cheaper in the future will the entrepreneur initially finance a long-term investment with short-term debt. Such short-term financing then takes the form of a current account bank credit which will later be replaced by the sale of securities. The shifting to and fro between the short and the long market is, in so far as the entrepreneurs are concerned, by no means as frequent in practice as a theory based on the assumptions of single-valued expectations and absence of transaction costs would make us believe. Realistically speaking, we shall not commit a gross error if the method of financing is made dependent on the type of investment good: short-term in the case of "circulating" capital; long-term in the case of fixed capital assets.

III. Flow Analysis: The Term Structure of Interest Rates

After having dealt separately with supply and with demand in the capital market, we shall now bring the two together. During the period under consideration, we now have a new demand for funds from entrepreneurs who issue new securities to satisfy their demands; and, at the same time, households are building up new financial assets by saving. Hence the problem is no longer simply to find the equilibrium at a certain moment with given financial assets.

We have seen that one can determine, for each hypothetical structure of interest rates, how much individual suppliers of funds will offer in each of the markets and how much individual entrepreneurs will demand. Both supply and demand are functions of the existing and the expected long and short rates of interest. Equilibrium in the short-term and long-term capital market requires a structure of interest rates satisfying the following conditions: On the supply side, each household must obtain the same utility from the last unit of money spent in consumption, held in cash, or invested in securities. On the demand side, the present value – computed in the manner described in the preceding section – of the quasi-rents from the "last" purchase which an entrepreneur makes of a durable capital good must for each entrepreneur be equal to the price of the capital good. For circulating capital, the present value of the marginal product of productive inputs must be equal to the price of these inputs. Finally, the market in which the entrepreneur finances his investments must be chosen so that the expenses of financing are minimized.

If we want to retain the usual rule that in equilibrium the marginal efficiency of investment has to be equal to "the interest rate", we shall have to use the approach presented in our treatment of Fisher's theory (p. 96 ff.). We shall explain it once more, using the example of a durable producer good (a machine). The investment decision is to be made at moment t_0. The current short rate is assumed to be valid for the period from t_0 to t_1. We now discount back to t_1 all quasi-rents which arise after t_1, using the method described in the preceding section; together with the quasi-rent which falls due at t_1 this yields us the present value V_1 for the end point of the first period. This "present" value will now be discounted to t_0 with the internal rate of return and equated to the cost C of the machine – i.e., $V_1/(1+i)=C$, where i is the internal rate of return. The investment will then be continued until $i=r$, i.e., until i is equal to the current short-term rate of interest of the period.

Roughly speaking we can state that any increase in the quasi-rents relative to the prices of durable capital goods will drive up the demand for funds for investment in fixed capital assets, and that any increase of product prices relative to factor prices will drive up the demand for funds for investment in circulating capital; both effects tend to raise the level of interest rates. Which rates will be affected most strongly depends on the interest rate expectations of entrepreneurs and suppliers of funds. This last point we shall revert to in the next section. A lowering of the discount factor – which, as we know, does not have to be identical with a lowering of the current short or long rates – will increase investment, and vice versa.

In the case of a single interest rate – as we have shown in the last chapter – the rate which results from market supply and demand during a period will be the same rate which is obtained from a stock analysis once all transactions have been effected. This is also true here. The term structure of interest rates resulting during the period on the basis of supply and demand is the same as that resulting at the end of the period from a stock analysis such as we used in the first section of this chapter. In view of the number of variables involved, a diagrammatic presentation of this result is here not possible. Yet it should be self-evident that every participant in the market, in selecting the composition of his assets – cash, short-term and long-term securities, real assets – so as to be constantly in accord with the evolving structure of interest rates, will be "content" with the structure of rates that finally emerges in the sense that he will not undertake new transactions unless some of the data of the system change. The stock equilibrium obtained in this manner for the end point of the period under consideration now comprises the real assets also.

IV. Changes in the Term Structure of Interest Rates

It will be helpful for an understanding of the term structure of interest rates, if we consider the process of changes in this structure. We shall again start from the assumption that at the beginning of the period – at point t_0 – equilibrium prevails, meaning that no participant in the market has cause to alter the composition of his assets as long as the data in the system do not change. We then introduce such a change of data and analyse its effects under the *ceteris paribus* condition.

Let us first assume that expectations as to the future price of consols become more optimistic, so that the liquidity preference declines. In the initial situation the short-term interest rate r_0 is assumed to lie below the long rate R_0, as is normally the case. Since holders of bills will now try to shift into consols, the short rate will rise and the long rate will fall; the difference between the two rates will decrease and, depending on how strongly the liquidity preference falls, may even be reversed so that the short rate could come to lie above the long rate. Conversely, if the liquidity preference increases, the short rate will fall and the long rate will rise; the difference between the two rates thus will increase. In short, changes in the liquidity preference change the structure of rates.

Let us next assume an increase in the demand for short-term funds through the issue of additional bills. In the initial situation we again posit that $r_0 < R_0$. Now r_0 will increase, and as a result of arbitrage operations between the two markets the long rate will also rise. We now ask which of the two rates will rise more. It will be simplest to put the question in the form: at which long rate will the present owners of consols be willing to hold on to their consols? Since owners of consols are more optimistic than non-owners with respect to the expected yield on consols, we will have to conclude that, unless changes in the expectations about the future long rate R_1 occur, in the new equilibrium after the rise of r_0 and R_0 the same people as before will be owners of consols, and that the additional bills will be entirely in the hands of former holders of cash for whom the acquisition of bills will now be advantageous. Our way of posing the question is thus justified.[11]

For the marginal holder of consols it was true up to now that $r_0 = R_0 + (R_0/R_1) - 1$, where by assumption $r_0 < R_0$, and hence $(R_0/R_1) - 1 < 0$. We neglect the transaction costs. If r_0 now rises to a new level r'_0, the marginal owner of consols will hold on to them only if, with an unchanged expectation of R_1, the long rate has risen to the level of R'_0 in the equation $r'_0 = R'_0 + (R'_0/R_1) - 1$. Since R'_0 is greater than R_0, the expression $(R'_0/R_1) - 1$ will be greater than $(R_0/R_1) - 1$; in other words, it will be a negative expression of smaller absolute magnitude, or perhaps even be positive. But this means that r'_0 must be lying above r_0 by a larger amount than R'_0 lies above R_0; the short rate rises by more than the long rate. The more the short rate is driven up by the demand for short-term capital, the higher will the long rate rise and the sooner will a situation be reached in which even the marginal holder of consols will expect a capital gain, $(R'_0/R_1) - 1$ having become positive for him. Hence in this case the short rate will come to lie above the long rate.

These conclusions are based on the assumption that the expected rate R_1 will stay unchanged for every participant in the market. According to what was said in the preceding chapter, it is however reasonable to assume that with a higher present long rate the expectations with respect to the yield on consols will improve – i.e., that those who hitherto expected a

[11] It should be noted that we made the assumption here that all those holding cash in the initial situation are less optimistic with respect to the yield on consols than the holders of consols. This is not necessarily correct; cash holders might be more optimistic and yet consider the yield on consols too small to make the investment worth-while. We shall nevertheless retain the assumption.

capital loss will now reckon with a smaller loss or a gain, and those who up to now expected a gain will now anticipate a larger gain. If the long rate is 3 per cent, for instance, and an investor expects no change in this rate, he will anticipate neither a capital gain nor a capital loss. (For him $R_0+(R_0/R_1)-1=0.03+(0.03/0.03)-1=0.03$). If R_0 rises to 5 per cent, he may revise his expectation about R_1; let us say, he will expect a rate of 4 per cent. This means that he will now be counting on a capital gain, even though a smaller one than he would have anticipated with an unchanged expectation of $R_1=3$ per cent. If such an upward revision of R_1 is made by everyone down to the marginal holder of consols, the extent to which the short rate rises more than the long rate will be reduced, and the point at which the short rate comes to lie above the long rate will be shifted upward – i.e., it will be reached only at a higher level of both rates. A movement of the two interest rates in opposite directions would require that a rise in the short rate is associated with a fall in the expected long rate.

If the increased demand for funds impinges on the market for long-term capital, the immediate effect will be a rise in the long rate, a shift from bills into consols and from cash into bills and consols, with the further consequence that the short rate will also rise and cash holdings will be channelled into the transaction sphere. As a result of the rising long-term rate, more and more investors, each expecting a higher R_1 than his "predecessor", will be lured out of cash or bills and into consols. As far as we can see, the short rate can here rise more, less, or in step with the long rate even if we assume that none of the investors will change his expectations with respect to R_1. In the new equilibrium, it must again be true that at the margin $r_0'=R_0'+(R_0'/R_1')-1$, where R_0' is higher than R_0 (the long-term interest rate in the initial position), and R_1' – the long rate expected for t_1 by the new marginal holder of consols who has just shifted into consols from cash or bills – is higher than R_1, the long rate expected for t_1 by the previous marginal holder of consols. If R_0'/R_1' is higher than R_0/R_1 was in the initial situation, then r_0' must lie above r_0 by a larger amount than that by which R_0' lies above R_0; the short rate rises more than the long rate. The opposite will be true if $(R_0'/R_1')<(R_0/R_1)$. To state precisely under which conditions the one or the other would happen is hardly worth-while.

A movement of the short and the long rate in opposite directions may also occur. This is possible if a rise in the long rate induces expectations for a rise in R_1 such that all holders of consols down to the marginal one will anticipate sufficiently large capital losses.

We shall not analyse the case of a decrease in the demand for short or long funds or of an increase in the supply of investible funds, nor will we examine the case of an increase in the demand for funds on the short or long market accompanied by an increase in the supply of new funds out of savings. Let us instead summarize our results.

First we take over two results from section I:

1. The long rate will as a rule be lying above the short rate.

2. The long rate will lie below the short rate only when even the most pessimistic holder of consols still expects a capital gain (a fall of the long rate). This will be the more probable, the higher the long rate is.

To these conclusions we add, as result of the present section:

3. In general one ought to expect that the long and the short rate will change in the same direction, and that the short rate will fluctuate more strongly than the long rate.

4. A movement of the two rates in opposite directions will occur if a rise in the short rate, induced by an increased demand for short-term funds, is accompanied by a large enough downward change in the expectations about the future long rate; or a divergent movement may occur if a rise in the long rate, due to an increased demand for long-term funds, is accompanied by a large enough upward change in the expectations about the future long rate. Corresponding conditions can be formulated for the case of a decline in demand for short-term or long-term funds. The same conditions might, instead of inducing a movement in opposite directions, merely cause the short rate to fluctuate less strongly than the long rate.

These results do not fit too badly the course of the long and short rates of interest which is shown in Figure 39 for England and the United States of America for the years 1952–1961. The graph shows three characteristic features:

1. The short rate fluctuates more than the long rate.

2. Both rates as a rule move in the same direction, although deviations from this rule are not infrequent. In the 120 months of the period 1952–1961 the rates moved in opposite directions in England in 38 months and in the United States in 46 months.

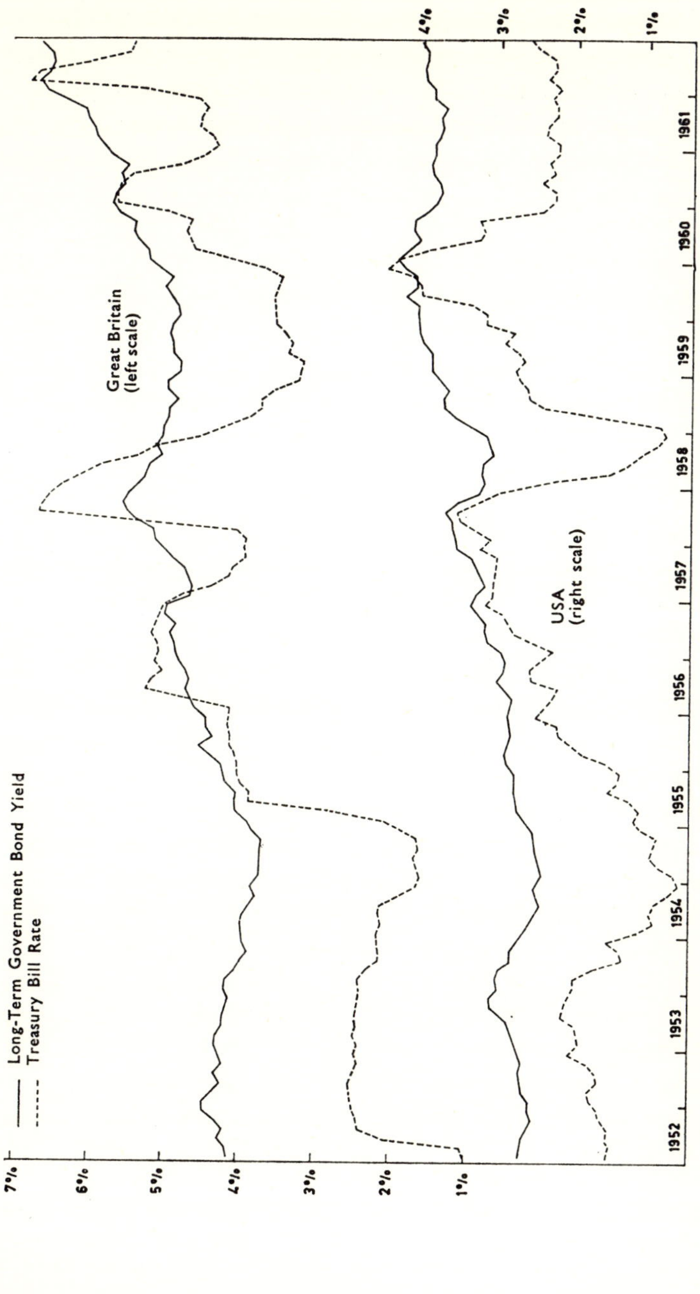

Fig. 39. Short-Term and Long-Term Interest Rate in Great Britain and in the United States, 1952–1961. Sources: *Monthly Digest of Statistics* (London) and *Federal Reserve Bulletin.*

3. The short rate lies above the long rate only if the latter is exceptionally high.

It should, however, be remembered that hitherto the banking system, which has a decisive influence on interest rates, has not yet been brought into the picture. This will be done in the next chapter.

CHAPTER 22

BANKING SYSTEM AND INTEREST RATES

Hitherto we have hardly even mentioned the banking system, although experience shows that, at least in the short run, it can exert a dominating influence on the level of interest rates. We must now make up for this sin of omission. The influence of the banking system stems above all from its capacity to create money; but before we discuss this, we must say a word about the interrelation between the long-term rate of interest and the rate on short-term bank loans. In our previous analysis of the interdependence of the short and long interest rates, we have assumed that entrepreneurs in need of short-term funds issue marketable bills. The most important form of short-term financing, however, consists in borrowing from the banks.

I. Loan Rate and Long-Term Interest Rate

If we could assume that the interest rate on short-term loans is a free market rate as is the rate on Treasury bills in the Anglo-Saxon countries, we could conclude that each bank – given its yield expectations, its evaluation of the risks involved and its attitude to risk – will choose that combination of bank loans and longer-term bonds[1] which leaves it indifferent at the margin between investing a dollar in short-term loans or in securities. The time horizon underlying the yield comparison between short-term loans and bonds may, of course, be different for different banks. If a rise in the yield on long-term bonds is expected, the composition of assets would shift in favour of bonds with the consequence of a rise in the loan rate and a fall in the long-term rate, and vice versa if the expectations should move in the opposite direction. An increased demand

[1] For simplicity's sake we restrict the analysis here to these two types of assets, since the relationship between investment in long and in short-term securities has been discussed earlier.

by entrepreneurs for bank loans would raise the interest rate on these loans; and, since the banks would (on the assumption of a given volume of loanable funds) shift from bonds into loans, it would also raise the rate on bonds. Under the assumption of a competitive loan market, we would come to exactly the same conclusion as in our analysis of the choice between cash and bonds or between bonds and bills, and we would not have to repeat this analysis as applied to the choice between bank loans and bonds.

The rate on bank loans, however, is not a free market rate like that on long-term bonds or on Treasury bills.[2] Nor is it uniform; it varies according to the client, according to the magnitude of the loan, and other criteria. We shall do best to assume here that the entire range of loan rates is determined directly by the discount rate and lies above the latter.

Under these circumstances it is possible that the banks will not be able to reach the optimum mixture of loans and bonds, because, when the loan rate is tied to the discount rate, there may not be enough demand for bank credit. The rate on long-term bonds will then be lower, and the loan rate higher, than they would be if the loan rate were a free market rate. If an additional demand for bank credit arises in such a situation, the bank will shift from bonds into loans even though the loan rate has not changed. The sale of bonds causes the long rate to rise, and ultimately the point may be reached at which the expectations with respect to the yields on long-term bonds have improved so much that further "shifting" ceases because the optimum combination of loans and bonds has been attained. At this point Roosa's "locking-in effect" takes hold.[3]

It is, of course, theoretically possible that, with appropriately optimistic yield expectations for long-term bonds, the banks will shift from loans into bonds even though the demand for credit at the given loan rate has not yet been satisfied. But the observation of banks' management of funds leads us to conclude that, as a rule, the ratio of loans to bonds deviates from the optimum in favour of bonds, so that banks are always ready to

[2] In Germany the loan rate set by the banking system (at 4.5 per cent above the discount rate) is a maximum rate which can be underbid. In England most clients pay a rate of one per cent above the discount rate. In the United States the loan rate is not tied in any such way, but even there it is relatively immobile compared with the rate on long-term securities.

[3] See Robert V. Roosa, 'Interest Rates and the Central Bank', in *Money, Trade, and Economic Growth*, in honor of John Henry Williams (New York, 1951), pp. 270–295.

sell bonds if the demand for credit increases.[4] Banks will shift into bonds only if the demand for credit falls off. It follows that an increase in the demand for bank credit will not cause the loan rate to rise so long as the discount rate remains unchanged; the increase will, instead, cause the long-term rate to increase because the banks will sell bonds. Conversely, the long rate but not the loan rate will fall if the demand for bank loans declines. If the liquidity of the banks is reduced and the banks must contract their assets, the banks will sell bonds rather than reduce their loans so that the loan rate will remain unchanged while the long rate will rise.[5]

II. Bank Liquidity and Short-Term Interest Rates

We shall now turn to the effect of bank liquidity on interest rates, an effect which ultimately stems from the fact that this liquidity determines the lending capacity of the banks. The liquidity of the banking system is increased whenever commercial banks experience an inflow of cash in the form of central bank money: liquidity is decreased by an outflow. We should thus expect that an inflow of central bank money would lower the level of interest rates and an outflow would raise it. However, such textbook platitudes, which are not even entirely correct, do not suffice for our purpose. We have to go a little further afield in order to analyse the relationship between bank liquidity and the level of interest rates. In undertaking this, we have to introduce a new rate of interest, the interbank rate on day-to-day loans of central bank money which in the United States is called the "Federal Funds rate".

A bank that is or expects to be short in its holding of those forms of reserve money which it must legally, or conventionally, keep as a per-

[4] For example, between January 20th and June 15th, 1960 – a period during which Bank Rate did not change – the English clearing banks sold government bonds worth £ 326 million, or 21 % of their investment in such bonds, and expanded their "advances" by roughly £ 300 million. The interest rate on long-term government bonds (maturities of 15–25 years) rose considerably during the same period, undoubtedly under the influence of these sales (January average 5.34, June average 5.65 per cent).

[5] From the point of view of the central bank, it is of course important that a restrictive monetary policy can push up the long rates by inducing the banks to sell securities when the demand of entrepreneurs for bank credits is rising; and vice versa in the case of an expansive monetary policy. Essentially, this is the manner in which an increase in the discount rate pulls the long rates up.

centage of its deposits can obtain such funds in various ways.[6] It might borrow central bank money for a day from other banks; it might let short-term assets – especially bills – "run off" without replacement, or it might sell them off prematurely; it might, thirdly, borrow money from the central bank. Conversely, a bank might use inflowing central bank funds to lend to other banks, to purchase bills, or to repay central bank credit. The existence of these three alternatives implies that the interbank rate on central bank money (Federal Funds) for a day, the rate on bills, and the official discount rate are interdependent. The following conclusions can be drawn.

1. The rate on central bank money borrowed for a day from other banks cannot rise above the discount rate in any banking system in which the central bank does not set a limit to the rediscount facilities of each bank and in which, in addition, the central bank is ready to lend to banks for one day. If this rate did rise higher, borrowing from the central bank would become advantageous. The discount rate thus forms the upper limit for the rate on day-to-day funds. The "Federal Funds rate" in fact only once[7] exceeded the official discount rate during the period 1952–1961. (Figure 40 shows the deviations of the Federal Funds rate from the discount rate during this period.) In banking systems in which the rediscounting facilities of the individual banks are restricted and/or in which a bill to be rediscounted must have at least several days before maturity – both conditions apply to the Federal Republic of Germany – it can, of course, happen that the rate on day-to-day funds rises above the discount rate. For once the rediscounting facilities of a bank are exhausted, rediscounting as an alternative no longer exists, and the discount rate can therefore no longer be considered the upper limit of what the bank is willing to pay for central bank money. If a bill is required to have several days left until maturity in order to be eligible for rediscounting, it is also possible that a bank would be willing to pay a rate higher than the discount rate for one-day central bank money, provided it expects that the

[6] In what follows we have in mind a banking system of the type existing in the Federal Republic of Germany and in the United States of America. For England the presentation would have to run along different lines.

[7] In August, 1957. In 1966 the Federal Funds rate was frequently above the discount rate. The explanation for this phenomenon is probably the aversion of the banks to be indebted to the Federal Reserve Banks, an aversion which is likely to grow with their indebtedness.

day-to-day rate will drop again in the very near future. If, besides the discount rate, there exists a higher rate on central bank advances against collateral security (*Lombard* loans), and if such advances are to be had for a single day and are not part of the rediscounting facilities, then the rate for day-to-day money can rise above the discount rate but not above this *Lombard* rate. This, too, can be empirically verified.[8]

2. Since Treasury bills and day-to-day loans of central bank funds are closely related assets, the prices of these two – i.e., the interest rates – have to move, on the whole, parallel to each other. However, since they are not perfect substitutes, it is quite possible that the rate on day-to-day funds may come to lie either above or below that on Treasury bills. But the difference between the two rates can never become very large. This can also be verified empirically.[9] The parallelism of the two rates has been shown graphically so often, both for the United States and for the Federal Republic of Germany, that we can here do without presenting empirical evidence.[10]

Since the Treasury bill rate can thus come to lie somewhat above the rate on day-to-day money, and since the latter rate can rise up to the level of the discount rate (or the *Lombard* rate), the bill rate can rise somewhat above the discount rate (or the *Lombard* rate). A definite upper limit cannot be given.

Let us now start from a situation in which the commercial banks are in debt to the central bank – i.e., in which their so-called "free reserves" (excess reserves less debts to the central bank) are negative – and let us

[8] In 1966 however, the rate for day-to-day money in Frankfurt was occasionally above even the *Lombard* rate.

[9] One reason for the absence of perfect substitutability between Treasury bills and loans of day-to-day money is the difference in the length of their term to maturity; in this respect only bills one day short of redemption are exactly equal to day-to-day money. In Germany the repurchase of Treasury bills by the central bank is effected at a discount rate higher than the rate at which it sells bills, so that it is advantageous for a bank which is short of cash to go into the market for day-to-day money even if the rate charged there is a little above the issue rate on Treasury bills. Finally, not all banks participate in both markets. In the United States, for instance, many banks never enter the market for "Federal Funds", so that for them day-to-day money is never considered as a substitute for Treasury bills. A whole series of such reasons explain the imperfectness of substitutability between the two types of assets and accordingly also the difference which may arise between the two rates.

[10] We refer the reader to Figs. 4 and 5 in F. A. Lutz, 'Die Liquidität des Banksystems und die Zinssätze', *Weltwirtschaftliches Archiv*, **87** (1961) 273–305.

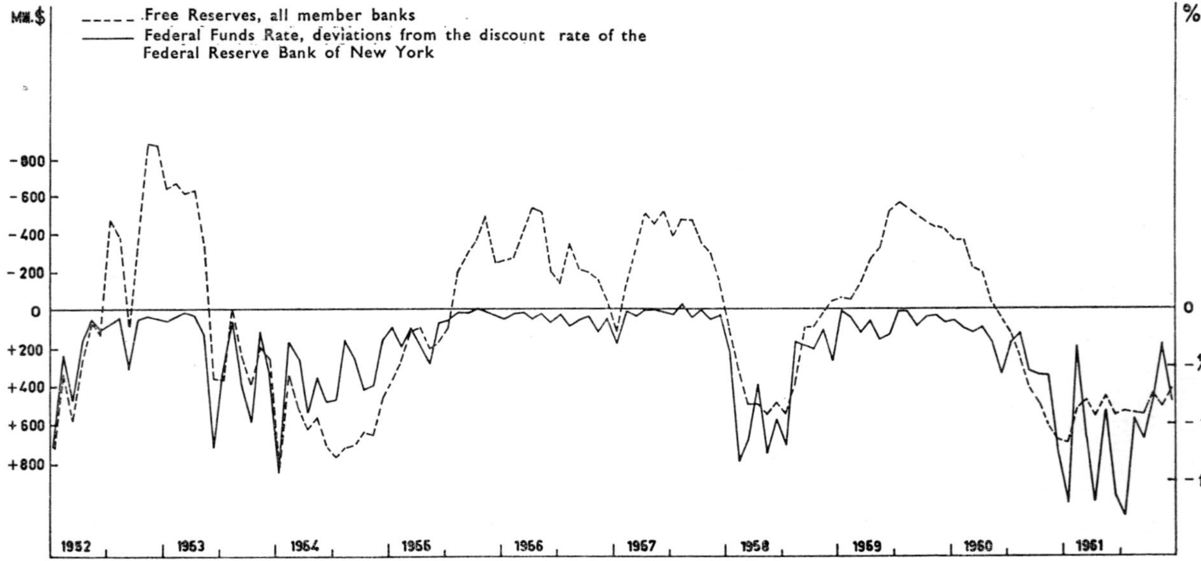

Fig. 40. Free Reserves and Federal Funds Rate (Deviations from the Discount Rate) in the United States of America, 1952–1961. Sources: *Federal Reserve Bulletin* and *New York Times.*

assume that central bank money is now flowing into the commercial banks. The most important causes of such inflows are: the acquisition of gold or of foreign exchange and open-market purchases by the central bank or a net inflow of bank notes into the commercial banks. A reduction of the minimum reserve requirements, by freeing reserves, would have the same effect.

In the initial situation the rate on day-to-day money and the Treasury bill rate will lie at the level of the discount rate. The first two rates, as we know, cannot be lower than the discount rate because, if they were, it would be advantageous for a bank to sell bills or borrow day-to-day money in order to discharge its debt to the central bank. These two rates cannot be significantly higher because, again, a bank managing its funds will do what is most advantageous. If central bank money now flows into the banking system for one of the reasons indicated, the rate on day-to-day interbank loans and the bill rate will not immediately fall below the discount rate, because as long as the system is on balance in debt to the central bank – i.e., as long as free reserves are negative – the demand of the indebted banks for central bank money with which they can liquidate their debt to the central bank is perfectly elastic at the given discount rate. The influx of central bank money – the increase in the banking system's liquidity – will here bring about a decline in the banks' indebtedness to the central bank; but it will not, so long as the discount rate remains unchanged, cause a fall in the interest rates. Only when free reserves have become positive will the increased liquidity of the banks lead to a larger supply of funds in the money markets and thus to a decline of the two interest rates.[11] These conclusions can be verified for the United States. In Figure 40 the solid line shows the deviations of the Federal Funds rate from the discount rate, and the dashed line represents the volume of free reserves on an inverted scale (i.e., an increase of the free reserves will appear as a decline in the curve, and vice versa). It can be seen that the Federal Funds rate sticks to the discount rate whenever free reserves of the banking system are negative.[12] It can also be observed that if free

[11] It must here be borne in mind that not all banks in the United States make use of the Federal Funds market, so that the free reserves can become positive while there is still some indebtedness to the Federal Reserve banks left.

[12] In the Federal Republic of Germany, in contrast to the United States, the rate for day-to-day money occasionally falls below the discount rate even if free reserves are negative. The reason for this may be that the banks which had borrowed from the

reserves are positive, their movement fairly closely determines the movement of the rate on Federal Funds.

An outflow of central bank money and the resulting decline in the liquidity and lending capacity of the banks will, should it occur when commercial banks are not in debt to the central bank and when the discount rate lies above the two money market rates, drive these rates up to the level of the discount rate. One might perhaps expect that the money market rates would not rise so long as the free reserves are positive – so long as net excess reserves exist; and one might think that they would jump abruptly to the ceiling given by the discount rate as soon as the free reserves become negative. But the facts contradict this hypothesis. The gradual rise of the money market rates has a rational explanation under the assumption that banks attach a positive utility to the liquidity of excess reserves, with the result that they ask for ever higher rates, the more reserves they sacrifice. While the outflow of central bank money continues, the banks will begin to borrow from the central bank once the Federal Funds rate and the Treasury bill rate reach the discount rate. The money market rates will rise no further so long as the discount rate is not raised. When it is raised, the money market rates will follow at once. While they remain below the discount rate, it will be advantageous for banks to sell Treasury bills or to borrow day-to-day funds rather than to continue borrowing from the central bank. In such a case, accordingly, discount rate policy will be effective without the support of open-market policy or changes in the reserve requirements. Empirical investigations indeed show that sudden sharp rises of the short-term rates are always attributable to changes in the discount rate.

We can thus draw the following preliminary conclusions, taking the official discount rate as a datum. The discount rate or the *Lombard* rate is (roughly) the upper limit for the money market rates on one-day funds and on bills. If the commercial banks are in debt to the central bank, these

---

central bank can replace the rediscounted bills (which in Germany have to have at least 5 days to maturity in order to be eligible) by day-to-day funds only as the bills mature; consequently, at a rate equal to the discount rate, the demand for day-to-day money for the purpose of discharging debts to the central bank may be smaller than the supply from banks which have day-to-day funds to offer, even though the central bank is still holding rediscounted bills. Nevertheless, the connection between free reserves and the rate on day-to-day money is also in the Federal Republic very close. See Figure 7 in the paper mentioned in footnote 10, *supra*.

rates will be at the level of the discount (or *Lombard*) rate. Increases in the liquidity of the banking system through an inflow of central bank money will not cause a fall of the money market rates so long as the indebtedness to the central bank has not been liquidated. Once this has been done, further increases in liquidity will cause a fall in the money market rates. If we start from a situation in which the banks are not indebted to the central bank, a decline in bank liquidity will force the money market rates up to the level of the discount (or *Lombard*) rate. Once this level is reached, the money market rates will stick to it unless the discount rate itself is changed.

III. Bank Liquidity and Other Factors Affecting Interest Rates

Our conclusions in the last section may be reformulated and expanded to include some of our earlier results simply by saying that the level of bank liquidity, as measured by the free reserves, determines the money market rates – subject to the ceiling given by the discount (or *Lombard*) rate – while the expectations of the market participants determine the relationship of the long-term rates to the short-term rates. This statement should not be interpreted to mean that all those factors which, in our preceding analysis, were shown to have an influence on the short rates could in practice be neglected. They influence the interest rates via their effect on bank liquidity as measured by the free reserves. Free reserves are, directly or indirectly, linked to all the interactions that occur whenever there is a change in any of those factors which, according to our previous analysis, affect the interest rates. We shall illustrate this by a few examples.

In the preceding chapter we investigated how an increase in the demand for short-term funds – e.g. through an increased issue of Treasury bills – raises the short-term interest rate and, as a rule, also the long-term rate. If the banking system is included in the analysis, the rise in interest rates takes place in the following manner. If free reserves are positive in the initial situation, each individual bank having excess reserves will be induced by the upward tendency of the Treasury bill rate to acquire additional bills. Banks without excess reserves – and also those with excess reserves, even though perhaps only at a later stage – may see cause to sell longer-term securities in favour of Treasury bills, with the effect that the longer rates will also rise. The purchase of Treasury bills by the banks having excess reserves reduces the level of these reserves – in the first instance because of the expansion of deposits associated with such purchases, and secondly because such expansion is normally accompanied by a withdrawal of bank notes from the banking system. The increase in the demand for short-term funds is thus accompanied by a reduction of free reserves; but this decline in bank liquidity is clearly not the final cause of the rise in interest rates. Once the Treasury bill rate has reached the level of the discount rate, a further increase in demand for short-term funds can no longer raise the short-term rates, since the banks can borrow from the central bank at the given discount rate. However, in such a situation the central bank will, as a rule, raise the discount rate, so that a continued increase in the demand for short-term funds will raise the short rates still further. Thus the results obtained in the previous chapters remain valid even when the banking system is taken into account.

Let us take a second example. The government or the entrepreneurs issue long-term securities. The long rate begins to rise. If the banks themselves, on the basis of their excess reserves, begin to buy such new securities, the process will develop as in the last example: the free reserves will shrink for the two reasons discussed above. The increasing tightness of central bank money together with the desire to shift from short paper into longer maturities will have the effect of driving up the short rate as free reserves shrink. If the "public" alone and not banks buy the newly issued securities, possibly because the latter are not of the type eligible for bank investment, the same effects will occur but as indirect consequences of the public's security purchases. One such repercussion would be arbitrage operations between securities of different types so that ultimately there is an effect on those securities that banks are interested in, at which point banks will start buying, thus reducing their free reserves. Another possible repercussion is that, in purchasing the newly issued securities, the public will most likely transform saving balances and time deposits into demand deposits, with the immediate effect of a reduction in the excess reserves of banks since demand deposits have a higher reserve requirement than time deposits. Finally, cash will flow out of the banking system because in an expanding economy cash in circulation usually increases.

A third example: the public increases its demand for long-term bonds, paying for them with funds that stem either from dishoarding or from additional saving. The long-term rate falls, changing the configuration of the financial market in such a way that short-term paper becomes relatively more profitable for individuals as well as for banks. Sales of long-term bonds by banks contract the volume of deposits and have the immediate effect of increasing free reserves. The banks' increased purchases of short-term paper, which now follow, cause the deposits to expand again and the short rates to fall. It should be noted that the very temporary expansion of free reserves – since the shift from long into short assets requires little time – can rarely be caught in the statistics. After all, not *every* change in the short rate has been accompanied by a change in the opposite direction in the statistical data showing free reserves. (See Figure 40.) Such exceptions are, however, relatively rare.

These examples should suffice to show that changes in free reserves or changes in the short-term rates which accompany them do not necessarily originate in the inflow or outflow of central bank money into or out of the commercial banks. It is true that cases in which this is so are in reality particularly important since the inflow of central bank money through open-market purchases or purchases of gold and foreign exchange by the central bank (and vice versa) belong to the most frequent and quantitatively most significant causes of changes in the free reserves of the banking system. But it would be wrong to believe that the correlation between changes in the amount of free reserves and changes in the short rates justifies the conclusion that, as determinants of short-term rates, we may consider only the banks' supply of central bank money and neglect all other factors determining interest rates. Hence the analysis of changes in the level and term structure of rates, such as we conducted in the preceding chapter, remains applicable also when the banking system is drawn into the analysis. The existence of banks even intensifies the interdependence of interest rates. Suppose, for instance, that by buying bonds the central bank lowers the long rate and at the same time creates excess reserves (or increases existing excess reserves) in the commercial banks. As a result the short rates will also decline. The fall in the long rate thus spreads to the short rates, even though it does not induce a single individual investor or bank to shift from long-term bonds into short paper – that is, even though direct arbitrage operations between the markets for short-term and long-term funds are entirely absent.

CHAPTER 23

THE RATE OF INTEREST IN GENERAL EQUILIBRIUM

In a general equilibrium analysis it is not possible to take account of all those variables which we considered in our partial equilibrium analysis. To avoid having the system of equations become unmanageable, we must construct a model which is drastically simplified in comparison with reality.

I. The Model

Since our main concern is with investment and the interest rate, our model will reflect, not a stationary economy, but a progressive one in which investment is taking place.

Let us imagine a closed economy in which only one consumer good and one capital good are produced. Let the latter – as well as all pre-existing capital goods – have a perpetual "life" once produced, so that we can neglect depreciation and replacement. Thus all investments are net investments. The capital goods existing at the beginning of the period supply services which have a price just like the services of labour. We could imagine that the capital goods are leased to the entrepreneurs; but even if this is not the case, the entrepreneurs have to impute to their capital goods a contribution to the product which corresponds to the price they would have to pay if they were lessees. Hence we shall simply speak of the price of capital services. Like labour, capital goods can be used in both the consumer goods and the producer goods industry. In other words, the two factors of production are not specific, that is, not tied to a given industry. We also assume that in each of the two branches labour services and capital services can be used in varying combinations – i.e., that the technical coefficients are not fixed. Since we have only one type of capital good, we have to imagine that more or less labour can be combined with a unit of capital. We neglect circulating capital.

In our system of equations, we start out from a given capital stock in the form of a given *number* of capital goods yielding productive services. Thereby, we satisfy, in principle, one of the requirements for an adequate theory which emerged from the analysis of the interest theories of Böhm-Bawerk, Wicksell and Åkerman. Their use of a capital stock in the form of a sum of *value* was found to be inadmissible. The assumption of a given quantity of capital services, which brings us close to Walras, allows us, as we shall see, to trace the effect of the existing capital stock on the interest rate, an effect which was neglected by all those authors (Fisher, Keynes and his followers) in whose systems only current investment in value terms appears explicitly.

However, our model radically simplifies the investment process by assuming only one kind of capital good which has, moreover, an infinite length of life. If we were to try to include in the general equilibrium system all the possible investment types which were defined in the course of the debate on the interest problem – the "point input–point output" case with or without variability of the time span between input and output, the "point input–continuous output" case with or without variability of the lifetime of the durable capital good, etc. –, our model would become so complicated, and the tracing of the effects of changes in the data so difficult, that we would find ourselves thrown back to investigating such changes within a framework of partial equilibrium analysis, as we did in Chapter 21. It was certainly not by accident that Böhm-Bawerk, Wicksell and Åkerman based their general equilibrium analysis on only *one* type of investment.

The interest rate in our system of equations is identical with the marginal rate of return on new investments. Like most authors (from Böhm-Bawerk to Modigliani) we have omitted the equations reflecting the market for securities, but we shall later indicate, how this market can be introduced. Meanwhile the reader may, if he so wishes, identify the interest rate in our system of equations with the rate on the consols that are being issued during the period under consideration for the purpose of financing new investments.

We assume the quantity of money to be constant. The central bank is holding the commercial banks by a tight rein. This presupposes, as we know from the discussion in the preceding chapter, that the commercial banks are in debt to the central bank. The assumption further implies that, for the quantity of money to remain constant in the case of changes in data – as, e.g., a shift in the saving function – the central bank must let its discount rate follow the market very closely. Thus the discount rate in a general equilibrium analysis can not be taken as a datum, as it was in the preceding chapter, but must be considered one of the variables. Since we work with only one rate of interest, we must imagine that the central bank sets a buying (selling) rate for consols which exactly and at all times reflects the market rate, so that no sales of securities to the central bank (purchases from the central bank) will occur. The central bank rate will then simply be identical with the long-term market rate. Discount policy in this system thus is purely passive. If for any reason we want to investigate the effects of a change in the datum "quantity of money", we have to assume that the bank temporarily does not simply follow the market; instead – if it wants to increase the quantity of money – it sets the buying rate for securities below the level which would have resulted from the market forces determining the interest rate under the assumption of a constant money supply. A dependent variable is thus, so to speak, turned into an independent one.

We neglect problems of uncertainty about the future and hence of risk by assuming subjective certainty.

Following Walras, we express all values in our system of equations in real terms by taking one good – here the consumer good – as the unit of account (*numéraire*). Hence the price of this good in terms of the *numéraire* is equal to unity. The price of the unit of account in terms of money, and hence the price level, will then be determined by the money equation.

After this description of the most important features of our model, we shall now turn to the presentation of the system of equations. Further assumptions underlying certain features of the model will be discussed as we explain the system itself.

II. The System of Equations

In our system of equations we use the following symbols:

x_c = Quantity of consumer goods produced

x_k = Quantity of capital goods produced

x_k^c = Capital goods sold to the consumer goods industry

x_k^k = Capital goods sold to the capital goods industry

q_c^0 = Capital services used in the consumer goods industry in the current period
q_k^0 = Capital services used in the capital goods industry in the current period
q_c^1 = q_c^0 *plus* the capital services made available to the consumer goods industry during the current period through the purchase of x_k^c, but utilized only from the next period on
q_k^1 = q_k^0 *plus* new capital services available in the next period in the capital goods industry through the purchase of x_k^k
$\bar{q}^0$ = Total supply of capital services in the current period (given)
l_c = Labour services used in the consumer goods industry
l_k = Labour services used in the capital goods industry
$\bar{l}$ = Total supply of labour services (given)
p_c = Price of the consumer good in terms of money
p_k = Price of the capital good
p_l = Price of the labour service (wage rate)
p_q = Price of the capital service in the current period
p_q' = Price of the capital service in the next period
i = Rate of interest
I = Investment
S = Saving
Y = National income
$\bar{M}$ = Quantity of money (given)

ϕ_{l_c}, ϕ_{l_k}, $\phi_{q_c^0}$, $\phi_{q_k^0}$, $\phi_{q_c^1}$, $\phi_{q_k^1}$ are first partial derivatives of the function ϕ and stand for the marginal products of the productive factors.

The unknowns in the system of equations which now follows are: x_c, x_k, x_k^c, x_k^k, q_c^0, q_k^0, q_c^1, q_k^1, l_c, l_k, p_c, p_k, p_l, p_q, p_q', i, S, I, and Y – hence 19 unknowns altogether.

The system of equations, arranged by markets, is as follows:
Consumer goods market:

$$x_c = \phi(l_c, q_c^0) \tag{1}$$

$$x_c = l_c \frac{p_l}{p_c} + q_c^0 \frac{p_q}{p_c} \tag{1a}$$

$$x_c = \bar{l} \frac{p_l}{p_c} + \bar{q}^0 \frac{p_q}{p_c} - \frac{S}{p_c} \tag{1b}$$

Capital goods market:

$$x_k = a\phi(l_k, q_k^0) \tag{2}$$

$$x_k \frac{p_k}{p_c} = l_k \frac{p_l}{p_c} + q_k^0 \frac{p_q}{p_c} \tag{2a}$$

$$\phi_{q_c^1} = \frac{p_q'}{p_c} \tag{3}$$

$$a\phi_{q_k^1} \frac{p_k}{p_c} = \frac{p_q'}{p_c} \tag{4}$$

$$q_c^1 = q_c^0 + x_k^c \tag{5}$$

$$q_k^1 = q_k^0 + x_k^k \tag{6}$$

$$\frac{\dfrac{p_q'}{p_c}}{i} = \frac{p_k}{p_c} \tag{7}$$

$$x_k^c + x_k^k = x_k \tag{8}$$

Labour market:

$$\phi_{l_c} = \frac{p_l}{p_c} \tag{9}$$

$$a\phi_{l_k} \frac{p_k}{p_c} = \frac{p_l}{p_c} \tag{10}$$

$$l_c + l_k = \bar{l} \tag{11}$$

Market for capital services:

$$\phi_{q_c^0} = \frac{p_q}{p_c} \tag{12}$$

$$a\phi_{q_k^0} \frac{p_k}{p_c} = \frac{p_q}{p_c} \tag{13}$$

$$q_c^0 + q_k^0 = \bar{q}^0 \tag{14}$$

Capital market:

$$\frac{I}{p_c} = x_k \frac{p_k}{p_c} \tag{15}$$

$$\frac{S}{p_c} = s\left(\frac{Y}{p_c}, i, \frac{\bar{M}}{p_c}\right) \tag{16}$$

$$\frac{I}{p_c} = \frac{S}{p_c} \tag{17}$$

Money market:

$$\frac{\bar{M}}{p_c} = m\left(\frac{Y}{p_c}, i, \frac{\bar{M}}{p_c}\right) \tag{18}$$

Definition:

$$\frac{Y}{p_c} = x_c + x_k \frac{p_k}{p_c} \tag{19}$$

Consumer goods market: The first equation expresses the production of the consumer good, x_c, as a function of the quantity of labour used in the production, l_c, and of the capital services used, q_c^0, where the unit of capital services is the service produced by one unit of the capital good. We assume that this production function is linearly homogeneous. Equation (1a) equates the value of consumer goods produced with their costs, consisting of wages and payments for capital services. (Since we use the consumer good as the *numéraire*, the value of consumer goods produced is identical with the quantity produced.) This equation can be derived from others, so it cannot be counted as an independent equation.[1] Equation (1b) states the equality between the quantity of consumer goods demanded and national income (sum of wage income and income from capital services) *less* current saving. This equation, too, can be derived from others and hence may not be counted.[2]

Capital goods market: Equation (2) expresses the production of capital goods as a function of labour services and capital services used. For simplicity's sake[3] we shall assume that the production function is again linearly homogeneous, and also that it is different from the production function of the consumer goods industry only by a multiplicative factor a; this merely means that the conventional unit of the investment good can be produced with an a-fold multiple of the quantity of factors used in the consumer goods industry to produce a conventional unit of the consumer

[1] It can be obtained from (1) by Euler's theorem for linearly homogeneous functions, and from (9) and (12) which equate the marginal products of the two factors to their prices.

[2] It follows from (1a), (2a), (11), (14), (15) and (17).

[3] This assumption simplifies considerably the mathematical treatment contained in Section 6 of our Mathematical Appendix, which is tedious enough as it is.

good. Circulating capital will be disregarded. The assumption that two products are being produced with identical production functions is preferable to the still more unrealistic assumption that only one product is produced which can be used either as a consumption or as an investment good. Since the factor prices – that is, p_l and p_q – are equal in both industries, our assumption of identical production functions signifies that both production processes are always equally capital- and labour-intensive.

Equation (2a) sets the value of capital goods produced equal to the cost of labour services and capital services used. Like its counterpart (1a), it cannot be counted as an independent equation since it can be derived from other equations.

Equations (3) and (4), which refer to the consumer goods and producer goods industries respectively, require a somewhat more extensive explanation. In these equations the value of the marginal products of the capital services q_c^1 and q_k^1 – i.e., the value of the marginal products of the capital services after these have been expanded by the services yielded by capital goods produced during the current period – are set equal to the price of a capital service in the next period. We obviously have to assume that the value of the marginal product of the expanded quantity of capital services available in the next period (p_q'/p_c) is lower than the current price (p_q/p_c) of the services of capital goods used during the current period. With respect to all other prices, we assume that the entrepreneurs expect them to be constant. The price of capital services is an exception. The entrepreneurs are assumed to anticipate a fall in the marginal product, and therefore in the price of capital services for the next period, because the stock of capital goods will be larger. It follows that capital goods, all of which have the same price whether they are old or new, must yield a higher return in the current period than in the next period. If we wanted to avoid the conclusion that p_q'/p_c expected for the next period will be lower than p_q/p_c in the current period, we would have to assume either: (1) that the entrepreneurs figured with an increase in the supply of labour services proportional to the increase in capital, in which case the rate of return on capital (the marginal product of capital) would not drop; or, (2) we would have to neglect the time-lag between the production and utilization of new capital goods so that the marginal product of capital services appearing in equations (12) and (13) would include the effects of services from the capital goods produced during the current period.

We can illustrate these relationships with the help of Figure 41. The curve $\phi_{q_c}(l_c, q_c)$ represents the first partial derivative with respect to q_c of the production function for x_c. It thus shows the marginal product of capital services in the consumer goods industry. At q_c^0 we can read off the marginal product of the capital services currently used in the consumer goods industry as q_c^0G. At q_c^1 the marginal product of capital services, after these have been increased by x_k^c, can be seen to be q_c^1G'. (We remember that one unit of the capital good throws off one unit of capital service during the unit period.) The marginal product at q_c^0 is equal to the price p_q/p_c (equation (12)), and the marginal product at q_c^1 is equal to the price p_q'/p_c expected for the next period. Corresponding statements can be made for the capital goods industry.

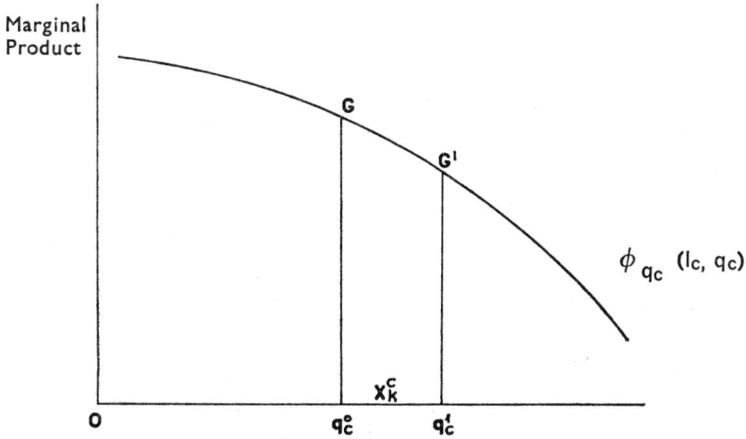

Fig. 41.

Equations (5) and (6) offer no special difficulties. Since one unit of capital services corresponds to each unit of the capital good, we can measure the capital services due to the production of new capital goods by the quantity of these capital goods.

Equation (7) equates the expected next-period price of a unit of capital service, capitalized at the interest rate, to the price of the capital good. By capitalizing the price of this service (or, what amounts to the same thing, the value of the marginal product of newly produced capital services) in the same way in which the coupon yield on consols is capitalized with "the" interest rate, we implicitly assume that entrepreneurs figure from the second period on with a constant marginal product of capital services. But, on the assumption that the supply of labour services is constant and that no inventions are made, this marginal product would stay unchanged only were the economy to be stationary from the second period on. This, however, would contradict some of our other equations. Equation (4) in particular implies that capital services will be used in the next period in the production of capital goods, while under our assumption of infinite durability of capital goods, the productive factors in a stationary state would all be used in the production of consumer goods.[4] We shall thus have to argue that, while the entrepreneurs indeed expect the events of the next period to be different from those of the current period, they erroneously figure with no further changes after that. If we wanted to avoid this assumption, we would have to follow Lindahl in developing a system which from the beginning contains all expected changes up to a stationary state after *n* periods. We would then obtain a series of successive short interest rates for all periods up to the stationary state, and the longer rates for terms to maturity from 2 to *n* periods as averages of these short rates. In the stationary state after *n* periods, the rates on bonds of all terms to maturity would be equal. Those perpetual capital goods produced in the current period would, in the stationary state, render an infinite series of identical marginal products. This series of marginal products would first have to be discounted to the beginning of the stationary state at the ruling interest rate. The value so obtained would then have to be discounted to the present with the long rate for *n* periods; and, to this value, we would have to add the present values of the successive decreasing marginal products of the services during the *n* periods up to the stationary state, each discounted at the rate applicable to the time span from the present to the period in which the marginal product emerges. In this manner we would obtain the present value of the capital good, which would have to be equated to its price, as in equation (7). But an all-encompassing system of equations of this type would be so complicated that the effects of changes in data on the variables in the system, the analysis of which is our main interest here, could no longer be traced with precision.

Equation (8) expresses the equality of the number of capital goods sold

[4] From this point of view it would have been better not to assume infinite durability of the capital goods.

to the consumer goods industry and to the capital goods industry with the total number of capital goods produced.

Labour market: Equations (9) and (10) equate the value of the marginal product of labour in consumer goods production and capital goods production to the price of labour services, i.e. to the wage rate. Equation (11) equates the sum of labour services used in the two industries to the total supply of labour services.

Market for capital services: As in the case of the labour market, the value of the marginal product of capital services used in the current period in the two industries is equated in (12) and (13) to the price of capital services; and in (14) the sum of the capital services used in both industries to the given quantity of capital services.

Capital market: While equations (2) to (8) relate to the market for capital goods, equations (15) to (17) refer to the market for capital. Equation (15) sets investment equal to the value of the capital goods demanded. Equation (16) is the saving function which shows the volume of saving as depending on national income, the interest rate, and the magnitude of real cash balances. With larger real balances less will be saved and hence – equation (1b) – more will be consumed (Pigou effect). Equation (17) expresses the equality between saving and investment. The capital market equations, as we see, do not include the usual equation showing investment as a function of the interest rate and national income: $I=f(i, Y)$.

The capital market and the capital goods market have to be considered together. We shall clarify these relationships by taking the relevant equations out of the general system and analysing them separately. The money price of the *numéraire* will here be taken as unity.

In the left-hand panel of Figure 42 we show the price of the capital good on the y-axis and the quantity x_k produced during the period on the x-axis. Since the production of capital goods is taken to follow a linearly homogeneous function, marginal and average costs of capital goods are constant with given factor prices. We have accordingly drawn a horizontal supply curve for the capital goods at the level p_k^0. For each given i we can now draw a demand curve for x_k^c and one for x_k^k which reflect the functions $x_k^c=h(p_q'/i)$ and $x_k^k=g(p_q'/i)$, where p_q'/i is equal to the demand price. These

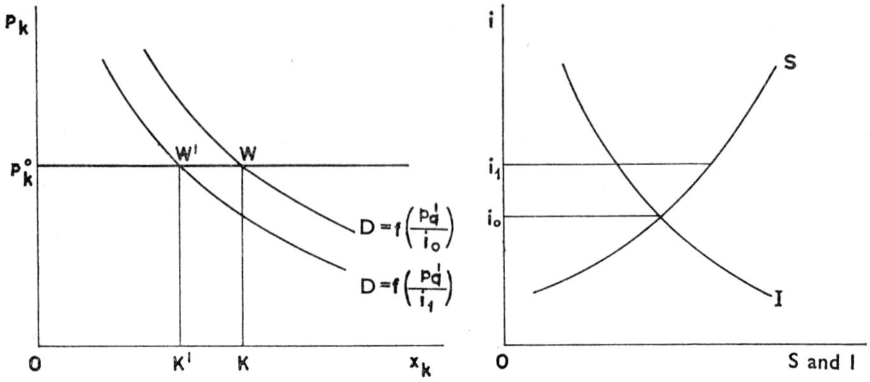

Fig. 42.

two demand curves of the two industries can be added to yield an aggregate demand curve for x_k. In the left-hand panel of Figure 42 we have drawn two such aggregate demand curves for two different levels of i, where the higher curve rests on a lower level of the interest rate ($i_0 < i_1$). At the interest rate i_0 the equilibrium demand for the capital good would be equal to OK, and at i_1 it would be OK'. In the right-hand panel we show the saving function as the supply of funds (national income and real cash balances are assumed to be given); and we show the investment schedule as the demand for funds. The latter curve we obtain by taking from the left-hand panel the value of capital goods demanded at each interest rate. At the rate i_0 this value is represented by the quadrangle $OKWp_k^0$, and at the rate i_1 by $OK'W'p_k^0$. In this manner we determine simultaneously p_q', the interest rate, saving, investment, and the quantity of capital goods demanded and supplied (x_k).

Money market: Equation (18) equates the real supply of money, $\bar{M}/p_c$, to the demand for it which is shown as a function of real income, real cash balances, and the interest rate. In including the real cash balances in the function we follow Patinkin.

At this point let us make clear, with the help of Figure 43, how the phenomenon of so-called hoarding or dishoarding appears in our system. The income recipients divide their money incomes between consumption and saving. In Figure 43 consumption is not shown; saving, which for simplicity's sake is assumed to be insensitive to the interest rate, is set at

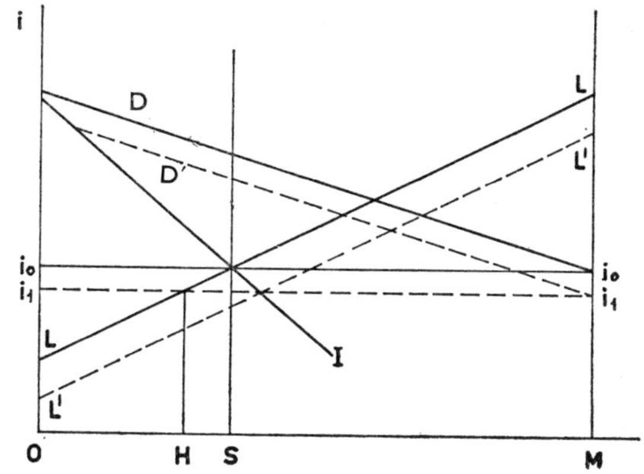

Fig. 43.

the level *OS*. It is assumed that the income recipients have the newly earned money at hand and are free to dispose of it. The period is chosen so that the velocity of circulation of money is equal to unity.

The total cash balances of the income recipients are larger than the money incomes received and utilized during the period. Money incomes received are equal to planned consumption and saving. The total cash balances are assumed to exceed this amount by *SM*. The curve *LL* shows how much the income recipients intend to invest. At the interest rate i_0 this amount is exactly equal to their total current saving. At a lower interest rate i_1 they would invest only *OH* and hoard *HS* out of current income, while at an interest rate higher than i_0 they would dishoard. The *LL*-curve thus is a supply curve of investible funds. If one views the same curve from the vertical over *M* – thus taking *M* as the origin –, it is obviously a liquidity preference curve telling how much cash the income recipients will be wanting to hold at different interest rates. If we add the horizontal difference between the *LL*-curve and the vertical over *M* to the demand for cash by entrepreneurs seeking investment funds, represented by the *I*-curve, we obtain the *D*-curve. Transaction money in the consumption sphere is not shown, as noted, since it is assumed to be a fixed amount. The intersection of the *D*-curve with the vertical over *M* yields the same interest rate i_0 as the demand and supply curves for investment funds. If the *LL*-curve is situated as drawn, we are in equilibrium: Saving equals investment and the demand for money equals the supply. If, however, the liquidity preference curve shifts downward to the position of the $L'L'$-curve, the interest rate will fall below the equilibrium level, investment will be larger than saving, and an inflationary process will set in.

Definition: Equation (19) says that national income is equal to national output. Under our assumptions there can be no difference between gross and net national product. National income is, of course, also equal to the sum of all wage and capital incomes. But we cannot introduce the equation $Y = \bar{l}p_l + \bar{q}^0 p_q$ as an independent equation in our system since it follows from equations (1a) and (2a), which in turn are derived from some of the other equations.

We have no securities market in our system of equations, but it would be easy to insert one between investment and saving. Since the "lifetime" of the capital goods is considered eternal, it is reasonable to assume that the securities consist in perpetual bonds (consols). The value of newly issued securities has to be equal to the volume of investment. A perpetual bond which yields one money unit per period has a price of $1/r$, where r denotes the rate of interest on the security. If we denote the supply (in units) of new securities by B_s, the following must thus be true:

$$\frac{1}{r} \cdot B_s = p_k \, x_k \qquad (20)$$

Furthermore, the interest rate on these securities must be equal to the marginal rate of return on capital after the addition of new capital goods, so that

$$r = i \qquad (21)$$

In Figure 43 above, the I-curve would represent the value of newly issued securities which, at the interest rate i_0, is equal to the volume of current saving.[5]

[5] In our model there is really more than one interest rate. We have seen that the marginal rate of return on the existing capital goods is higher than it will be on those in which the entrepreneurs are investing in the current period ($p_q/p_k > p_q'/p_k$). Let us now first imagine that the old capital goods as well as the new ones are financed by the issue of securities with a term to maturity of only one period so that these securities must continually be replaced. Because $p_q/p_k > p_q'/p_k$ the securities issued in the beginning of the current period to refinance the old equipment will carry a higher

The data of the system of equations presented here are the quantity of money $\bar{M}$, the supply of labour $\bar{l}$ and that of services from existing capital goods, $\bar{q}^0$. Further there are the following functions: the production functions for the consumer good and capital good industries, the saving function, and the demand function for money. The task now is to show how changes in these data affect the rate of interest.

III. The Effects of Changes in Data

Before we begin to investigate the effects of changes in data on the interest rate we should point out that in a system of 19 equations these effects will go in so many directions and may cause so many kinds of feed-back reactions that an exact verbal description of these processes is hardly possible. With the help of a rather lengthy mathematical procedure, it can in certain cases be unambiguously shown in which direction the variables of the system, including the interest rate, will change in consequence of changes in data. In the Mathematical Appendix this procedure and its results will be presented for four types of changes – changes in the quantity of money, in the demand for money, in the saving function, and in the existing capital stock. Here in the text we shall have to restrict ourselves to a rather impressionistic demonstration.

The first datum to be changed is the quantity of money. The system of equations shows us immediately that the interest rate will not change, if the quantity of money changes. Suppose the money supply is doubled. Households and business firms, in attempting to equalize the marginal utility of money held in cash balances with the marginal utility of money spent on consumption and investment goods, will use the bulk – even though not the whole – of the additional cash for consumption and investment. The price level will rise. The attempt to acquire additional goods will not succeed. So long as the price level has not risen proportionally to the expansion of the money supply, real balances will be larger than they were prior to the increase in the quantity of money. Hence the equalization

interest rate than the securities issued towards the end of the period for the purpose of acquiring the newly produced capital goods. Let us secondly assume that the existing capital goods had been financed by the issue of consols. It follows that the rate of return obtained on them in the current period $[R_0 + (R_0/R_1) - 1]$ is higher than the interest rate on the new consols (R_1 or i in our system of equations) issued to finance current investments.

of marginal utilities will require further attempts to obtain goods in exchange for cash, with the consequence of further price increases. The process will come to an end only when the price level has doubled and real balances have thus again reached the initial magnitude. All other variables stay unchanged in real terms.

This result presupposes that no transactions are executed during the period until equilibrium prices in the Walrasian sense have been found in all markets. If, by contrast, one should attempt to trace through successive steps the reactions to a change in data such as an expansion of the money supply, one must introduce time-lags in the adjustment process; and the above result will not be obtained. But in that case our formulation of the question – namely, what the equilibrium in the current period would be if only one of the data is assumed to have changed – becomes meaningless. An expansion in the money supply, for instance, can produce forced saving during the transition phase if the prices of factors of production lag behind the prices of finished goods; and the result will be that the new equilibrium differs from the old not only by the change in the money supply with its consequences, but also by the effect of time-lags which, in this case, consist in a larger output of capital goods and a lower interest rate. The changes in the variables of the system between the old and the new state of equilibrium are thus the result of the change in the datum "money supply" *and* of the introduction of time-lags, not solely the result of the former. Hence, in our mathematical presentation we assume a simultaneous adjustment of all variables to the given change in data. It hardly needs mentioning that the step-by-step discussion of the effects of a change in data, which is unavoidable in a verbal presentation, should not be taken to mean that the adjustment of the variables stretches over several time periods.

Let us now, as a second illustration, change the demand for money, supposing individuals wish to hold larger real balances. As equation (18) shows, their desire will be realised through a fall in the price level. The reduction of money expenditures which individuals make in order to increase their cash balances has its effects on prices. If the individuals reduce their expenditures on consumption and investment goods by an amount sufficient to equalize *at the initial price level* the marginal utility of the last money unit spent on these goods with the now higher marginal utility of cash balances, they will overshoot their goal, since the fall in the price level which is the consequence of the reduction of their money expenditures will make the real cash balances larger than originally desired. But this overshooting can be corrected again by increasing the expenditures on goods.

If the real balances were not represented as an independent variable in the saving function, the fall of the price level would be the only effect of an increase in the demand for money. But since we in fact assume that with larger real balances real saving from current income will be smaller owing to the Pigou effect, we have to conclude that in the new equilibrium (at which saving equals investment and the entire money supply is absorbed) the interest rate is higher than it was in the initial equilibrium. From this it follows that, while the price level will indeed be lower than it was prior to the intensification of the demand for money, it will, because of the higher interest rate, not be quite so low as it would have been had we not made saving dependent also on the level of real balances.

The important further effects of an increased demand for money are as follows:

1. Investment in value terms, which must be equal to saving, will be smaller. Since investment is equal to the production of capital goods times the price (expressed in the *numéraire*) of capital goods, p_k/p_c, and since this price stays unchanged because of the unchanged real costs in capital goods production, the production of capital goods will be smaller. The marginal product of capital services after the capital stock has been expanded by newly produced capital goods will thus be larger; accordingly, p_q'/p_k will be larger, which follows also from the fact that the interest rate, to which p_q'/p_k must be equal, will be higher.

2. The production of consumer goods will be larger.

3. The increase in consumer goods production and the decrease in capital goods production imply a different allocation of the available labour and capital services – a reallocation in favour of the production of consumer goods.

As a third illustration, let us change the saving function. We assume that more will be saved at each hypothetical interest rate. To show the immediate effect of this shift in the saving function, we use a graphical presentation similar to Figure 43; but this time we explicitly show the quantity of money used for consumption expenditures (Figure 44). We again choose our period so that the velocity of circulation of money is equal to unity. *OC* is the quantity of money used for consumption, and *CS* is the amount saved. As in Figure 43, saving will for simplicity's sake be assumed insensitive to the interest rate. The *LL*-curve is the supply curve for investible funds and, if read from the right to the left, the demand curve for money. If we add the horizontal difference between the *LL*-curve and the vertical erected over *M* to the demand for funds – i.e., to the *I*-curve –, we obtain the *D*-curve which intersects the vertical over *M* in the point *R*. The interest rate, $MR = SR$, is the equilibrium rate at which saving equals investment and at which the demand for money equals the supply. Now let us increase saving to $C'S$ at the expense of consumption so that consumption shrinks to OC'. The demand-for-funds curve – the *I*-curve – we leave unchanged to keep matters simple[6], but we will have to let it begin at the vertical over C'. Let us also leave the liquidity preference curve unchanged. By adding the demand for cash (the distance between the *LL*-curve and the vertical over *M*) to the demand for funds in the same manner as above, we obtain the D'-curve and the interest rate MR' which is identical with the rate NR' at the intersection of the demand-for-funds curve with the corresponding supply curve (the *LL*-curve read from the left to the right). This interest rate is

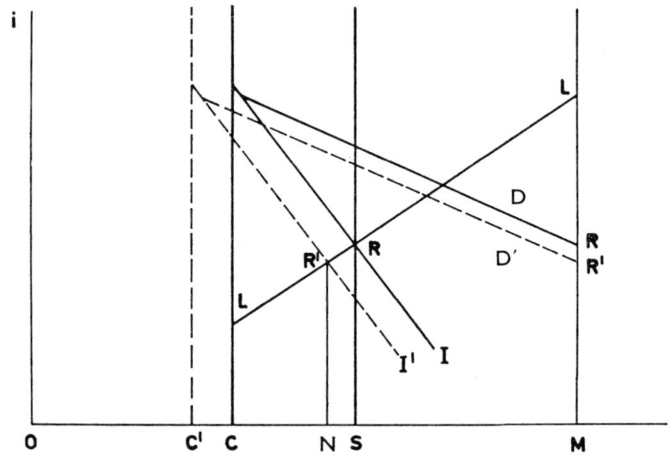

Fig. 44.

[6] It should actually be lowered because of the decline in consumption.

lower than the old rate SR or MR; but it is no longer an equilibrium rate, because saving is now larger than investment by the amount NS.

Since the nominal supply of money $\bar{M}$ (OM in Figure 44) stays unchanged, the price level will have to fall. This will happen as a consequence of the deflationary gap due to the positive discrepancy between saving and investment – in other words, due to the fact that part of the money income will be hoarded. The real balances will thus be increasing; and as a consequence, saving will diminish somewhat and consumption will increase, both factors contributing to the removal of the discrepancy between saving and investment. We could show this in Figure 44 by shifting the C-vertical to a position between C' and C, thereby shifting the demand curve for investment funds to the right towards the I-curve. Simultaneously the demand for money will diminish because it is codetermined by the level of real balances. Therefore we also have to lower the LL-curve. All these movements help to reach a level of the interest rate at which saving and investment and the demand for and supply of money are simultaneously in equilibrium. The new interest rate will, of course, lie below the old one. The price level will stay lower than in the initial position because the lower interest rate induces an increase in the demand for cash.

The higher level of investment is, as we know, associated with greater production of capital goods and thereby with a lower p'_q/p_k, which corresponds to the fall in the interest rate. The expansion of capital goods production, which occurs at the expense of consumer goods production, implies a redistribution of the available labour and capital services in favour of the capital goods industry.[7]

Having investigated a change in the quantity of money, a shift in the demand for money, and a shift in the saving function, we have dealt with those changes in data which are most frequently discussed in connection with the interest problem.

Finally, let us assume a larger initial capital stock. Then the marginal product of the capital services available during the period, and thus also

[7] If we had assumed that the production functions of the two goods are different, the increase in saving would free labour and capital in the consumer goods industry in proportions which do not correspond to those at which these factors are needed in the capital goods industry. If the consumer goods industry should be the less capital intensive, the result of increased saving might even be that the interest rate would rise.

the price p_q/p_c of these services, will be smaller than it would be with a smaller initial capital stock. It follows that the marginal productivity curve of the services of currently produced new capital goods starts out from a lower level, so that even with the same volume of capital goods production a lower p'_q/p_c will result (see Figure 41). But since saving will be larger because of the increased national income, the capital goods production will also be larger; this provides an additional cause for a lower marginal product of capital services after the expansion of the capital stock, and thus for a lower interest rate. Since national income is larger and the interest rate lower, the price level will also be lower (see the money equation). It is true that the Pigou effect, which is greater the lower the price level, will now work in the direction of smaller saving; but it seems realistic to assume that this effect will not offset the effect on saving of the increase in national income.

The results of our analysis show that changes on the monetary side have an influence on the interest rate only when they cause changes in the real variables. Under the comparative-statics approach, a shift in the demand for money causes a change in the interest rate because it has an effect on real saving. An increase or decrease in the money supply, however, exerts no "real" effect. Changes in non-monetary data cannot always be shown to have unambiguous effects on the interest rate. An increase in the propensity to save – meaning that more will be saved at the same interest rate, national income and level of real balances – will definitely cause a fall in the interest rate. An increase in the initial capital stock will not, of necessity, have this effect on the interest rate, although it is more likely than not that it will.

MATHEMATICAL APPENDIX

§ **1.** For the mathematical presentation of Böhm-Bawerk's theory[1] we make use of the following symbols:

p = product of a worker per unit period
w = wage of a worker per unit period
i = rate of interest per unit period
τ = average period of production
K = capital per worker
A = number of workers, given
S = subsistence fund (in value terms), given

The unit of output is used as the unit of account.

To begin with, we have the productivity function:

$$p = f(\tau) \tag{1}$$

From the definition of the "original" interest as internal yield per unit of time it follows that the wage of a worker plus the interest accrued during the average period of production on this wage is equal to the product of the worker:

$$p = w(1 + i\tau) \tag{2a}$$

or

$$i = \frac{p - w}{w\tau} \tag{2b}$$

Given the wage, the individual entrepreneur chooses the average period of production so as to maximize the rate of return or rate of interest. Accordingly, we differentiate equation (2a) or (2b) with respect to τ and set $\mathrm{d}i/\mathrm{d}\tau = 0$, whence we obtain:

$$i = \frac{1}{w}\frac{\mathrm{d}p}{\mathrm{d}\tau} \tag{3a}$$

[1] Cf. Wicksell, *Value, Capital and Rent* (New York, 1954), p. 120 ff.

or

$$\frac{dp}{d\tau} = \frac{p - w}{\tau} \tag{3b}$$

The condition for the maximization of i, namely that $(d^2i/d\tau^2) < 0$, is satisfied by the assumption that $f(\tau)$ increases at a decreasing rate. Equation (3b) states that at the point where i is maximized the marginal product of the roundabout process of production is equal to the internal return or interest yield per unit of time. Equation (3a) shows that the interest rate is equal to the marginal product of the extension of the process of production divided by the wage.

Given the wage, equations (1) to (3) suffice to determine for the individual entrepreneur the three unknowns p, τ, and i.

In the analysis of the economic system as a whole the wage becomes an unknown. The necessary additional equation can be obtained from the condition that in equilibrium the entire subsistence fund must be absorbed by wage payments during the average period of production:

$$S = Aw\tau \tag{4}$$

The capital required per worker is equal to the wage multiplied by the average period of production:

$$K = w\tau \tag{5}$$

By differentiating equation (5) with respect to τ we obtain:

$$\frac{dK}{d\tau} = \tau \frac{dw}{d\tau} + w \tag{6}$$

For the individual entrepreneur $dw/d\tau = 0$, and thus

$$\frac{dK}{d\tau} = w \tag{6a}$$

i.e., the amount of capital required by him for a lengthening of the production process is equal to the wage. Equation (3a) can in this case be interpreted to mean that the interest rate is equal to the marginal product of the lengthening of the process of production divided by the capital which makes this lengthening possible. By inserting equation (6a) into

(3a), we obtain:

$$i = \frac{\dfrac{\mathrm{d}p}{\mathrm{d}\tau}}{\dfrac{\mathrm{d}K}{\mathrm{d}\tau}} = \frac{\mathrm{d}p}{\mathrm{d}K} \tag{7}$$

i.e., the interest rate is, for the individual entrepreneur, equal to the marginal internal rate of return or the marginal product of capital.

For the economic system as a whole, $\mathrm{d}w/\mathrm{d}\tau$ is positive; this was explained in the text where it was shown that an extension of the average period of production is accompanied by a rise in the wage. The capital required for such lengthening is thus larger than w (equation (6)). Equation (3a) in connection with equation (6) gives us in this case:

$$i = \frac{1}{w}\frac{\mathrm{d}p}{\mathrm{d}\tau} > \frac{\dfrac{\mathrm{d}p}{\mathrm{d}\tau}}{\dfrac{\mathrm{d}K}{\mathrm{d}\tau}} \quad \text{or} \quad i > \frac{\mathrm{d}p}{\mathrm{d}K}$$

For the economy as a whole the interest rate is greater than the marginal product of the roundabout process of production divided by the capital which renders the lengthening of this process possible, or larger than the marginal product of capital.

As we already stated in the text, the value of the subsistence fund must be found by capitalizing its yield. This value is $S = (Ap\tau)/(1 + i\tau)$. Hence we cannot take S as a datum, for its value can only be known when the interest rate and the average period of production have been determined.

§ **2.** For the presentation of Wicksell's first contribution to the theory of interest we use the same symbols as in § 1 and the following additional ones:

h = number of land services combined with one worker
r = rent for a unit of land services per unit period
B = total number of land services, given

We assume initially, as did Wicksell, that only one good is being produced, P_1; the unit of this good is taken as the unit of account.

To begin with, we again have the productivity function which expresses the product of a worker as a function both of the number of land services combined with the worker and of the average period of production:

$$p = f(h, \tau) \tag{1}$$

In addition, we know that the product per worker is equal to the sum of his wage and the payments for the land services combined with him *plus* the interest accrued on this sum during the average period of production:

$$p = (w + rh)(1 + i\tau) \tag{2}$$

or

$$i = \frac{p - (w + rh)}{\tau(w + rh)} \tag{2a}$$

The individual entrepreneur, for whom wage and rent are given, will choose the average period of production and the number of land services to be combined with a worker in such a manner as to maximize the rate of return or rate of interest. The interest rate will be maximized if the two partial derivatives of equation (2a) with respect to τ and to h are equal to zero.

Let us first take the derivative with respect to τ:

$$\frac{\partial i}{\partial \tau} = \frac{\tau(w + rh)\dfrac{\partial p}{\partial \tau} - [p - (w + rh)](w + rh)}{\tau^2 (w + rh)^2} = 0$$

whence we obtain:

$$\frac{\partial p}{\partial \tau} = \frac{1}{\tau}[p - (w + rh)] \tag{3}$$

or, by inserting equation (2) into (3):

$$\frac{\partial p}{\partial \tau} = i(w + rh) \quad \text{or} \quad i = \frac{1}{w + rh}\frac{\partial p}{\partial \tau} \tag{3a}$$

Equation (3) states that when i is at a maximum the marginal product of the average period of production is equal to the interest (yield per unit of time) earned per worker; equation (3a) states that the interest rate is equal to the marginal product of the average period of production divided by the capital which is absorbed by the lengthening of this period. For the individual entrepreneur the sum of the wage and of the rent on the land that is combined with a worker represents the entire outlay (capital) required for an extension of the average period of production. Therefore, he maximizes the interest rate if it is equal to the marginal internal rate of return or the marginal product of the capital that is absorbed by the lengthening of the process of production.

Let us now put the partial derivative of equation (2a) with respect to h equal to zero, which gives us:

$$\frac{1}{r\tau}\frac{\partial p}{\partial h} = \frac{p}{(w + rh)\tau} \tag{4}$$

This equation states that at the maximum value of i the marginal product of land divided by the capital tied up in this last unit of land is equal to the average product obtained on the entire capital invested per worker. If we insert the expression for p from equation (2) into (4), we obtain:

$$\frac{\dfrac{\partial p}{\partial h}}{1 + i\tau} = r \tag{4a}$$

i.e., the discounted marginal product of land must be equal to the rent.

Wicksell, who proceeds by partial differentiation of equation (2) with respect to τ and h as if i were a constant, immediately obtains (3a) and (4a); he does not have equation (4) which served as the basis for the verbal presentation in the text.

The four equations (1) to (4) suffice to determine the four unknowns p, τ, i, and h for the individual entrepreneur. For the economic system as a whole we need two more equations for the determination of wage rate and rent.

One of these equations expresses the fact that the number of land services combined with one worker must be equal to the total supply of land services divided by the total number of workers:

$$h = \frac{B}{A} \tag{5}$$

The second equation states that in equilibrium the entire subsistence fund must be absorbed by wage and rent payments during the average period of production:

$$S = (Aw + Br)\tau \tag{6}$$

Instead of taking as our starting point equation (1), which reflects the product of one worker, we could also have started out from an equation which gives the total product of an entrepreneur, P, as a function of the number of workers a, the number of land services b used by this entrepreneur and the average period of production τ:

$$P = F(a, b, \tau) \tag{7}$$

Equation (2) will in this case be replaced by:

$$P = (aw + br)(1 + i\tau) \tag{8}$$

The interest rate is maximized if

$$\frac{\partial i}{\partial \tau} = \frac{\partial i}{\partial a} = \frac{\partial i}{\partial b} = 0$$

which gives us the three conditions mentioned in the text:

$$\frac{\partial P}{\partial \tau} = \frac{1}{\tau}[P - (aw + br)] \tag{9}$$

$$\frac{\dfrac{\partial P}{\partial a}}{1 + i\tau} = w \tag{10}$$

$$\frac{\dfrac{\partial P}{\partial b}}{1 + i\tau} = r \tag{11}$$

Furthermore, we know that the entrepreneur can employ only as many workers and land services as his share in the total subsistence fund, S_0, permits:

$$S_0 = (aw + br)\tau \tag{12}$$

Equation (8) is not an independent equation: if we assume that P is a linearly homogeneous function of a and b, equation (8) can be obtained by Euler's theorem from the two marginal productivity equations for labour and land, equations (10) and (11). Equations (7) and (9) to (12) suffice, given the wage and the rent, to determine for the entrepreneur the five unknowns: P, τ, a, b, and i.

If we now introduce a second good P_2, we have the two productivity functions $p_1 = f_1(h_1, \tau_1)$ and $p_2 = f_2(h_2, \tau_2)$ and correspondingly two equations for each of the above equations (2), (3), and (4). The wage, the rent, and the rate of return must be the same in both industries. We have 8 equations, to which we add the following seven additional ones:

$$h_1 = \frac{B_1}{A_1} \tag{13}$$

$$h_2 = \frac{B_2}{A_2} \tag{14}$$

$$S_1 = (A_1 w + B_1 r)\tau_1 \tag{15}$$

$$S_2 = (A_2 w + B_2 r)\tau_2 \tag{16}$$

$$A = A_1 + A_2 \tag{17}$$

$$B = B_1 + B_2 \tag{18}$$

$$S = S_1 + S_2 \tag{19}$$

We thus have 15 equations for 15 unknowns ($p_1, p_2, \tau_1, \tau_2, i, r, w, h_1, h_2, A_1, A_2, B_1, B_2, S_1, S_2$).

These equations, however, hide one more unknown – namely the price of good P_2. Only if we know this price, π, can S_1 and S_2 be added up.

If we continue to use good P_1 as the unit of account, the productivity function $p_1 = f_1(h_1, \tau_1)$ can remain unchanged. But p_2 now represents the *value* produced by a worker. If we call the quantity of the second good produced by him q_2, then $p_2 = \pi \cdot q_2$, where π is the price of a unit of P_2 expressed in units of good P_1. We thus need one further equation to determine π.

We can derive the demand of each individual for each of the two goods from the marginal utility functions, assumed to be known, and the incomes which are determined once w, r, and i are found. The aggregate demand of all individuals for the second good must in equilibrium be equal to the supply. Let us denote the quantity demanded of the second good by Y. It must then be true that

$$Y = \frac{A_2 p_2}{\pi} \tag{20}$$

The equality of supply and demand for good P_1 follows from the other equations.

§ 3. In his *Lectures on Political Economy* Wicksell first takes up a case in which the productive inputs consist only of labour services which are all applied at the beginning of the period of production. The production and the sale of the wine occur continuously; the time which elapses between production and sale is the absolute period of production.

We use the following symbols:

V_0 = cost of the grape juice produced by one worker = wage
W = value of the wine produced by one worker
ρ = interest rate, continuous compounding being assumed
t = absolute period of production
A = number of workers, given
S = aggregate value of capital (subsistence fund), given

To begin with, we have the function which shows how the value of the wine increases with the length of the storage period:

$$W = f(t) \tag{1}$$

In addition, we know that the wage of a worker (which is identical with the cost of the grape juice produced by him) plus the accrued and compounded interest must equal the value of the product. If we assume perfectly continuous compounding, we have the equation

$$W = V_0 e^{\rho t} \tag{2}$$

or

$$\rho = \frac{\log W - \log V_0}{t} \tag{2a}$$

For the individual entrepreneur V_0 is given; he will maximize ρ. The interest rate will be at a maximum if

$$\frac{d\rho}{dt} = \frac{t\dfrac{W'}{W} - (\log W - \log V_0)}{t^2} = 0$$

where W' designates the first derivative of (1) with respect to t. We obtain:

$$\frac{W'}{W} = \frac{\log W - \log V_0}{t} = \rho \tag{3}$$

This result is, of course, identical with Jevons' formula

$$\rho = \frac{F'(t)}{F(t)}$$

Given the wage or V_0, these three equations are sufficient to determine t, W, and ρ. For the system as a whole, however, V_0 is not given. But we have a further equation which states that the aggregate value of capital – assumed by Wicksell to be known – must in the case of perfectly continuous production, storing and selling be equal to the wage times the number of labour services used during the entire period of production plus the accrued and compounded interest:

$$S = AV_0 \int_0^t e^{\rho x}\, dx = A\frac{W - V_0}{\rho} \tag{4}$$

In this connection Wicksell also proves that for the economic system as a whole the marginal rate of return on a small increase in capital is smaller than the rate of interest. As this result, for the case of simple interest, is already known to us from Böhm-Bawerk's theory, we do not need to demonstrate it here anew.

The second case discussed in the text – two different productive inputs being applied at two different points in time – is also given a mathematical presentation by Wicksell. We use the following symbols:

a = number of workers employed
b = number of land services employed
t_1 = investment period of the labour services
t_2 = investment period of the land services

l = wage of a worker
r = rent for a unit of land services
W = total product
The unit of product is again the unit of account.

We have the production function:

$$W = f(a, b, t_1, t_2) \tag{5}$$

W must be equal to the sum of rents and wages paid plus the compounded interest accrued on both, hence:

$$W = ale^{\rho t_1} + bre^{\rho t_2} \tag{6}$$

In order to maximize ρ, Wicksell proceeds by partial differentiation of (6) with respect to a, b, t_1 and t_2, as if ρ were a constant; this approach is simpler than the more tedious one of first isolating ρ in (6) and then equating the four partial derivatives of ρ to zero. We obtain:

$$\frac{\partial W}{\partial a} e^{-\rho t_1} = l \tag{7}$$

i.e., the marginal product of a worker, discounted to the moment of the input of his service, must be equal to the wage.

$$\frac{\partial W}{\partial b} e^{-\rho t_2} = r \tag{8}$$

The marginal product of land, discounted over the investment period of the land service, must be equal to the rent on land.

$$\frac{\frac{\partial W}{\partial t_1}}{ale^{\rho t_1}} = \rho \tag{9}$$

$$\frac{\frac{\partial W}{\partial t_2}}{bre^{\rho t_2}} = \rho \tag{10}$$

Equations (9) and (10) state that the interest rate must be equal to the marginal product of the lengthening of the investment period of each of the two productive inputs divided by the contribution (compounded) of these inputs to the value of output.

As the production of wine is assumed to be a linearly homogeneous function of a and b, equation (6) cannot be counted as an independent equation in addition to the marginal productivity equations (7) and (8) from which (6) can be derived. We thus have five equations as compared with the eight unknowns W, a, b, t_1, t_2, ρ, l, and r. We need three more equations. The first one expresses the condition that all labour must be employed, so that

$$a = A \tag{11}$$

Correspondingly we have for the services of land

$$b = B \tag{12}$$

In addition we have the condition that the subsistence fund must be absorbed by wage and rent payments:

$$S = al\int_0^t e^{\rho t_1}\,\mathrm{d}t_1 + br\int_0^t e^{\rho t_2}\,\mathrm{d}t_2 \tag{13}$$

§ **4.** Let us assume that the durable good throws off a continuous constant income stream of $m = i_1 b$ per unit of time. The present value V of a machine which lasts t units of time is:

$$V = \int_0^t me^{-\rho x}\,\mathrm{d}x = \frac{m}{\rho}(1 - e^{-\rho t}) \tag{1}$$

where ρ represents the interest rate, continuous compounding being assumed. This present value must be equated to the cost of the good, consisting of the quantity of labour a times the wage rate w, where a is a function of the length of life of the machine. We thus obtain the equation

$$aw = \frac{m}{\rho}(1 - e^{-\rho t}) \tag{2}$$

We have to maximize ρ. We differentiate equation (2) with respect to t, as if ρ were a constant, and obtain:

$$w\frac{\mathrm{d}a}{\mathrm{d}t} = me^{-\rho t} \tag{3}$$

The right-hand side of equation (3) represents the present value of the income received in the last small unit of time; this present value must be equal to the cost of extending the length of life by this last unit of time (left-hand side of the equation). We have thus obtained Åkerman's result.

The general mathematical proof that the durability of a machine increases as the ratio m/w decreases is difficult. In his review of Åkerman's book Wicksell dealt with this problem.[2] He gave the proof for the special cost function

$$a = kt^{v}$$

where a represents the quantity of labour required to produce a machine with the length of life t; k is a constant and v a rational fraction. It is assumed that the time required to construct the machine can be neglected. This cost function for extending the durability of a machine can be presented by a curve which is concave to the t-axis throughout – in other words, its rate of increase decreases continuously as t increases.

By differentiating equation (4) with respect to t, we obtain

$$\frac{\mathrm{d}a}{\mathrm{d}t} = vkt^{v-1} = \frac{va}{t} \tag{5}$$

If we insert the expression for $\mathrm{d}a/\mathrm{d}t$ from equation (5) into equation (3), we have

$$\frac{vaw}{t} = me^{-\rho t} \tag{6}$$

and by solving (6) for aw and inserting it into equation (2) we obtain

$$e^{\rho t} = 1 + \frac{\rho t}{v} \tag{7}$$

[2] Wicksell, *Lectures on Political Economy* (London, 1934-1936), Vol. 1, p. 293 ff.

The product ρt here is obviously a constant, because ρt is the root of an equation which contains only v as a "variable"; v, however, is constant.

Now we can write equation (3) as follows:

$$\frac{\mathrm{d}a}{\mathrm{d}t} = \frac{m}{w} e^{-\rho t} = i_1 \frac{b}{w} e^{-\rho t}$$

As ρt is constant, it follows that as long as m/w or b/w are rising, $\mathrm{d}a/\mathrm{d}t$ will also be rising. But this means that the length of life of the machine must become shorter (and vice versa for a decreasing m/w) because the first derivative of the cost function decreases continuously with an increasing t or increases with a decreasing t.

§ **5.** We shall present Fisher's theory on the assumption that the time horizon extends over three unit periods (years). Fisher himself formulated his theory mathematically on the assumption of m years. As the addition of further years raises no new problems, we can confine ourselves to three years.

We first consider an individual who can change his income stream through investing. He attempts to maximize the present value of the income stream. The optimum investment possibilities can be represented by the equation

$$F(y', y'', y''') = 0 \tag{1}$$

where y', y'', y''' are the incomes of the successive years which are to be determined. It is presumed that y' is available immediately, y'' at the beginning of the second year, and y''' at the beginning of the third. The present value V of the income stream is

$$V = y' + \frac{y''}{1 + i'} + \frac{y'''}{(1 + i')(1 + i'')} \tag{2}$$

where i' stands for the interest rate of the first year and i'' for that of the second year. The necessary condition for the maximization of this income stream, relative to equation (1), is, in accordance with a well-known rule of the differential calculus, that

$$\frac{\dfrac{\delta V}{\delta y'}}{\dfrac{\delta F()}{\delta y'}} = \frac{\dfrac{\delta V}{\delta y''}}{\dfrac{\delta F()}{\delta y''}} = \frac{\dfrac{\delta V}{\delta y'''}}{\dfrac{\delta F()}{\delta y'''}} \tag{3}$$

It follows from (2) that

$$\frac{\delta V}{\delta y'} = 1 \qquad \frac{\delta V}{\delta y''} = \frac{1}{1+i'} \qquad \frac{\delta V}{\delta y'''} = \frac{1}{(1+i')(1+i'')}. \tag{2a}$$

By substituting we obtain for the first pair in (3):

$$\frac{1}{\dfrac{\delta F()}{\delta y'}} = \frac{\dfrac{1}{(1+i')}}{\dfrac{\delta F()}{\delta y''}} \quad \text{or} \quad \frac{\dfrac{\delta F()}{\delta y'}}{\dfrac{\delta F()}{\delta y''}} = 1 + i' \tag{3a}$$

It follows from (1) that

$$\frac{\dfrac{\delta F()}{\delta y'}}{\dfrac{\delta F()}{\delta y''}} = -\frac{\delta y''}{\delta y'} \tag{1a}$$

so that equation (3a) becomes

$$-\frac{\delta y''}{\delta y'} = 1 + i' \tag{3b}$$

The left-hand expression in equation (3b) represents the growth of the income of the second year if a small amount of this year's income is used for investment; this increment is by definition equal to $1+r'$, where r' represents the marginal rate of return of the investment in the first year. Thus we ultimately obtain the result that

$$r' = i' \tag{4}$$

In an analogous manner we obtain from the second pair in (3) for the marginal rate of return in the second year, r'', the equation

$$r'' = i'' \tag{5}$$

From the equality of the first and third expression in (3) it also follows that

$$1 + r_2 = (1 + i')(1 + i'') \tag{6}$$

where r_2 is the marginal rate of return over a period of *two* years.

Let us assume that $1+r_2$ equals 1.1025; i.e., a unit of money invested "at the margin" must after two years have grown into the amount 1.1025. Its *annual* growth rate is thus 5%; $1+r_2$ is equal to $(1+R)^2$ if R represents the rate of return on an *annual* basis.[3] Accordingly we can rewrite equation (6):

$$R = \sqrt{(1 + i')(1 + i'')} - 1$$

This expression for R, as we can see, is identical with the formula for the rate of interest on a two-year contract if the market rate of interest for the first year is i' and that for the second year is i''. An investment which matures after two years must on a *per annum* average yield the interest rate for a two-year contract. But as this equation follows from the equality of the first and the last term of equation (3), it cannot be used as an independent equation. Fisher does not mention it at all. With given market rates of interest, equations (1), (2), (4), and (5) are sufficient to determine the unknowns y', y'', y''', and V.

The maximum income stream obtained in this manner through investment can now be changed in its time structure by borrowing or lending. How the income stream will be changed is determined by the desire of the individual to maximize the utility of his income stream; it should be noted here that the present value V of the income stream cannot be changed through loans and repayments. Accordingly, the maximization of the utility of the income stream must be obtained subject to the side relation

$$y' + x' + \frac{y'' + x''}{(1 + i')} + \frac{y''' + x'''}{(1 + i')(1 + i'')} = y' + \frac{y''}{(1 + i')} + \frac{y'''}{(1 + i')(1 + i'')} \tag{7}$$

or

$$x' + \frac{x''}{(1 + i')} + \frac{x'''}{(1 + i')(1 + i'')} = 0 \tag{7a}$$

[3] $(1.05)^2 = 1.1025$.

where x', x'', and x''' designate the additions to and subtractions from the incomes of the first, second, and third year – income changes which reflect lending and borrowing, repayments and interest payments. Some of these magnitudes are positive, others negative.

The utility function is

$$W = \rho(y' + x', y'' + x'', y''' + x''') \tag{8}$$

This utility function is maximized relative to equation (7a) in the same manner in which the income stream through investing was maximized subject to the side relation of equation (1); therefore we do not demonstrate it here in full, but proceed immediately to the result. The marginal time preference in the two years denoted by g' and g'' respectively, where

$$g' = \frac{\frac{\delta W}{\delta x'}}{\frac{\delta W}{\delta x''}} - 1 \quad \text{and} \quad g'' = \frac{\frac{\delta W}{\delta x''}}{\frac{\delta W}{\delta x'''}} - 1$$

must be equal to the interest rate in the corresponding year, so that

$$g' = i' \tag{9}$$

$$g'' = i'' \tag{10}$$

Given the market rates of interest, equations (7a) to (10) suffice to determine x', x'', x''', and W. The magnitudes x', x'', and x''' are thus determined as functions of the interest rate. Incidentally, a relationship analogous to that demonstrated above for r_2 and i', i'' (see equation (6)) exists here between the marginal time preference over *two* years and the interest rates for two successive years.

If we are dealing with n individuals, we have $8n$ equations to determine for all individuals the unknowns y', y'', y''', x', x'', x''', V, and W.

The interest rates i' and i'' were hitherto assumed to be given. In order to determine them we have to add a group of equations stating that the capital market must in each period be in equilibrium, i.e., that all amounts lent or repaid by individuals must be equal to all amounts borrowed or received. Hence:

$$x_1' + x_2' + \cdots + x_n' = 0 \tag{11}$$

$$x_1'' + x_2'' + \cdots + x_n'' = 0 \tag{12}$$

$$x_1''' + x_2''' + \cdots + x_n''' = 0 \tag{13}$$

where the subscripts denote the individuals 1, 2,... *n*.

This seems to yield three additional equations for only two new unknowns. But it can be seen from (7a) that one of the three equations (11) to (13) can be obtained from the other two in connection with (7a). If we want to calculate the interest rate on two-year contracts in the first year, we can add the equation

$$I = \sqrt{(1 + i')(1 + i'')} - 1 \tag{14}$$

§ 6. For the sake of simplicity, we introduce the following abbreviations in our system of equations[4]:

$$\frac{p_l}{p_c} = P_l \qquad \frac{p_q'}{p_c} = P_q' \qquad \frac{Y}{p_c} = Y_1$$

$$\frac{p_q}{p_c} = P_q \qquad \frac{S}{p_c} = S_1$$

$$\frac{p_k}{p_c} = P_k \qquad \frac{I}{p_c} = I_1$$

The four changes in data to be dealt with will be introduced in the following manner. A shift in the saving function will be designated by β, so that the saving function – equation (16) – now reads:

$$S_1 = s\left(Y_1, i, \frac{\bar{M}}{p_c}\right) + \beta$$

A shift in the demand for real cash balances will be denoted by γ, so that the equilibrium condition for the money market – equation (18) – now reads:

$$\frac{\bar{M}}{p_c} = m\left(Y_1, i, \frac{\bar{M}}{p_c}\right) + \gamma$$

[4] Cf. *supra*, p. 290 ff.

Furthermore, we shall treat the quantity of money M and the quantity of available capital services q^0 as variables.

First we present the system of equations in differentiated form. ϕ_x denotes, as is usual, the first partial derivative of ϕ with respect to the variable x, ϕ_{xx} the second partial derivative with respect to the variable x, and ϕ_{xy} the "cross" second partial derivative with respect to the variables x and y.

$$\mathrm{d}x_c = \phi_{l_c}\mathrm{d}l_c + \phi_{q_c^0}\mathrm{d}q_c^0 \tag{1'}$$

$$\mathrm{d}x_k = a\phi_{l_k}\,\mathrm{d}l_k + a\phi_{q_k^0}\,\mathrm{d}q_k^0 \tag{2'}$$

$$\phi_{l_c q_c^1}\,\mathrm{d}l_c + \phi_{q_c^1 q_c^1}\mathrm{d}q_c^1 = \mathrm{d}P_q' \tag{3'}$$

$$P_k a\phi_{l_k q_k^1}\,\mathrm{d}l_k + P_k a\phi_{q_k^1 q_k^1}\,\mathrm{d}q_k^1 + a\phi_{q_k^1}\,\mathrm{d}P_k = \mathrm{d}P_q' \tag{4'}$$

$$\mathrm{d}q_c^1 = \mathrm{d}q_c^0 + \mathrm{d}x_k^c \tag{5'}$$

$$\mathrm{d}q_k^1 = \mathrm{d}q_k^0 + \mathrm{d}x_k^k \tag{6'}$$

$$\mathrm{d}P_q' = i\,\mathrm{d}P_k + P_k\mathrm{d}i \tag{7'}$$

$$\mathrm{d}x_k^c + \mathrm{d}x_k^k = \mathrm{d}x_k \tag{8'}$$

$$\phi_{l_c l_c}\mathrm{d}l_c + \phi_{l_c q_c^0}\mathrm{d}q_c^0 = \mathrm{d}P_l \tag{9'}$$

$$P_k a\phi_{l_k l_k}\mathrm{d}l_k + P_k a\phi_{l_k q_k^0}\,\mathrm{d}q_k^0 + a\phi_{l_k}\mathrm{d}P_k = \mathrm{d}P_l \tag{10'}$$

$$\mathrm{d}l_c + \mathrm{d}l_k = 0 \tag{11'}$$

$$\phi_{l_c q_c^0}\mathrm{d}l_c + \phi_{q_c^0 q_c^0}\mathrm{d}q_c^0 = \mathrm{d}P_q \tag{12'}$$

$$P_k a\phi_{l_k q_k^0}\,\mathrm{d}l_k + P_k a\phi_{q_k^0 q_k^0}\,\mathrm{d}q_k^0 + a\phi_{q_k^0}\mathrm{d}P_k = \mathrm{d}P_q \tag{13'}$$

$$\mathrm{d}q_c^0 + \mathrm{d}q_k^0 = \mathrm{d}q^0 \tag{14'}$$

$$\mathrm{d}I_1 = P_k\mathrm{d}x_k + x_k\mathrm{d}P_k \tag{15'}$$

$$\mathrm{d}S_1 = \frac{\delta s}{\delta Y_1}\mathrm{d}Y_1 + \frac{\delta s}{\delta i}\mathrm{d}i + \frac{1}{p_c}\frac{\delta s}{\delta \frac{M}{p_c}}\mathrm{d}M - \frac{M}{p_c^2}\frac{\delta s}{\delta \frac{M}{p_c}}\mathrm{d}p_c + \mathrm{d}\beta \tag{16'}$$

$$\mathrm{d}I_1 = \mathrm{d}S_1 \tag{17'}$$

$$0 = \frac{\delta m}{\delta Y_1}\mathrm{d}Y_1 + \frac{\delta m}{\delta i}\mathrm{d}i + \frac{1}{p_c}\left[\frac{\delta m}{\delta \frac{M}{p_c}} - 1\right]\mathrm{d}M - \frac{M}{p_c^2}\left[\frac{\delta m}{\delta \frac{M}{p_c}} - 1\right]\mathrm{d}p_c + \mathrm{d}\gamma \tag{18'}$$

$$\mathrm{d}Y_1 = \mathrm{d}x_c + P_k\mathrm{d}x_k + x_k\mathrm{d}P_k \tag{19'}$$

Our assumptions are the following:

$$\phi_{l_c},\ a\phi_{l_k} > 0$$

The marginal product of labour is positive both in the consumer goods and in the capital goods industry.

$$\phi_{q_c^0},\ a\phi_{q_k^0} > 0$$

The marginal product of the capital services available in the current period is positive in both branches of production.

$$\phi_{q_c^1},\ a\phi_{q_k^1} > 0$$

The marginal product of capital services in the next period – after expansion of the available capital services due to capital goods production in the current period – is positive in both branches of production.

$$\phi_{l_c l_c},\ \phi_{q_c^0 q_c^0},\ \phi_{q_c^1 q_c^1},\ a\phi_{l_k l_k},\ a\phi_{q_k^0 q_k^0},\ a\phi_{q_k^1 q_k^1} < 0$$

The marginal products of the factors decrease with the increase in their employment.

$$\phi_{l_c q_c^0},\ \phi_{l_c q_c^1},\ a\phi_{l_k q_k^0},\ a\phi_{l_k q_k^1} > 0$$

The marginal product of a factor increases with increasing applications of the other factor.

$$0 < \frac{\delta s}{\delta Y_1} < 1$$

The marginal propensity to save from real income is positive and smaller than unity.

$$\frac{\delta s}{\delta i} > 0$$

Saving increases with an increasing interest rate.

$$\frac{\delta s}{\delta \dfrac{M}{p_c}} < 0$$

Saving decreases with increasing real cash balances (Pigou effect).

$$0 < \frac{\delta m}{\delta Y_1} < 1$$

The demand for real cash balances increases with growing real income, but at a lesser rate than real income.

$$\frac{\delta m}{\delta i} < 0$$

The demand for real cash balances falls with an increasing rate of interest.

$$0 < \frac{\delta m}{\delta \frac{M}{p_c}} < 1$$

The demand for real cash balances increases with increasing real balances, but at a lesser rate (real-balance effect).

Let us first consider a change in the quantity of money alone. Hence we assume that $\mathrm{d}\beta = \mathrm{d}\gamma = \mathrm{d}q^0 = 0$. By solving the 19 equations, we get for the change of the interest rate:

$$\left(P_k U - \frac{\delta s}{\delta i} + \frac{1}{V} \frac{\delta m}{\delta i} \frac{\delta s}{\delta \frac{M}{p_c}} \right) \frac{\mathrm{d}i}{\mathrm{d}M} = 0$$

where

$$U = \frac{P_k}{\phi_{q_c^1 q_c^1}} + \frac{1}{a \phi_{q_k^1 q_k^1}} < 0$$

and

$$V = \frac{\delta m}{\delta \frac{M}{p_c}} - 1 < 0$$

The coefficient of $\mathrm{d}i/\mathrm{d}M$ is negative on our assumptions; hence $\mathrm{d}i/\mathrm{d}M$ must be equal to zero – i.e., the interest rate does not change in consequence of a change in the quantity of money:

$$\frac{\mathrm{d}i}{\mathrm{d}M} = 0$$

As a further result we obtain:

$$\frac{\mathrm{d}p_c}{\mathrm{d}M} = \frac{p_c}{M} > 0 \quad \text{or} \quad \frac{\mathrm{d}p_c}{p_c} = \frac{\mathrm{d}M}{M}$$

i.e., the money price of the consumer good, our unit of account, and with it the price level rise or fall proportionally to the change in the quantity of money. All real magnitudes remain unaffected by the change in the quantity of money.

As a second change in data we consider a shift in the demand for real cash balances. Here we obtain for the change of the interest rate the equation:

$$\frac{\mathrm{d}i}{\mathrm{d}\gamma} = -\frac{1}{V}\left[\frac{\dfrac{\delta s}{\delta \dfrac{\bar{M}}{p_c}}}{P_k U - \dfrac{\delta s}{\delta i} + \dfrac{1}{V}\dfrac{\delta m}{\delta i}\dfrac{\delta s}{\delta \dfrac{\bar{M}}{p_c}}}\right] > 0$$

where U and V are as defined above. A shift of the demand for real balances to the right ($\mathrm{d}\gamma$ is positive) thus will cause the interest rate to rise, and a shift to the left will cause it to fall. But if we were to neglect the influence of the size of real balances on saving (the Pigou effect), i.e. if we were to put

$$\frac{\delta s}{\delta \dfrac{\bar{M}}{p_c}} = 0$$

the numerator in the above equation would become zero while the denominator in the brackets would remain negative; the interest rate would not change in consequence of the shift in the demand for real balances, i.e. $\mathrm{d}i/\mathrm{d}\gamma = 0$.

For the change of the money price of the *numéraire* and hence for the change of the price level we obtain the following equation in the case of a shift in the liquidity preference:

$$\frac{\mathrm{d}p_c}{\mathrm{d}\gamma} = \frac{p_c^2}{\bar{M}V}\left[\frac{P_k U - \dfrac{\delta s}{\delta i}}{P_k U - \dfrac{\delta s}{\delta i} + \dfrac{1}{V}\dfrac{\delta m}{\delta i}\dfrac{\delta s}{\delta \dfrac{\bar{M}}{p_c}}}\right] < 0$$

i.e., with a shift of the demand for real balances to the right (dγ is positive) the price level will fall, and vice versa. This result occurs even if we neglect the Pigou effect

$$\left(\frac{\delta s}{\delta \dfrac{\bar{M}}{p_c}} = 0\right)$$

If, in addition to the Pigou effect, we also neglect the real-balance effect

$$\left(\frac{\delta m}{\delta \dfrac{\bar{M}}{p_c}} = 0\right)$$

then it turns out that a relative change in the demand for money leads to an equal relative change in the value of money: a doubling in the demand for money, for instance, will reduce the price level to half of what it was.

The most important results of a shift in the liquidity preference are, in summary, as follows (with the verbal description always relating to a positive dγ):

$\dfrac{\mathrm{d}i}{\mathrm{d}\gamma} > 0$	The interest rate rises.
$\dfrac{\mathrm{d}p_c}{\mathrm{d}\gamma} < 0$	The money price of the *numéraire* and hence the price level falls.
$\dfrac{\mathrm{d}Y_1}{\mathrm{d}\gamma} = 0$	Real income remains unchanged.
$\dfrac{\mathrm{d}P_k}{\mathrm{d}\gamma} = 0$	The price of the capital good in terms of the *numéraire* remains unchanged.

$\dfrac{dl_c}{d\gamma} > 0$, $\dfrac{dq_c^0}{d\gamma} > 0$	The quantities used in the consumer goods industry of the factors labour and capital services increase.
$\dfrac{dx_c}{d\gamma} > 0$	The production of consumer goods increases.
$\dfrac{dl_k}{d\gamma} < 0$, $\dfrac{dq_k^0}{d\gamma} < 0$	The quantities used in the capital goods industry of the factors labour and capital services decline.
$\dfrac{dx_k}{d\gamma} < 0$	The production of capital goods declines.
$\dfrac{dI_1}{d\gamma} < 0$	Real investment declines.
$\dfrac{dS_1}{d\gamma} < 0$	Real saving declines.
$\dfrac{dP_l}{d\gamma} = \dfrac{dP_q}{d\gamma} = 0$	The prices of the factors labour and capital services, expressed in terms of the *numéraire*, remain unchanged.
$\dfrac{dP_q'}{d\gamma} > 0$	The price of capital services in the next period, expressed in terms of the *numéraire*, rises.

For the third change in data, the shift of the saving function, we obtain:

$$\frac{di}{d\beta} = \frac{1}{P_k U - \dfrac{\delta s}{\delta i} + \dfrac{1}{V} \dfrac{\delta m}{\delta i} \dfrac{\delta s}{\delta \dfrac{\bar{M}}{p_c}}} < 0$$

and

$$\frac{dp_c}{d\beta} = \frac{p_c^2}{\bar{M}V} \left[\frac{\dfrac{\delta m}{\delta i}}{P_k U - \dfrac{\delta s}{\delta i} + \dfrac{1}{V} \dfrac{\delta m}{\delta i} \dfrac{\delta s}{\delta \dfrac{\bar{M}}{p_c}}} \right] < 0$$

Interest rate and price level fall with a shift of the saving function to the right ($d\beta$ is positive), and vice versa. The other most important results are as follows (the verbal description relating to the case of a positive $d\beta$):

$\frac{dY_1}{d\beta} = 0$ Real income remains unchanged.

$\frac{dP_k}{d\beta} = 0$ The price of the capital good, expressed in terms of the *numéraire*, remains unchanged.

$\left.\begin{array}{l}\frac{dl_c}{d\beta} < 0 \\ \frac{dq_c^0}{d\beta} < 0\end{array}\right\}$ The quantities of the factors labour and capital services used in the consumer goods industry decline.

$\frac{dx_c}{d\beta} < 0$ The production of consumer goods declines.

$\left.\begin{array}{l}\frac{dl_k}{d\beta} > 0 \\ \frac{dq_k^0}{d\beta} > 0\end{array}\right\}$ The quantities of the factors labour and capital services used in the capital goods industry increase.

$\frac{dx_k}{d\beta} > 0$ The production of capital goods increases.

$\frac{dI_1}{d\beta} > 0$ Real investment increases.

$\frac{dS_1}{d\beta} > 0$ Real saving increases.

$\frac{dP_l}{d\beta} = \frac{dP_q}{d\beta} = 0$ The prices of the factors labour and capital services, expressed in terms of the *numéraire*, remain unchanged.

$\frac{dP_q'}{d\beta} < 0$ The price of capital services in the next period, expressed in terms of the *numéraire*, falls.

Let us finally have a short look at a change in the original endowment with capital services, q^0. For the change of the interest rate resulting from this change we obtain the following equation:

$$\frac{\mathrm{d}i}{\mathrm{d}q^0} = \frac{P_k + \phi_{q_c^0}\left(\frac{\delta s}{\delta Y_1} - \frac{1}{V}\frac{\delta m}{\delta Y_1}\frac{\delta s}{\delta \frac{\bar{M}}{p_c}}\right)}{P_k U - \frac{\delta s}{\delta i} + \frac{1}{V}\frac{\delta m}{\delta i}\frac{\delta s}{\delta \frac{\bar{M}}{p_c}}}$$

The denominator of the right-hand side of this equation is negative; the sign of the numerator is undetermined. If we were to neglect the Pigou effect, putting

$$\frac{\delta s}{\delta \frac{\bar{M}}{p_c}} = 0$$

the numerator would be positive and the interest rate would have to fall with an increase in the capital stock, i.e. $(\mathrm{d}i/\mathrm{d}q^0) < 0$. As we noted in the text, this result must also be expected even if saving declines with increasing real cash balances due to the Pigou effect – i.e., even if

$$\frac{\delta s}{\delta \frac{\bar{M}}{p_c}} < 0$$

– because the effect of real income on saving overcompensates that of real cash balances.

As further results we obtain:

$$\frac{\mathrm{d}p_c}{\mathrm{d}q^0} = \frac{p_c^2}{\bar{M}V}\left[\frac{\frac{\delta s}{\delta Y_1}\frac{\delta m}{\delta i}\phi_{q_c^0} + P_k\frac{\delta m}{\delta i} + \left(P_k U - \frac{\delta s}{\delta i}\right)\frac{\delta m}{\delta Y_1}\phi_{q_c^0}}{P_k U - \frac{\delta s}{\delta i} + \frac{1}{V}\frac{\delta m}{\delta i}\frac{\delta s}{\delta \frac{\bar{M}}{p_c}}}\right] < 0$$

and

$$\frac{dY_1}{dq^0} > 0$$

i.e., the price level falls in consequence of an increased capital stock, which is to be explained by the fact that real national product increases simultaneously.

AUTHORS' INDEX